Bases of
the Plantation Society

Bases of
the Plantation Society

Edited by
AUBREY C. LAND

UNIVERSITY OF SOUTH CAROLINA PRESS
Columbia, South Carolina

BASES OF THE PLANTATION SOCIETY

Introduction, editorial notes, and compilation copyright
© 1969 by Aubrey C. Land.

Printed in the United States of America.

First edition: HARPER PAPERBACKS, 1969,
Harper & Row, Publishers, Incorporated,
49 East 33rd Street, New York, N.Y. 10016.

This edition published by the University of South Carolina Press, Columbia, S.C.,
1969, by arrangement with Harper Paperbacks, from whom a paperback edition is
available (HR/1429).

Standard Book Number: 87249-162-5.

Library of Congress Catalog Card Number: 70–625504.

Contents

Introduction

In a sense all the American colonies were plantation colonies. The English-speaking world of Elizabeth I and her Stuart successors meant by "plantation" a settlement that was "planted" overseas. And those who established such a colony were "planters." New Englanders, Pennsylvanians, and Virginians were all planters. These terms continued to have this reference throughout colonial times. But gradually a second and technical meaning became attached to "planting"—a reference to the cultivation of the great staple crops: tobacco, rice, indigo. Those areas where such prized commodities grew took on special value in the eyes of British merchants and statesmen. They were the plantations par excellence, the jewels of the trade empire, the nursery of seamen, the source of mercantile wealth. In short they represented the good features of empire. As the years passed, the second meaning became the foremost: the planting colonies comprised the seaboard provinces from Maryland on to the south.

It is the second meaning of "planting" that has survived. The derivative terms, "planter" and "plantation," have acquired connotations directly related to the economic and social system that rested on the raising of the great staple crops. The planting society calls up various images according to the reader's background and interest. For some, slavery comes first to mind. To others, landed estates, mansion houses, gentlefolk, and the leisurely life. For still others, improvident planters deeply in debt to British merchant houses. The planting society was all of these and much more besides. In fact the most appropriate descriptive term for the planting society is "variety." In every aspect—the economic arrangements, social relations, culture, ethnic stocks, commodities produced—the range between extremes is wide. To bring such variety to a short statement is an almost impossible task: what simple or single unifying factor can the student use to bind together a paragraph that will encompass the planting society? A great scholar who gave a lifetime to the study of this subject professed to find a key: Ulrich B. Phillips opens his *Life and Labor in the Old South* with the sentence, "Let us begin by talking about the weather."

But something more than climate made the planting domain, and of course Phillips knew that. He went on to discuss many other matters that in his view gave a special character to the Old South. Perhaps the student who has not already made a thorough study of the subject would be well advised to jettison his notions and go back in imagination to the time when there was no South, no planting society in the common meaning of the term, and follow the development over a century and a half. Such a method of study would disclose a process—the dynamics—as well as the variety. For not only was the planting order richly varied by the time it reached its golden age around the middle of the eighteenth century, but it was forever changing. The scene Virginians saw about them in 1650 was different from that which they perceived a hundred years later. The plan of this book invites this study of change over time; and the time was long, almost half of our history, from Jamestown in 1607 down to the revolutionary troubles.

One fringe benefit of organic study of this sort is a truer conception of the texture of society. And it is to this end that the student is advised to begin without preconceptions and to build his ideas anew as he watches the system evolve. This is particularly true if his notions of the planter follow the usual stereotypes of gracious gentlemen, cultured ladies, Negro family retainers, great houses, lavish hospitality, and the like. Families like these of course do appear in the planting colonies. But they are hardly typical of the whole social order. Possibly they constituted as many as one twentieth of the families in the tidewater by the decade before the War for American Independence. Statistics plainly tell a story of a population composed mainly of smaller producers, thousands upon thousands who over the decades of our colonial dependence lived their allotted spans and disappeared from the scene leaving hardly a trace: no monumental houses, no archives of family letters upon which historians of later years could draw for illustrations, no proud descendants who revered the memory of great-grandfather so-and-so. Fortunately the slight trace they did leave—inventories and accounts in the public records—has enabled us to reconstruct with accuracy the social context of their world.

These small fry, then, are the typical planters of the southern colonies. They have been difficult to see because they left no records, at least not much of a record, of their existence. Consequently they have been the invisible people of the southern colonies. By any standards their lives were drab. Their houses more nearly resembled shacks than the mansions of tradition, and almost all of them have disappeared. Their stocks of worldly goods comprised the bare essentials of daily living: bedding, a few cooking utensils, a gun, knife, weeding hoes, and personal clothing. The drama of marketplace and political forum passed them by. The county courthouse, the tavern, and the store bounded their social and business outlook. Most were literate, without being lettered. If they had books at all, these were the Bible, a volume of sermons or pietistic literature, perhaps a home medical guide. The produce of their small plantations included meat, grain, and vegetables for subsistence and tobacco, rice, or other staple that could be sold for cash. Even their plantations hardly extended beyond the dimensions of a small farm. Probably the portion of the population falling into this lowest economic group could be set at one half to two thirds. The total assets of families in this bracket amounted to less than £100.

Above them were other planting families, somewhat better off in worldly goods, education, and manners. The most obvious distinction of these families was their property, which ranged from estates of £100 up to £1,000. Neither poor nor rich, they were families of substance—a description that carried definite meaning to the eighteenth-century mind.

Finally, at the top of the scale, the grandees of legend possessed the great estates in slaves, land, houses, and luxuries. Some of them, a very few, counted their worth in tens of thousands of pounds.

It would be false to think of these as "classes" set above one another in some sort of pecking order. Top to bottom they were all planters, a wide spectrum ranging from very rich to very poor in the mid-eighteenth century. To think of these strata as classes is to venture into a social analysis that invites the notion of class conflict, which men of the time would have repudiated indignantly.

The absence of class conflict can be put to the test in two ways: by examining the political picture of the eighteenth century and by noting the social mobility in the society of the southern colonies. In politics the most fortunate group economically had a near monopoly on public office, both elective and appointive positions. It is often said that the southern colonies were "dominated" by an aristocracy, sometimes called the squirearchy. In the sense that the upper crust held the posts of trust and profit, this statement is correct. But the squires did not obtain their political positions in defiance of the less fortunate, but rather by their votes. If the squirearchy set political style and invariably enjoyed the fruits of office, they can be said to "dominate" only in the sense of "predominate." They stood out. Probably never since then in American history have the favored few enjoyed such harmony with the less fortunate. Put in another way, never since then has top wealth had such a harmonious relationship with the rest of society. Like their less fortunate brethren they were planters, bound to the cycle of the annual field crop, subject to the vagaries of weather, the state of the market, and the nuisances of agricultural pests. In the fullest sense they represented the interests of small producers, who were their neighbors and their political clients and who put them in office.

Similarly, by the test of social mobility and all that the term implies, the division between lower and upper economic strata was one of degree and not one of kind. Few people of great means migrated to the colonies. The rich won their wealth by their talents and by hard work. And they never became a closed group, their hands against those who like themselves were scaling the economic ladder. There are cases of men who came to these shores as indentured servants, or not much better economically, and who rose to the top rank of wealth and social position within their life's span. Such persons were exceptional, to be sure, but they illustrate the opportunities open to talent and the tolerance of society to movement upward.

The planting society—its people, its goods, and its way of life— was the work of colonials themselves. Of course the settlers came from Europe originally, and they represented a human investment by the mother country. But once the stock was here, it bred its own increase, fed by continual trickles of new blood from overseas. Similarly, considerable initial investment of capital was necessary to set the colonial economies going in the first place. But English investment did not bring the immediate and large returns expected by investors from the days of the Virginia Company onward. Consequently capital investment was a trickle also. Colonials themselves created the capital that was their wealth: they cleared the land, they built the fences, the roads and wharves, the barns and mills, and the public structures such as courthouses and forts.

The process began at Jamestown and continued through the entire period of colonial dependency. The parallel accomplishment of building stable social mechanisms completes the record of achievement for the first segment of our national history.

Framework and Selection of Documents

The story of the planting order can be told in two sets of terms. First, the economic side can be described through an examination of the way colonials combined the factors of production: land, labor, capital, and enterprise. This is the study of an unfolding colonial economy. It is fair to say that the characteristic use of each of the factors of production gave the plantation domain the plangent modality that so easily lures the tender-minded from realities into myth and romance. The antidote is to consider each factor in sufficient detail to show lights and shadows of real life. The documents for each of the chapters were chosen to reflect not only the direction of development but also the experimentation and the sense of uncertainty that accompanied the process of adaptation to a new land.

A second set of terms must also figure in this delineation, namely the social arrangements made to carry on essential production. To put it so seems almost to predicate the primacy of production, to place the business of making a living as the aim and the end of a society. Actually the economic and the social intertwine to the point of inseparability, without regard to ancient disputes about means and ends. Only for purposes of clarity are they separated at all. Analytically the laws and rules, institutions and behavior must be, and are here, considered separately. These define the special style of life and the tissue of social relations that were, as truly as land or labor, bases of the planting society.

I

Beginnings of a
Planting Society

THE ENGLISH came late to planting in the New World. Spain had
established beachheads in America during the reign of the first
Tudor monarch, Henry VII, and had expanded over major parts of
both American continents by the time of his granddaughter Elizabeth, last of the Tudors. All Europe saw the results in trade, in
treasure fleets returning to ports of Spain, and in the splendor and
power of the Spanish monarchs. Stirred by Spanish and Portuguese
overseas enterprise, English imaginations projected ventures into
these little-known but obviously promising lands beyond the seas.

English promoters of American colonization could not prevision
in any exact way the details of their enterprises. At best they foresaw the thrust their efforts would take. As managers of colonial
undertakings they had to have some plans and goals to present to
backers and investors. Not unnaturally they turned to persons who
could produce promotional tracts. The promotional literature of
the seventeenth century is among our most revealing sources on
motives and maneuvers of promoters. Many hands produced it:
Captain John Smith, William Penn, Joseph Alsop. Some were
little more than literary hacks; others were scholars of the first
order, like the Richard Hakluyts, the geographers.

In 1585 the elder Richard Hakluyt wrote a set of "Inducements"
for colonizing Virginia, a document so appropriate for promotion
that it was later (1602) printed as part of the effort to get still
another venture in motion after earlier failures of Raleigh. The
"Inducements" show at once how fully Hakluyt realized the
amount of work ahead for the adventurers, and how little he, or
any other promoter, foresaw the planting order as it developed.
Yet Hakluyt puts the case in far more practical terms than the
more famous *Discourse on Western Planting*, his nephew's widely

7

quoted writing, which was essentially an argument in mercantile terms for overseas expansion. The elder Hakluyt specifically recognized the importance of artisans and laborers and saw a range of possible returns. But even he did not fully comprehend the realities of the raw wilderness that stretched back hundreds of miles from the Atlantic coast.

The first planters came to American shores as employees of the Virginia Company of London, a joint-stock company whose shareholders expected immediate and handsome returns on their investments—from treasure, as they called gold and silver; from trade with natives; or from exploitation of products of the country. Painfully the planters learned the limitations and later the potentialities of the Chesapeake. Instead of treasure they found trees. Hope of profitable trade with the Indians died early; the primitive natives had nothing in common with the Indians of Asia or the Chinese, both producers of commodities prized by Europeans. The rich soil promised bounteous cereal crops and kitchen gardens, but these sustained rather than supported. Subsistence agriculture could keep the planters from starving but offered no hope of profit to them, much less to English investors.

The man who reported at length on the beginnings of English mainland colonization is perhaps the most famous name in the annals of our early history, and for years one of the most controversial: Captain John Smith. Through his writings run a sense of the overpowering wilderness, the dangers from natives, the perversity of adventurers seeking quick wealth, and his own determination to keep the enterprise afloat by attending to the grubby details of needful work. Though he participated actively in the first settlement and kept up with Virginia affairs long after he left the colony, Smith lacked a sense of where the main chance lay. He, as well as many others, knew about the beginnings of tobacco culture without really grasping its importance. He was not a crystal-gazer but a driving realist who lived in a hard present with one eye cocked for tomorrow's meal.

The first years in Virginia were bleak and often harrowing. Yet the commentators, who were often promoters themselves, maintained an optimistic tone. They spoke enthusiastically of the natural resources—the immense forests, the deep loamy soil—and predicted a great future ahead. But for the planters themselves the mere conquest of nature, bringing a raw country under cultivation, was hard and frustrating. So it was for years to come. A hundred years after Jamestown, settlers in new regions of the southern seaboard told of toil and heartbreak, which even the clergy shared. Pioneering was a continuing process, and its exactions left marks on generation after generation while the early battle with nature was being won.

A turning point occurred, however, toward the end of the first decade of Virginia history, when tobacco culture set the colony on a course that Virginians followed for three centuries. John Rolfe, an enterprising adventurer, introduced the crop, which shortly became a craze. Settlers planted tobacco in every cleared place, even in the streets of Jamestown. Rolfe's successful experiments transformed the planters of settlements into planters of tobacco, a cash crop that brought fabulous returns in the first years. Furthermore, from the English point of view, tobacco ideally fitted the requirements of mercantile theory. Virginia tobacco replaced the Spanish product in English pipes and stopped the drain of English money into Spain. For the Virginia planters tobacco opened the way to commercial agriculture. After a minimum of fumbling they discovered a suitable foundation upon which to build a society. Tobacco was a crop that almost anyone could produce, and almost everyone did. Briefly, tobacco was a staple crop, and Virginia an early staple colony, the first in the seaboard south and an example to those that followed.

Approximately a quarter-century after the founding of Jamestown, the first contingent of settlers reached Maryland, first of the great proprietary colonies. The planters immediately adopted the Virginia staple, which grew as well north of the Potomac as south of it. Maryland planters had no period of search for a profitable crop. In the 1660's Carolina had less good fortune. But after three decades of fumbling, settlers in Carolina found the tidal and riverine swamps ideal for rice, which after 1700 was shipped in ever-increasing quantities from the port of Charleston. Some forty years later the persistent efforts of a remarkable woman gave South Carolina a second staple, indigo. Finally Georgia, founded in the 1730's on the southern flank of Carolina, adopted the ways of her neighbor as soon as the trustees of the colony revoked their prohibition on slavery and permitted planters to buy Negroes for field duty.

By the end of the seventeenth century, settlers in the southern colonies had established a pattern of life that distinguished them in important ways from other areas of British America. The story was similar in each colony. An imaginative, enterprising individual or a small group took the initiative in introducing a crop that became the foundation of the economy. Over and over again the process of clearing and planting occurred as settlement pushed away from sea or bay up the rivers and into the interior. What had been originally a broken line of settlements precariously perched on the rim of Christendom became burgeoning commonwealths. The bases on which the planter built were the traditional factors of production: land, labor, capital, and enterprise. Combining these in distinctive ways, planters developed a viable economy and a congruent social order.

The heyday of the planting society—the golden age—was the eighteenth century. But already toward the end of the seventeenth, special characteristics were becoming apparent. These are treated in the following chapters.

1. The Vision of Plantation

Promoters of overseas planting used every device at hand, from lotteries and stock sales to literary effusions, to raise the necessary capital and to recruit settlers for their enterprises. The promotional literature ranges from propaganda pieces like the elder Hakluyt's "Inducements," directed at a specific object, to the prose epic of his nephew, known to students as Hakluyt's Voyages. The "Inducements" give concrete details of what possibilities the promoters saw in the New World. The appeal was to merchants and prospective investors, who of course wanted informed opinion about possible profits. Dozens of such pieces passed from hand to hand in manuscript copies, as this one did before its rich detail caught the eye of an enterprising promoter who had it published in 1602 when plans for colonization of Virginia were maturing. Hakluyt used the term "Virginia" to indicate the Atlantic seaboard from Spanish Florida north to Labrador.

Source: Eva G. R. Taylor (ed.), *The Original Writings and Correspondence of the Two Richard Hakluyts* (London, Cambridge University Press for the Hakluyt Society, 1936), II, 327–338.

Inducements to the Liking of the Voyage
Intended Towards Virginia in 40. and 42. Degrees of Latitude,
Written 1585, by M. Richard Hakluyt the Elder,
Sometime Student of the Middle Temple

1. The glory of God by planting of religion among those infidels.
2. The increase of the force of the Christians.
3. The possibilitie of the inlarging of the dominions of the Queenes most excellent Maiestie, and consequently of her honour, revenues, and of her power by this enterprise.
4. An ample vent in time to come of the Woollen clothes of England, especially those of the coursest sorts, to the maintenance of our poore, that els sterve or become burdensome to the realme. . . .
6. By returne thence, this realme shall receive (by reason of the situation of the climate, and by reason of the excellent soile) Oade, Oile, Wines, Hops, Salt, and most or all the commodities that we receive from the best parts of Europe, and we shall receive the same better cheape, than now we receive them, as we may use the matter.

9. Whatsoever commodities we receive by the Steelyard merchants, or by our owne merchants from Eastland, be it Flaxe, Hempe, Pitch, Tarre, Masts, Clap-boord, Wainscot, or such like; the like good may we receive from the North and Northeast part of the countrey neere unto Cape Briton, in returne for our course Woollen Clothes, Flanels and Rugges fit for those colder regions.

15. The great plentie of Buffe hides, and of many other sundry kinds of hides there now presently to be had, the trade of Whale and Seale fishing, and of divers other fishings in the great rivers, great bayes, and seas there, shall presently defray the charge in good part or in all of the first enterprise, and so we shall be in better case than our men were in Russia, where many yeeres were spent, and great summes of money consumed, before gaine was found.

16. The great broad rivers of that maine that we are to enter into so many leagues navigable or portable into the maine land, lying so long a tract with so excellent and so fertile a soile on both sides, doe seeme to promise all things that the life of man doth require, and whatsoever men may wish, that are to plant upon the same, or to trafficke in the same.

17. And whatsoever notable commoditie the soile within or without doth yeeld in so long a tract that is to be carried out from thence to England, the same rivers so great and deepe, do yeeld no small benefit for the sure, save, easie and cheape cariage of the same to shipboord, be it of greate bulke or of great weight.

20. Where there be many petie kings or lords planted on the rivers sides, and by all likelihood mainteine the frontiers of their severall territories by warres, we may by the aide of this river ioine with this king heere, or with that king there, at our pleasure, and may so with a few men be revenged of any wrong offered by any of them; or may, if we will proceed with extremity, conquer, fortifie, and plant in soiles most sweet, most pleasant, most strong, and most fertile, and in the end bring them all in subiection and to civilitie.

21. The knowen abundance of Fresh fish in the rivers, and the knowen plentie of Fish on the sea coast there, may assure us of sufficient victuall in spight of the people, if we will use salt and industrie.

22. The knowen plentie and varietie of Flesh, of divers kinds of beasts at land there, may seeme to say to us, that we may cheaply

victuall our navies to England for our returnes, which benefit every where is not found of merchants.

25. The navigating of the seas in the voyage, and of the great rivers there, will breed many Mariners for service, and mainteine much navigation.

26. The number of raw Hides there of divers kindes of beasts, if we shall possesse some Island there, or settle on the firme, may presently imploy many of our idle people in divers severall dressings of the same, and so we may returne them to the people that can not dresse them so well; or into this realm, where the same are good merchandize. . . .

27. Since great waste Woods be there, of Oake, Cedar, Pine, Wall-nuts, and sundry other sorts, many of our waste people may be imployed in making of Ships, Hoies, Busses and Boats; and in making of Rozen, Pitch, and Tarre, the trees naturall for the same, being certeinly knowen to be neere Cape Briton and the Bay of Menan, and in many other places there about.

28. If mines of white or gray marble, Jet, or other rich stone be found there, our idle people may be imployed in the mines of the same, and in preparing the same to shape, and so shaped, they may be caried into this realm as good balast for our ships, and after serve for noble buildings.

29. Sugar canes may be planted aswell as they are now in the South of Spaine, and besides the imploiment of our idle people, we may receive the commodity cheaper, and not inrich infidels or our doubtful friends, of whom now we receive that commoditie.

31. This land that we purpose to direct our course to, lying in part in the 40 degree of latitude, being in like heat as Lisbone in Portugall doth, and in the more Southerly part as the most Southerly coast of Spaine doth, may by our diligence yeeld unto us besides Wines and Oiles and Sugars, Orenges, Limons, Figs, Resings, Almonds, Pomegranates, Rice, Raw-silks such as come from Granada, and divers commodities for Diers, as Anile and Cochenillio, and sundry other colours and materials. Moreover, we shall not onely receive many precious commodities besides from thence, but also shal in time finde ample vent of the labour of our poore people at home, by sale of Hats, Bonets, Knives, Fish-hooks, Copper kettles, Beads, Looking-glasses, Bugles, & a thousand kinds of other wrought wares, that in short time may be brought in use among the people of that countrey, to the great

reliefe of the multitude of our poore people, and to the woonder-full enriching of this realme. . . .

Sorts of Men Which Are to Be Passed in This Voyage

1. Men skilfull in all Minerall causes.
2. Men skilfull in all kinde of drugges.
3. Fishermen, to consider of the sea fishings there on the coasts, to be reduced to trade hereafter: and others for the fresh water fishings.
4. Salt-makers, to view the coast, and to make triall how rich the sea-water there is, to advise for the trade.
5. Husbandmen, to view the soile, to resolve for tillage in all sorts.
6. Vineyard-men bred, to see how the soile may serve for the planting of Vines.
7. Men bred in the Shroffe in South Spaine, for discerning how Olive trees may be planted there.
8. Others, for planting of Orenge trees, Figge trees, Limon trees, and Almond trees; for iudging how the soile may serve for the same.
9. Gardeners, to proove the severall soiles of the Islands, and of our setling places, to see how the same may serve for all herbs and roots for our victualling. . . .
10. Lime-makers, to make lime for buildings.
11. Masons, Carpenters, etc. for buildings there.
12. Bricke-makers and Tile-makers.
13. Men cunning in the art of fortification, that may chuse out places strong by nature to be fortified, and that can plot out and direct workemen.
14. Choise Spade-men, to trench cunningly, and to raise bul-warks and rampiers of earth for defence and offence.
15. Spade-makers, that may, out of the Woods there, make spades like those of Devonshire, and of other sorts, and shovels from time to time for common use.
16. Smithes, to forge the yrons of the shovels and spades, and to make blacke billes and other weapons, and to mend many things.
17. Men that use to breake Ash trees for pike-staves, to be imploied in the Woods there.
18. Others, that finish up the same so rough hewd, such as in London are to be had.

19. Coopers, to make caske of all sorts.

20. Forgers of pike heads and of arrow heads, with forges, with Spanish yron, and with all maner of tooles to be caried with them.

21. Fletchers, to renew arrowes, since archerie prevaileth much against unarmed people: and gunpowder may soone perish, by setting on fire.

22. Bowyers also, to make bowes there for need.

23. Makers of oares, since for service upon those rivers it is to great purpose, for the boats and barges they are to passe and enter with.

24. Shipwrights, to make barges and boats, and bigger vessels, if need be, to run along the coast, and to pierce the great Bayes and Inlets.

25. Turners, to turne targets of Elme and tough wood, for use against the darts and arrowes of Salvages.

26. Such also as have knowledge to make targets of horne.

27. Such also as can make armor of hides upon moulds, such as were woont to be made in this realme about an hundred yeeres since, and were called Scotish jacks: such armor is light and defensive enough against the forces of Salvages.

28. Tanners, to tanne hides of Buffes, Oxen, etc. in the Isles where you shall plant.

29. White Tawyers of all other skinnes there.

30. Men skilfull in burning of Sope ashes, and in making of Pitch, and Tarre, and Rozen, to be fetched out of Prussia and Poland, which are thence to be had for small wages, being there in maner of slaves. . . .

31. A skilfull painter is also to be caried with you, which the Spaniards used commonly in all their discoveries to bring the descriptions of all beasts, birds, fishes, trees, townes, etc.

2. Realities of Early Planting

THE EXPEDITION that founded Jamestown, the first permanent British colony in North America, arrived in Virginia in 1607. All the personnel of the expedition were employees of the Virginia Company, and their assigned mission was to seek out the opportunities Hakluyt and others had suggested. Captain John Smith's exploits have become a part of

American folklore, but his account of the Virginia scene has the ring of authority. Through his eyes the confusion and the groping for solutions to problems of early planting days show up clearly. Smith took Hakluyt's advice seriousy and turned his energies to exploiting the products of the country, while many of the adventurers dissipated theirs in visionary schemes which produced neither return cargoes demanded by the company officers back home nor food to ward off the starving time ahead. Optimistic about the future, Smith saw and reported to the company in letters, which he paraphrases here, the errors and dangers of the present. His second account, written some twenty years later, indicates how slowly men of his day realized the direction plantation life would take. Tobacco had already won the day in Virginia, but Smith still talks about iron, naval stores, hemp, and potash as the objects that should be of major concern.

SOURCE: Captain John Smith, *The Generall Historie of Virginia, New England, and the Summer Isles* (Glasgow, James MacLehose and Sons, 1907), I, 148–150, 172–173, 288–289; and *The True Travels, Adventures and Observations* (Glasgow, James MacLehose and Sons, 1907), II, 178–179.

The Generall Historie of Virginia

[While others explored] I followed the new begun workes of Pitch and Tarre, Glasse, Sope-ashes, and Clapboord, whereof some small quantities we have sent you. But if you rightly consider, what an infinite toyle it is in Russia and Swethland, where the woods are proper for naught els, and though there be the helpe both of man and beast in those ancient Commonwealths, which many an hundred yeares have used it, yet thousands of those poore people can scarce get necessaries to live, but from hand to mouth. And though your Factors there can buy as much in a week as will fraught you a ship, or as much as you please; you must not expect from us any such matter, which are but a many of ignorant miserable soules, that are scarce able to get wherewith to live, and defend our selves against the inconstant Salvages: finding but here and there a tree fit for the purpose, and want all things els the Russians have. . . .

When you send againe I intreat you rather send but thirty Carpenters, husbandmen, gardiners, fishermen, blacksmiths, masons, and diggers up of trees, roots, well provided; then a thousand of such as we have: for except wee be able both to lodge

them, and feed them, the most will consume with want of necessaries before they can be made good for any thing. . . . For in
over-toyling our weake and unskilfull bodies, to satisfie this desire
of present profit, we can scarce ever recover our selves from one
Supply to another. And I humble intreat you hereafter, let us
know what we should receive, and not stand to the Saylers cour-
tesie to leave us what they please, els you may charge us with what
you will, but we not you with any thing. These are the causes that
have kept us in Virginia, from laying such a foundation, that ere
this might have given much better content and satisfaction; but as
yet you must not looke for any profitable returnes. . . .

It was the Spanyards good hap to happen in those parts where
were infinite numbers of people, who had manured the ground
with that providence, it affoorded victualls at all times. And time
had brought them to that perfection, they had the use of gold and
silver, and the most of such commodities as those Countries
afforded: so that what the Spanyard got was chiefely the spoyle and
pillage of those Countrey people, and not the labours of their owne
hands. . . .

But we chanced in a Land even as God made it, where we found
onely an idle, improvident, scattered people, ignorant of the
knowledge of gold or silver, or any commodities, and carelesse of
any thing but from hand to mouth, except bables of no worth;
nothing to incourage us, but what accidentally we found Nature
afforded. Which ere we could bring to recompence our paines,
defray our charges, and satisfie our Adventurers; we were to discover the Countrey, subdue the people, bring them to be tractable,
civill, and industrious, and teach them trades, that the fruits of
their labours might make us some recompence, or plant such
Colonies of our owne, that must first make provision how to live of
themselves, ere they can bring to perfection the commodities of
the Country: which doubtlesse will be as commodious for England
as the west Indies for Spaine, if it be rightly managed. . . .

Therefore let us not be discouraged, but rather animated by
those conclusions, seeing we are so well assured of the goodnesse
and commodities may bee had in Virginia, nor is it to be much
doubted there is any want of Mines of most sorts, no not of the
richest, as is well knowne to some yet living that can make it
manifest when time shall serve: and yet to thinke that gold and
silver Mines are in a country otherwise most rich and fruitfull, or

the greatest wealth in a Plantation, is but a popular error, as is the opinion likewise, that the gold and silver is now the greatest wealth of the West Indies at this present. True it is indeed, that in the first conquest the Spaniards got great and mighty store of treasure from the Natives, which they in long space had heaped together, and in those times the Indians shewed them entire and rich Mines, which now by the relations of them that have beene there, are exceedingly wasted, so that now the charge of getting those Metals is growne excessive, besides the consuming the lives of many by their pestilent smoke and vapours in digging and refining them, so that all things considered, the cleere gaines of those metals, the Kings part defraied, to the Adventurers is but small, and nothing neere so much as vulgarly is imagined; and were it not for other rich Commodities there that inrich them, those of the Contraction house were never able to subsist by the Mines onely; for the greatest part of their Commodities are partly naturall, and partly transported from other parts of the world, and planted in the West-Indies, as in their mighty wealth of Sugarcanes, being first transported from the Canaries; and in Ginger and other things brought from the East-Indies, in their Cochanele, Indicos, Cotton, and their infinite store of Hides, Quicksilver, Allum, Woad, Brasill woods, Dies, Paints, Tobacco, Gums, Balmes, Oiles, Medicinals and Perfumes, Sassaparilla, and many other physicall drugs: These are the meanes whereby they raise that mighty charge of drawing out their gold to the great & cleare revenue of their King. Now seeing the most of those commodities, or as usefull, may be had in Virginia by the same meanes, as I have formerly said, let us with all speed take the priority of time, where also may be had the priority of place, in chusing the best seats of the Country, which now by vanquishing the salvages, is like to offer a more faire and ample choice of fruitfull habitations, then hitherto our gentlenesse and faire comportments could attaine unto.

The True Travels

Now the most I could understand in generall, was from the relation of Mr. Nathaniel Cawsey, that lived there with mee, and returned Anno Dom. 1627. . . . Their numbers then were about 1500, some say rather 2000, divided into seventeene or eighteene severall Plantations; the greatest part thereof towards the falls, are so inclosed with Pallizadoes they regard not the Salvages; and amongst those Plantations above James Towne, they have now found meanes to take plentie of fish, as well with lines, as nets, and where the waters are the largest; having meanes, they need not want.

Their Cattle, namely oxen, Kine, Buls, they imagine to be about 2000. Goats great store and great increase; the wilde Hogs, which were infinite, are destroyed and eaten by the Salvages: but no family is so poore, that hath not tame Swine sufficient; and for Poultrie, he is a verie bad husband breedeth not an hundred in a yeere, and the richer sort doth daily feed on them.

For bread they have plentie. . . . For drinke, some malt the Indian corne, others barley, of which they make good Ale, both strong and small, and such plentie thereof, few of the upper Planters drinke any water: but the better sort are well furnished with Sacke, Aquavitae, and good English Beere.

Their servants commonly feed upon Milke Homini, which is bruized Indian corne pounded, and boiled thicke, and milke for the sauce; but boiled with milke the best of all will oft feed on it, and leave their flesh. . . .

For Discoveries they have made none, nor any other commodities than Tobacco doe they apply themselves unto, though never any was planted at first. And whereas the Countrey was heretofore held most intemperate and contagious by manny, now they have houses, lodgings and victuall, and the Sunne hath power to exhale up the moyst vapours of the earth, where they have cut downe the wood, which before it could not, being covered with spreading tops of high trees; they finde it much more healthfull than before; nor for their numbers, few Countreyes are lesse troubled with death, sicknesse, or any other disease, nor where overgrowne women become more fruitfull. . . .

James Towne is yet their chiefe seat, most of the wood destroyed, little corne there planted, but all converted into pasture and gardens, wherein doth grow all manner of herbs and roots we have in England in abundance, and as good grasse as can be. . . . Apples, Peares; Apricocks, Vines, figges, and other fruits some have planted, that prospered exceedingly, but their diligence about Tobacco left them to be spoiled by the cattell, yet now they beginne to revive. . . . Their Cities and Townes are onely scattered houses, they call plantations, as are our Country Villages.

. . . No discoveries of any thing more, than the curing of Tobacco, by which hitherto being so present a commodity of gaine, it hath brought them to this abundance; but that they are so disjoynted, and every one commander of himselfe, to plant what he will: they are now so well provided that they are able to subsist; and if they would joine together now to worke upon Sope-ashes, Iron, Rape-oile, Mader, Pitch and Tarre, Flax and Hempe; as for their Tobacco, there comes from many places such abundance, and the charge so great, it is not worth the bringing home.

3. Progress of the Staple

TOBACCO was not new to England when Virginians made their first shipments home. Spanish tobacco was already well known, though Englishmen had uneasy consciences about smoking it. High tobacco prices drained money out of England into Spanish pockets, and rumor had it that smoking sapped a man's virility. John Rolfe's success with tobacco changed the picture in both England and Virginia. Rolfe passed by the native tobacco (apooke), which Powhatan's people smoked, and imported the seed of Tobacum nicotinum from the Spanish West Indies. His tobacco caught on in England and before 1621 rivaled the Spanish product, which connoisseurs preferred. Virginia tobacco went to the growing mass market of undiscriminating addicts. London dominated the tobacco trade for a century until the rise of the port of Glasgow after 1720. But even the outports, a convenient name for all other English ports beside London, took small quantities from the outset. Import duties brought welcome revenues to the crown. Though James I damned the "sot-weed" publicly in his famous Counterblaste to Tobacco, he had no heart for destroying a trade that yielded handsome customs. Salved by the thought that Virginia tobacco at least kept money from trickling out to Spain, the consciences of mercantilist statesmen began to tolerate the idea of a "colony founded on smoake." Untroubled by such complexities, Virginia planters applied themselves to increasing production of a valuable cash crop, with results that show in cold statistics.

SOURCE: "Lord Sackville's Papers respecting Virginia, 1613–1631," American Historical Review, XXVII, 526–527.

An Abstracte of What Spanish Virginia and Bermudos Tobacco Hath Bin Imported into the Porte of London and the Out-Portes from Michaelmas 1614 to Michaelmas 1621, vizt.

| | LONDON | | OUT-PORTES | |
	Spanish	Virginia and Bermudos	Spanish	Virginia and Bermudos
1615	100926	00000	01351	0000
1616	56925	02300	01406	0200
1617	45279	18839	01797	0000
1618	57058	49518	08371	0150
1619	119634	45764	08493	0000
1620	97149	117981	12248	1040
1621	159873	73777	14520	0000
(Total)	636844	308179	48186	1390

The Medium [Average] per annum of Spanish Tobacco in London and the Outportes is	97861	3/7
The Medium per annum of the Virginia and Bermudos Tobacco etc. is	44223	1/7
Some Total	142084	4/7

	£.	s.	d.
97861 3/7 lb. of Spanish Tobacco at ii [2] s. per pound is	9786	03	00
44223 1/7 lb. of Virginia and Bermudos Tobacco at i s. per lb. is	2211	03	02
	11997	06	02
142085 at vi d. per Pound is	3552	02	06

[Endorsed:] The medium of Tobacco imported into the port of London and Out-portes for vii yeares endinge at Michaelmas 1621.

4. Persistent Difficulties of Beginnings

WHATEVER the colony, beginnings were hard and nearly always discouraging. Englishmen had neither confronted the immensity of primeval wilderness nor endured deprivation of commonplace amenities available back home. Immigrants who came to plant had not only the initial shock but successive jolts as they continued to battle perverse

conditions of a wild country. Whatever their calling back home—
whether tradesman, artisan, or intellectual—they immediately became
planters in the southern colonies, completely consumed by the labor of
establishing themselves. Conversely, the planters had to perform for
themselves the specialized services that were at their bidding even in
country villages back home. In brief, planters required a high degree of
self-dependence from the very outset of their careers in America. Small
wonder that newcomers looked enviously at established planters and
coveted their cleared fields, their buildings, and their laborers. The
Reverend Mr. Urmstone, though owner of a plantation larger than many
in the southern colonies, shared pretty much the common lot: small
clearing, few livestock, and the like. He had, of course, as a minister some
income, which his neighbors could not command. But for his subsistence, let alone improvement of his style of living, he worked like
them. His letter speaks for the inarticulate mass of planters winning their
way toward a competence.

SOURCE: The Reverend John Urmstone to the Secretary for Prop-
agating the Gospel, dated July 7, 1711, from North Carolina, in
Francis L. Hawkes, *History of North Carolina* (Fayetteville,
N.C., 1857–1858), II, 215. Reprinted in Ulrich B. Phillips (ed.),
A Documentary History of American Society (Cleveland, Ohio,
Arthur H. Clark, 1910), II, 271–272.

Workmen are dear and scarce. I have about a dozen acres of
clear ground, and the rest woods, in all, three hundred acres. Had I
servants and money, I might live very comfortably upon it, raise
good corn of all sorts, and cattle without any great labor or charges,
could it once be stocked; but for want thereof shall not make any
advantage of my land. I have bought a horse some time ago; since
that, three cows and calves, five sheep, and some fowls of all sorts,
but most of them unpaid for, together with fourteen bushels of
wheat, for all which I must give English goods. At this rate I might
have had any thing that either this government or any of the
neighboring colonies afford; but had I stock, I need not fear
wanting either butter, cheese, beef, or mutton, of my own raising,
or good grain of all sorts. I am forced to work hard with axe, hoe,
and spade. I have not a stick to burn for any use, but what I cut
down with my own hands. I am forced to dig a garden, raise beans,
peas, etc., with the assistance of a sorry wench my wife brought
with her from England.

Men are generally of all trades, and women the like within their

spheres, except some who are the posterity of old planters, and
have great numbers of slaves, who understand most handicraft.
Men are generally carpenters, joiners, wheelwrights, coopers,
butchers, tanners, shoemakers, tallow-chandlers, watermen, and
what not; women, soap-makers, starch-makers, dyers, etc. He or she
that cannot do all these things, or hath not slaves that can, over
and above all the common occupations of both sexes, will have but
a bad time of it; for help is not to be had at any rate, every one
having business enough of his own. This makes tradesmen turn
planters, and these become tradesmen. No society one with another, with all study to live by their own hands, of their own
produce; and what they can spare, goes for foreign goods. Nay,
many live on a slender diet to buy rum, sugar, and molasses, with
other such like necessaries, which are sold at such a rate that the
planter here is but a slave to raise a provision for other colonies,
and dare not allow himself to partake of his own creatures, except
it be the corn of the country in hominy bread.

5. The Planting Scene
at the End of the Seventeenth Century

How FAR had the planting society advanced by the end of the seventeenth century, the century of beginnings? To strike a fair balance is not
easy because the southern colonies were of different ages and consequently at different stages of maturity. Carolina had barely reached the
stage of staple production; Georgia was yet unborn; Virginia was nearly
one hundred years old. Accordingly, assessments of progress can easily
go too far toward extravagance or, on the contrary, err by failing to state
the case adequately. Fortunately in the last decade of the century three
well-informed Virginians attempted a balanced appraisal of the oldest
colony at the bidding of the Board of Trade. In October 1697, Henry
Hartwell, James Blair, and Edward Chilton produced a manuscript
report which they labeled The Present State of Virginia, and the College.
This short work, printed in 1727, gives a kind of still life that might be
entitled "Virginia as it stood at the century's end." Neither adulatory
nor carping, this striking paper shows the way the twig was bending. Already the prevailing type was the planter, who had acquired certain
agricultural skills and habits of mind. The absence of towns had in-
hibited growth of a class of tradespeople, simply because the genius of
an agrarian community was inhospitable to the calling of tradesmen.

And yet the merchant prospered—they "live best of any in that Country"
—even though he suffered real disabilities in the rural setting where he
did his business. In sum, the authors portray an order that closely resembles the unglamorized planting society as it was to be on a larger
scale a half-century in the future when the southern seaboard colonies
reached the pinnacle of affluence and self-conscious maturity.

SOURCE: Henry Hartwell, James Blair, and Edward Chilton, The
   Present State of Virginia, and the College (London, printed for
   John Wyat, 1727), 6–14. Reprinted and edited by Hunter D.
   Farish (Chapel Hill, N.C., University of North Carolina Press
   for the Institute of Early American History and Culture, 1940),
   8–16.

Of the Several Sorts of Inhabitants, and Cultivation of Virginia

So much for the natural (we cannot say Commodities, but)
disposition and advantageous Circumstances of the Country.

But now if it be enquir'd what sort of a Country it is after all
this, we must represent it after a quite different Manner from what
might be expected from the first and eldest of all the English
Plantations in America. As to the outward Appearance, it looks all
like a wild Desart; the High-Lands overgrown with Trees, and the
Low-Lands sunk with Water, Marsh, and Swamp: the few Plantations and clear'd Grounds bearing no Proportion to the rough and
uncultivated.

The Inhabitants are of three Sorts, Planters, Tradesmen, and
Merchants.

Tho' the Planters are the most numerous, perhaps not the
hundredth Part of the Country is yet clear'd from the Woods, and
not one Foot of the Marsh and Swamp drained. As fast as the
Ground is worn out with Tobacco and Corn, it runs up again in
Underwoods, and in many Places of the Country, that which has
been clear'd is thicker in Woods than it was before the clearing. It
is but in very few Places that the Plough is made use of, for in their
first clearing they never grub up the Stumps, but cut the Trees
down about two or three Foot from the Ground; so that all the
Roots and Stumps being left, that Ground must be tended with
Hoes, and by that time the Stumps are rotten, the Ground is worn
out; and having fresh Land enough, of which they must clear some

for Fire-Wood, they take but little Care to recruit the old Fields with Dung. Of Grain and Pulse they commonly provide only as much as they expect they themselves shall have Occasion for, for the Use of their Families, there being no Towns or Markets where they can have a ready Vent for them, and scarce any Money to serve for a common Exchange in buying and selling. The only Thing whereof they make as much as they can, is Tobacco, there being always a Vent for that at one Time of the Year or other; besides that their Want of Cloaths and Household-Furniture, and all their other Necessaries, instigate them to make as much To- bacco as they can, this being the Money of that Country which Answers all Things. But the great Labour about Tobacco being only in Summer time, they acquire great Habits of Idleness all the rest of the Year.

For want of Towns, Markets, and Money, there is but little Encouragement for Tradesmen and Artificers, and therefore little Choice of them, and their Labour very dear in the Country. A Tradesman having no Opportunity of a Market where he can buy Meat, Milk, Corn, and all other things, must either make Corn, keep Cows, and raise Stockes himself, or must ride about the Country to buy Meat and Corn where he can find it; and then is puzzled to find Carriers, Drovers, Butchers, Salting, (for he can't buy one Joynt or two) and a great many other Things, which there would be no Occasion for, if there were Towns and Markets. Then a great deal of the Tradesman's Time being necessarilly spent in going and coming to and from his Work, in dispers'd Country Plantations, and his Pay being generally in straggling Parcels of Tobacco, the Collection whereof costs about 10 per cent. and the best of this Pay coming but once a Year, so that he cannot turn his Hand frequently with a small Stock, as Tradesmen do in England and elsewhere, all this occasions the Dearth of all Tradesmen's Labour, and likewise the Discouragement, Scarcity, and Insuffi- cency of Tradesmen.

The Merchants live the best of any in that Country, but yet are subject to great Inconveniencies in the way of their Trade, which might be avoided, if they had Towns, Markets, and Money. For first they are obliged to sell upon Trust all the Year long, except just a little while when Tobacco is ready. 2dly, they likewise drive a pityful retail Trade to serve every Man's little Occasions, being all in Effect but Country Chapmen, for want of Towns to be a Center of Trade and Business. 3dly, Besides the Charge of it, they are necessitated to trust all their Concerns to their Receivers, who go about among the Planters that owe them Tobacco, and receive and mark it for them, which Receivers, if they want either Skill or Honesty, prove very fatal to the Merchant. 4thly, They are at the Charge of carting this Tobacco, so mark'd and receiv'd, to convenient Landings; or if it lyes not far from these Landings, they must trust to the Seamen for their careful rolling it on board of their Sloops and Shallops; and if the Seamen roll it in bad Weather, or dirty Ways, it is expos'd to a great deal of Damage. 5thly, It is a great while before the Ships can be loaded, their Freight lying at such a Distance, and being to be brought together in this scrambling Manner. By Reason of this it is an usual thing with Ships to lye three or four Months in the Country, which might be dispatch'd in a Fortnight's Time, if the Tobacco were ready at certain Ports; and this inhances the Freight to almost double the Price of what it needed to be, if the Ship had a quick Dispatch.

In New-England they were oblig'd at their first Settlement to settle in Towns, and would not permit a single Man to take up Land, till a certain Number of Men agreed together, as many as might make a Township; then they laid them out a Town, with Home-Lots for Gardens and Orchards, Out-Lots for Corn-Fields and Meadows, and Country-Lots for Plantations, with Overseers, and Gangs of Hands, which would have prov'd an excellent Way in such a Country as Virginia is. But this Opportunity being lost, they seated themselves, without any Rule or Order in Country Plantations, and being often sensible of the inconveniences of that dispers'd way of living, their General Assemblies have made several Attempts to bring the People into Towns, which have prov'd all ineffectual. One Error has generally run through all these Undertakings, viz. That they always appointed too many Towns, which will be still the Fault of them, if they are contriv'd by a General Assembly; for every Man desiring the Town to be as near as is possible to his own Door, and the Burgesses setting up every one of them for his own County, they have commonly contrived a Town for every County, which might be reasonable enough hereafter, when the Country comes to be well peopled, but at present is utterly impractical for want of People to inhabit them, and and Money to build them. And therefore we cannot but think the Governor and Assembly of Mary-Land have taken a much wiser

Course, who in their Law for Towns, have order'd only two Towns in that whole Province, viz. one on the eastern, and another on the western Shore. So perhaps two or three Towns in Virginia would be enough at first; the Country might add more afterwards, as they encrease in Wealth and People. Another Error they ran into in their last Law for Towns, was that they made it unlawful to buy or sell any Goods exported or imported, but at these Towns, under no less a Penalty than the Forfeiture of Ship and Goods, which was a great force upon Trade, and would have made all People very uneasy at present; tho' on the other hand there is this to be said for it, that their Merchants being already seated with their Stores in their Country Plantations, and having their Customers all round about them, without some considerable Force could not be induced to leave all these, and to come and live in Towns. Some are of Opinion that the King's constituting Ports for Exportation and Importation would do the Business, i.e. would bring the Trade to these Ports, and perhaps it would at the Long-run; for all that set up for Merchants after such a Constitution of Ports, would probably set up at these Places, but it would be a long Time before the old Merchants, who are in the present Possession of the Trade, would be perswaded to leave their Country-Houses and Stores, to come and live at Towns. Perhaps if there were great Care taken to encourage these Port-Towns with Privileges and Immunities, and likewise to discourage the Country Stores, the Thing would quickly be more effectual. However it is, hoc opus, hic labor est, if Towns and Ports can be brought to bear, the chief Obstruction to the Improvement of that Country will be removed. It is certain that little Help towards it is to be expected from their General Assembly, except they should come to have a Governor in whom they have a most mighty Confidence that he acts for the publick Good; which was the Case in Governor Nicholson's Time, when we see they were not only willing to have Towns, but to force them with many visible Inconveniences. But for their own Temper, they shewed it as soon as he was gone, i.e. they are daily more and more adverse to Cohabitation; the major Part of the House of Burgesses consisting of Virginians that never saw a Town, nor have no Notion of the Conveniency of any other but a Country Life: As a Proof whereof perhaps it may not be unfit to give an Account of an Argument which was brought against Towns by an Ingenious Virginian, who had never been out of the Country: His Argument was this, "That they might observe already, wherever they were thick seated, they could hardly raise any Stocks, or live by one another; much more, concluded he, would it be impossible for us to live, when a matter of an hundred Families are coop'd up within the Compass of half a Mile of Ground.

The want of Money, which is another great Obstruction of their Improvement, is chiefly occasion'd by the Governor who finds it his Interest to encourage the Tobacco, and discourage the Money Dealings, for by that Means he has as much of his Salary as he pleases paid him in Bills of Exchange, which is better for his Use to lay up in *England*, than that Country Money, being commonly Pieces of Eight at five Shillings. Then for what he wants to buy in the Country, he can buy it much cheaper for Quit Rent Tobacco, than for Money; e.g. an Ox which would cost him fifty Shillings or three Pounds, he can buy for six hundred Pounds of Tobacco, which buys of the King at four Shilling or Four and Six-pence the Hundred, so that he hath the Ox for about half Price of what it would cost him in Money. The Governor thus discouraging Money-Dealings, the Auditor is very scrupulous of taking Money of the Collectors, for the two Shillings an Hogshead; nor the People but to pay it to the Merchants for such Things as they have Occasion for; so that a positive Instruction that the two Shillings per Hogshead should be paid in Money, would cure all this, especially if the Value of Money were ascertain'd. Pieces of Eight are ascertained by Law at five Shillings, but that Law is very imperfect, for their being no Weight assign'd, they scruple a light Piece of Eight, alledging it is clipp'd, or a *Peru* Piece, as not being good Silver; and no other Coin is at all ascertain'd, except *English* Money, of which there is very little in the Country. "Last Assembly the House of Burgesses sent up a Bill for ascertaining all Coin, but it was thrown out in the Council, without so much as desiring a Conference about it, or offering any Amendments." It were good there were some common Standard of Money establish'd all over the *English* Plantations of *America*; for *Pensilvania* enhancing the Price of Money, and ordering a small Piece of Eight of twelve penny-weight to go for six Shillings, and so still for more, according to its Weight, does by that Means drain all the Money from *Virginia* and *Maryland*; the best Piece of Eight going in *Virginia* for five Shillings, and *Maryland* for four and Sixpence.

II

The Land Base

AN IMPORTANT base of the planting society was the land. Rich, tree-covered, and almost limitless, land was never entirely free. Englishmen were accustomed to the notion that all land had a lord, that it belonged to someone—either to a lord proprietor as in Maryland or early Carolina, or to a company as in Virginia during the first years. Accordingly, in order to enter into possession of their plantations, would-be planters had to acquire title from that someone. Every colony from Maryland to Georgia established procedures for granting title. In other words, they established land systems, which differed somewhat in details but in broad essentials were similar.

The first step was establishment of a right to acreage. Rights came into being on payment of a sum, about ten shillings per hundred acres, for a warrant. Next the purchaser of the warrant had the surveyor lay out the plantation and return a certificate of survey, which was entered on the land records. Finally, on the basis of the recorded certificate of survey the proper official issued the patent, or grant of ownership, duly inscribed on parchment and validated with a seal. Thus three steps usually sufficed to put a planter into possession.

The patent hardly created a plantation. A survey comprehended a certain number of acres of wild land, almost always with irregular metes and bounds: beginning at a tall white oak, thence north so many perches to a large rock, thence east to a stream, and so on around to the beginning point. The rectangular survey that imposed a neat checkerboard pattern on much of the United States came after the Revolution. In the planting colonies, boundary lines followed terrain features and landmarks in helter-skelter fashion. Within this vague mass of woodland the owner cleared a few acres, like Urmstone and thousands of others. The clearing became the "plantation"—literally the planted area—and on a patent of three hundred acres or larger, several such plantations might be made by the owner, his sons, or possibly tenants. Though "plantation" meant the planted area, it was understood to include surrounding woodlands where hogs and cattle foraged for food. Creation of a producing plantation depended on the investment of labor, the quality of husbandry, and capital.

Actually most of the land patents fell into the class of modest farms rather than of baronial holdings. Between 1660 and 1700, 72 per cent of all patents in Maryland were for tracts of less than 250 acres. Only 2 per cent were larger than 900 acres. The Virginia rent roll of 1704 shows a similar pattern of landholding in the family farm size.

The essentially simple land systems had refinements and complications. At every step of the procedure the patentee paid fees—for the survey, for recording documents, for use of the seal in validating the patent. Furthermore he had to locate the desirable land in the vast woodland that covered the tidewater—not an easy task. Those and other problems opened the door to professional land dealers, or speculators, to give them the usual name.

Around 1700 the land office business in larger patents picked up as a group of land dealers emerged. Traditionally, provincial men of substance had acquired land as a badge of station in the English manner, and a handful had amassed considerable acreage. But about the turn of the century the idea of treating land as a commodity to be sold for a profit began to appear—an idea alien to the settled and stable English. America was largely unsettled, and population was growing at an incredible rate. Opportunities to supply a commodity—the plantation—in this growing market did not go unheeded.

The land speculator became a fixture of the planting society. Indeed, speculators were among the wealthiest planters, and their land dealings helped build their fortunes. Many of the foremost families in the southern colonies owed their wealth to successful speculation. Perhaps the term "promoter" would more aptly describe them, for many of them did more than buy cheap and sell dear. No simple formula comprehends all their activities. They acquired land in enormous quantities, at first tens of thousands of acres, then hundreds of thousands. They leased small plantations to some of the landless men and sold to others. Their services spared tenants and customers both the complications and the expenses of dealing with the land office. Frequently they extended credit to buyers who could not purchase on any other terms; that is, they took mortgages on the properties they sold. Some of them actively promoted immigration to help dispose of their land and to enhance its value. Nearly all made specific provision for their tenants and purchasers to improve properties by clearing, fencing, building, and planting orchards. In brief, they forced the formation of capital.

In the early years of the eighteenth century the large landlords were typically individuals, or sometimes partnerships. They realized profits by selling to new immigrants, such as the Germans and the Scotch-Irish, or to newly freed indentured servants. From a large tract a speculator might dispose of half a dozen plantations and still have acreage left for another day when settlement drove land values even higher. A few individual speculators had immense holdings running well over one hundred thousand acres, like, for example, the Carters and the Byrds of Virginia. But they did not represent the ultimate in land operations. Toward mid-century the land companies—combinations of merchants, public officials, and wealthy colonials—sought grants to themselves as large as half a million acres and more.

Later generations have usually judged the land speculator harshly. Even in his own time he did not escape opprobrium as a person who reaped where he did not sow. More serious objections are found in some of the public records in the form of petitions and humble complaints. In substance the petitioners alleged that they, as humble individuals, could not obtain surveys because officials of the land system worked in collusion with speculators and land grabbers. When desirable areas were opened to survey, speculators made deals in advance with surveyors and judges to lay off their land first and to survey for Tom, Dick, and Harry later. Collusion did occur: the numbers of petitions in every colony attest it. Some cases became notorious. But not all land speculators can be fitted into these land office cliques or rings. Honest ones merit a different judgment. They were entrepreneurs in the first age of American enterprise.

6. Mechanics of the Land System

As a minor provincial official in Maryland, William Eddis learned the workings of most offices in the colony. His letter of 1772 to an English friend described the mechanics of obtaining a patent as simply and clearly as the procedure permitted. His elaboration of the basic three-step scheme of warrant-certificate-patent discloses some of the complications that drove many persons to large landholders and speculators for their land. Fees alone proved an obstacle. Officials collected them at each step of the proceedings, and the total came to a disproportionate sum for small plantations. Other complications called for legal skill, such as selecting the proper kind of warrant for improved land or escheated land. In the end, land seekers frequently went to landlord instead of land office. The quit rents, noted by Eddis, were paid in all the planting colonies but did not alter the character of tenure: grants were made in fee simple.

Source: William Eddis, Letters from America, Historical and Descriptive (London, 1792), 119–125.

Throughout the whole of the American provinces, there are immense tracts of unappropriated lands. In every government, offices are established under regal or proprietary authority, for the purpose of granting the same to adventurers on stipulated terms. As the method of proceeding in this business is nearly similar in every part of the continent, an account of the mode adopted with us will give you a general idea of this matter. Take, therefore, the following detail, which I have transcribed from an official record, for your information.

All papers relating to the granting of vacant land, within this province, issue out and are recorded in the land office; and the mode pursued to effect the grant of such vacant lands, is by warrants, either special or common. If the lands are cultivated or improved, they cannot be effected by any other than a special warrant, specifying the particular location and quantity to be effected. And all such warrants issue in consequence of an order from the proprietary's agent, intimating that the caution money of five pounds sterling, per hundred acres, is paid. The warrant is directed to the surveyor of the county where the land lies, who makes a survey, and returns a certificate thereof into the land office; from whence it is transmitted to the examiner general, and after examination, it is again sent back to the land office; a patent, or grant, then issues on the certificate, subject to the payment of an annual rent of four shillings sterling for every hundred acres. The fees attending granting the warrant; of the survey in consequence; of the examination of the certificate; issuing patent thereon; and affixing the great seal of the province thereto, will amount to about the sum of seven or eight pounds currency, per hundred acres.

The same mode is exactly pursued in common warrants, to effect uncultivated lands, but the expences are rather less.

It is to be observed, the aforesaid warrants are to effect lands never before taken up. There are other warrants that issue out of the land-office, such as warrants of re-survey, escheat warrants, and warrants under the proclamation.

The first of these are granted to re-survey a tract of land, already patented, and in which the petitioner has a fee-simple; and to add all, or any contiguous vacancy, whether cultivated or otherwise. This warrant, as well as all others, must be executed, or renewed within the first six months from the time of granting, otherwise they are of no force or effect; and any vacant land added, if not paid for within two years from the date of the warrant, (agreeable to sundry proclamations published) will become subject and liable to the benefit of the first discoverer thereof. And hence the proclamation warrants take their rise, for they, and no other warrants, can legally effect lands thus circumstanced.

Warrants of Escheat, are only granted in instances where the original patentees, or persons claiming under them, have died seised in fee, intestate, and without heirs, of tracts of land heretofore granted, with liberty given of effecting, as well such originall tracts of Escheat, as any vacant land thereto adjoining. The composition money [is] payable, as in the above cases; with this distinction, that the quality of the escheat land, and improvements thereon, are more particularly described by the surveyor, and from such description the agent, or receiver-general, ascertains the real value of the land so escheated. The petitioner is entitled to one third of the full valuation of the escheat for the discovery; and the residue, together with any vacancy added, must be paid for, to entitle him to a grant. The fees and expences incidental to all these warrants are considerably more than in primitive surveys, and cannot be particularly ascertained till the whole business is compleated.

By an instruction from the Board of revenue, no certificate whatever can be patented, though every requisite be complied with, till it has lain three months in the office. The intention of this instruction is to give persons who might be injured by the operation of secret surveys, an opportunity of contesting such surveys by a caveat.

The land-office, and all offices respecting the proprietary's revenue, are, in a great measure, subject to the control of the board of revenue, which was established by the late Lord Proprietary. Upon a declaration of a caveat in the land office, if it should be dissatisfactory to the parties, they may appeal to the board of revenue, and have the matter reheard and determined by them.

7. Sizes of Planter Holdings

IT IS always surprising to begin a search for plantations in colonial land records and to end by discovering mostly family farms. Elaborate statistical studies of the patent records or the most casual examination of debt books (quit rent accounts) lead to the same conclusion: the common planting unit was a holding of 250 acres or less. The following list of patents signed at the April General Court of 1706 in Virginia has several instructive features. Like similar reports, required by the Board of Trade, this one shows numerous patents of 250 acres or less, a much smaller but still respectable number of patents from 250 to 500 acres, and a scattering of tracts between 500 and 1,000 acres. But then at the thousand-acre level and above, almost a dozen appear, two of them around 5,000 acres. These call for some notice. Nearly all these patentees bear names of famous families: Harrison, Bland, Corbin, Digges. Already the larger landlords had started on the road toward speculation. On the rent roll of 1704 the estates of 10,000 acres and above could be numbered on the fingers of one hand. Twenty-five years later each of half a dozen Virginians counted their acreage above 100,000. Virginia had no monopoly on such engrossers: they appeared in every colony. North Carolina was notorious. Maryland had the Carrolls and the Dulanys. For some of the larger patentees on the list for April 1706 these tracts were merely a beginning, the earliest accumulations on the rolling snowball. For many smaller patentees the plantations here listed were the family holdings for a generation at least.

SOURCE: Public Record Office, CO 5: 1315 (Library of Congress Transcripts). Transcripts of Crown-copyright records in the Public Record Office appear by permission of H.M. Stationery Office.

List of Patents Signed in April General Court, 1706

COUNTYS	NUMBERS OF ACRES	TO WHOM GRANTED
Surry	1000	Francis Clements
Ditto	50	Joseph Procter
Do.	580	Wm. Cocke
Do.	150	Tho: Bentley
Do.	1000	Benja: Harrison Esqr.
Do.	180	Tho: King
Do.	150	Wm. Rhodes
Do.	200	Nicho. Smith
Prince George	16	Richd. Bland
Do.	43	Richd. Bland
Essex	171	Edwd. Barrow
Do.	1234	Gawin Corbin
Do.	65	Tho: Merriweather
Do.	103½	John Harper
Do.	100	John Harper
Eliza. City	1½	Robert Taylor
Do.	274	Wm. Mallory
New Kent	1900	Dudley Digges
Do.	850	Roger Thomson
Henrico	1468	Charles Evans
Do.	570	Richd. Cocke Junr.
Princess Anne	447	John Carraway Senr.
Do.	176	Thomas Wiles
Norfolk	150	William Maund
Norfolk	45	Thomas Cherry
King & Queen	211	Jane King
Do.	1245	John Major
Accomack	500	Tully Robinson
Gloucester	335	George Billops
Nanzemd.	250	Wm. Parker
Isle of Wight	380	Nicho. Fulgham
Northampton	330	Tho: Smith
King & Queen	546	John Hurt
James City	130	Nazth. Whitehead
King Wm.	107	Orlando Jones
Prince Geo:	351	Robert Munford

COUNTYS	NUMBERS OF ACRES	TO WHOM GRANTED
Do.	405	John Anderson & Robtt. Munford
Do.	1973	Collo Robt. Bolling, Senr.
Essex	145	Thomas Corbin
King Wm.	1091	John Kimbro
Henrico	190	John Worsham
Eliza. City	120	Robt. Beverly
King & Queen	2763	Collo. James Taylor &c.
Henrico	5644	Richd. Bland
New Kent	300	David Holt Minor
Prince Geo:	4583	Benja. Harrison Junr.

8. The Landlord at Work

THE LAND speculators, who appeared in every one of the planting colonies not long after 1700, felt their way along at first. By mid-century they had discovered most of the techniques of turning their holdings to a profit. In these later years the business became highly sophisticated and, for shrewder heads, extremely profitable. Many landlords who later became large speculators began by simply leasing their wild lands. Leaseholders were far commoner in the planting colonies than we realize. Indeed for newly freed indentured servants, for instance, the lease provided almost the only opportunity to attain the rank of planter. Ordinarily, leases ran for a long term (the eighteen-year lease was common) or for the life of the tenant. One curious arrangement, the lease for three lives, named three persons—ordinarily the head of the household, his wife, and his oldest son—who were to enjoy the leasehold until the last of them died. Most leases bound the tenant to make specified improvements: he must clear so many acres of land, he must plant and tend a certain number of fruit trees, or he must construct a house of such and such dimensions. Thus at the expiration of the lease the landlord's property was enhanced in value by these capital improvements. Daniel Dulany had field agents to manage his leased properties. In later years he acquired some 75,000 acres of choicest western land, which he leased or sold in family-size plots to new immigrants. His western land operations made him one of the wealthiest men in Maryland.

SOURCE: *The Maryland Gazette*, April 8, 1729, and March 10, 1747.

Annapolis, April 7, 1729

I the Subscriber, have several Tracts of Land lying in *Prince George's, Baltemore,* and *Kent* Counties; which I am desirous to let for Years, or lives, upon moderate Terms. Mr. Gilbert Falconar in *Kent*, and Mr. *John Bradford* in *Prince George's*, will shew the Lands in these Counties to, and agree upon the Terms, with any who desire to take Leases, if it be inconvenient for them to come to me: And whatever Terms they agree upon, I hereby promise to confirm, in Form. I intend (God willing) to be at *Baltemore* County, next June Court; where Any that want Land there, may apply to me. I will take the Rent in Tobacco, Corn, Wheat, or other the Produce of the Land, which the Tenants can best spare, at the Price current, and give a reasonable Time for making necessary Improvements.

DANIEL DULANY

March 9, 1746/7

The Subscriber has a Tract of Land called Williamsborough, in Prince George's County, above Capt. John's, of 14 or 1500 Acres, to rent on the following Terms: The Tenants to pay no Rent, except the Quit Rents, for 2 Years; and 800 weight of good Tobacco in Cask, yearly after the Expiration of the 2 Years, for every hundred Acres; to leave the Land and Improvements in good Order, at the Expiration of the Term.

D. DULANY

9. The Speculator as Promoter and Developer

THE UNDERSTANDABLE *desire of land speculators to increase population, especially in the vicinity of their holdings, led them into operations not always associated with their type. Several of the larger speculators became active promoters of immigration. William Byrd II had, among his other holdings, a tract in southern Virginia which he estimated at over 100,-000 acres. He made repeated efforts to attract Swiss and southern Germans to the area as a nucleus of settlement by offering the first band of* colonists free land. His terms of sale for later settlers, while not unreasonable, were high enough to give him returns of triple or quadruple his initial investment. Byrd leaned toward the southern Germans because they did not drift away from the land they seated but remained and applied their superior agricultural skills to improving their farms. Daniel Dulany offered similar inducements to Germans who would make initial settlements on his western lands. Dulany set up his son to act as American agent for a Dutch merchant house which brought immigrants from the upper Rhine to the New World.

SOURCE: "Letters of the Byrd Family," *Virginia Magazine of History and Biography,* XXXVI, 353, 361–362. Reprinted by permission of the Virginia Historical Society.

Letter of William Byrd II to Mr. Ochs, His Swiss Correspondent

Virginia, July 1736

If you will send over one hundred families to be here by the first day of May next, I will make a present to them of ten Thousand Acres of land lying on or under the South branch of Roanoke. Besides the 10,000 acres of land I propose to give to ye first Colony, I have much more Joining to that, which I propose to sell at the price of £3 pounds current money, per hundred acres. And if it should lye much in your way to help me to Customers for it, I should be obliged to you. If I should fail in my Intention, of planting a Swiss Colony, in this delightful part of the World (which are the People of the Earth I wou'd choose to have) I must then seat my land with Scots-Irish, who crowd from Pennsylvania in such numbers, that there is no Room for them. We have already a pretty many of them settled on the River Gerando, which neither the Clymate nor Soil is comparable to the Lands upon the Roanoke River. After I have so often repeated to you the good opinion we have of the Switzers, you will not question any good Offices, I shall be able to do them. Especially when they shall come recommended from my old Friend.

Letter of William Byrd II to Dr. Zwiffler, His German
Correspondent

Virginia, December 20, 1736

SIR,
Several Months ago I wrote to Mr. Henrick Harger concerning the Land I have for sale upon Roanoke River, I could dispose of it

to Such men, but I chuse rather to have a Colony of Germans to settle that Frontier. I have a fine Tract of Land on the South Branch of Roanoke River, which I discovered when I ran the Line between this Colony & North Carolina, & have since purchased it of His Majesty. It contains in all 105,000 acres, besides the River, which runs thro the Length of it, & includes a large quantity of good Land within Roanoke, on both sides, so that no Land, can be better watered. It lyes in a mild & temperate Clymate, about 36½° where the Winters, are moderate and short, so that there will not be much trouble to maintain the Cattle. The woods are full of Buffalo's, Deer, & Wild Turkeys, & the Rivers abound with Fish and Wild Fowl. It lyes 40 miles below the Mountains, & is a very level Road from thence to water carrage. It is within the Government of Virginia, under the King, where Liberty & Property is enjoyed, in perfection & the impartial administration of Justices hinders the Poor from every kind of Oppression from the Rich, & the Great. There is not the least danger from the Indians, or any other Enimy, & all we know of War is from Hearsay. The quit-rents we pay to the King, are no more than Two Shillings for every Hundred acres, & our Assembly hath made all Forreign Protestants, that will come, & inhabit this Land free from all other taxes, for the Space of Ten years, reckoning from the year 1738. And Last winter the Parliament of England, past an Act, to naturalize all strangers that shall live seven years in any of the British Plantations, so that Expence will be saved. The happiness of this Government, appears in nothing more than in its haveing Gold & Silver enough to Supply its occasions, without the vexation of Paper mony. The People too are hospitable to Strangers, nor is there that Envy, and aversion to them, that I have observed in other Places. Besides all these Recommendations of my Land, there is the cheapness of it, which makes it convenient to poor People. If any Person or Number of People will purchase 20,000 acres in one Tract, they shall have it for Three Pounds the Hundred, of this Currancy. Who so ever will purchase under that Quantity, & above 10,000 acres, shall have it for Four Pounds the Hundred of our mony. But if they will buy under that quantity, & buy only smaller Tracts, they must pay five Pounds, the Hundred of our mony, Because of the Trouble of laying off such small quantitys. They will be at no charge about the deeds of Conveyance, because I have had printed a great number, and unless they will have them re-corded, when there will be a small Fee to the Clerk.

10. Lease Practices in the Planting Colonies

LEASEHOLDERS in colonial times had little of the stigma attaching to tenants and sharecroppers of later periods in American history. Even in the most prosperous areas of the planting colonies, leaseholders formed a surprising percentage of the population. Though the figures vary considerably among localities, a limiting case appears in one of the prime tobacco-producing counties of Maryland where over 50 per cent of all producers leased their plantations. One hundred acres, the optimum holding, gave the tenant planter ample fresh land for tobacco and a surrounding area of woodland for cattle and swine. The variety of arrangements for paying rents can be brought to a simple statement: nearly all landlords allowed tenants some rent reduction for the first years of tenancy. Occasionally an owner waived rent payments altogether for the initial years of the lease. Charles Carroll scaled his rents so that the tenant paid least while he cleared and put the plantation into full-scale production. Daniel Dulany frequently took his rents in produce, but Carroll carefully specified sterling money. Most leases spelled out in minute detail the terms of improvements, whether orchards, buildings, or fences. Charles Carroll had a lease form printed for his rentals of plantations on his manor of Carrollton, a ten-thousand-acre tract in Prince George's County.

SOURCE: Prince George's County Land Records, Liber BB #1, folios 179–180 (Maryland Hall of Records, Annapolis).

This Indenture made this twenty fifth day of March in the Year of our Lord one thousand seven hundred and forty-four between Charles Carroll of the City of Annapolis Esquire of the one part and Thomas Matthews on the other part witnesseth that the said Charles Carroll for and in consideration of the yearly rents and covenants hereinafter reserved hath demised, let, and to farm let and by these presents doth demise, let, and to farm let unto the said Thomas Matthews all that part of a Tract of Land called Carrollton lying in Prince Georges county between Monocasi and Potowmack which is included in the following meets and bounds [here follows a description of the land] containing one hundred acres together with all and singular the premises with the appurtenances to the said land belonging,

To have and to hold the said parcel of land and premises unto the said Thomas Matthews his heirs and assigns for and during the term of seventeen years and half from the date hereof fully to be compleat and ended, yielding and paying therefor unto the said Charles Carroll his heirs or assigns at his dwelling house on the twenty-fifth day of March and the twenty-ninth day of September yearly by even and equal portions during the first three years and half of the said term the sum of eight shillings and four pence sterling, and paying during the term of the next seven years by even and equal portions on the days aforesaid yearly the sum of sixteen shillings and eight pence sterling, and paying during the term of the next seven years by even and equal portions on the days aforesaid yearly the sum of one pound thirteen shillings and four pence sterling over and above quit rents due and payable to the Lord Proprietary half yearly during the term hereby granted and the said Thomas Matthews doth bind himself his heirs, executors, and administrators to pay unto the said Charles Carroll, his executors, administrators, or assigns during the term aforesaid the rents hereinbefore reserved and the rents and services due and payable to the Chief Lord of the Fee,

And the said Thomas Matthews doth agree that if the rents and services herein reserved shall at any time during the term aforesaid be forty days in arrear that then it shall and may be lawful for the said Charles Carroll, his executors, and administrators into the demised premises to reenter and the same to hold as in his former estate and the said Thomas Matthews for himself, his executors, administrators, and assigns doth covenant and agree to and with the said Charles Carroll his heirs and assigns to plant on the premises before the expiration of six years from the date hereof one hundred good young apple trees in a regular orchard each tree being distant at least forty foot and by replanting from time to time to keep up the said number of trees and to keep them well inclosed under a tight fence and in case of nonperformance the said Thomas Matthews for himself, his executors, administrators, and assigns doth covenant to pay unto the said Charles Carroll, his executors, administrators, or assigns the sum of six pounds sterling,

And the said Thomas Matthews for himself, his executors, administrators, and assigns doth covenant grant and agree to and with the said Charles, his executors, administrators, and assigns that neither he or his executors, administrators, or assigns shall lease out to any under tenant any part of the demised premises nor make or suffer to be made on the demised premises more than one plantation or farm and the said Charles Carroll for himself and his heirs doth covenant and agree to and with the said Thomas Matthews, his executors, administrators, and assigns and every of them by these presents that he the said Thomas Matthews his executors administrators or assigns paying the rents above reserved and the rents and services due and payable to the chief Lord of the Fee and performing the covenants reserved on the part of the said Thomas Matthews shall and may according to the true intent and meaning of these presents peaceably and quietly have hold occupy possess and enjoy the said parcel of land with all and singular the demised premises with the appurtenances without any let, trouble, or interruption of the said Charles Carroll his heirs or assigns or any other persons whatsoever lawfully claiming by, from, or under him their right title or interest during the term aforesaid,

Provided the land herein leased be laid out within the bounds and courses of Carrollton and that the same run not into any land heretofore leased to any other person and that the beginning thereof stand and bear from the beginning of the original survey of the land referred to as is herein expressed and the said Thomas Matthews his executors administrators and assigns doth covenant grant and agree to and with the said Charles Carroll, his executors, administrators, and assigns that he the said Thomas Matthews, his executors, administrators, and assigns shall and will during the term aforesaid keep the house and plantation in good order and tenantable repair and at the expiration of the term aforesaid deliver the same in like good order and tenantable repair,

And lastly the said Thomas Matthews doth for himself his heirs and assigns covenant to and with the said Charles Carroll his heirs and assigns that neither he the said Thomas Matthews his heirs or assigns shall at any time sell or destroy any timber on the premises nor apply any but to the necessary repairs and use of the demised premises.

In witness whereof the parties to these presents have interchangeably set their hands and affixed their seals the day and year first above written.

CHARLES CARROLL [Seal]

Sealed and delivered in the presence of
JOHN DARNALL
WILLIAM BARKER

11. The Great Plantations

THE STORY-BOOK plantation, symbol of the southern colonies, came later rather than earlier in the eighteenth century. Such establishments were a far cry from the common run of plantations, which could boast little more than a house of one or two rooms and a few cleared areas. Behind the great plantations lay years of prudent management. Seats of the wealthier planters, the squires, those grand places were not usually objects of traffic and did not often change hands. Certain characteristics of these largest establishments are obvious: (1) their self-sufficiency in foodstuffs, (2) their capacity to produce and process the staple crop, and (3) their dependence on servile labor. Not so obvious but of the utmost importance, another feature is suggested here only by the phrase, "a well accustomed mill." The country seats of the squires were small cogs in the mechanism of provincial commerce. The owners provided essential services for the commercial agriculture about them: merchandising, milling, land distribution, moneylending. Such nonplanting activities accounted for the affluence of the great planters as much as the tobacco their hands produced. The land here advertised for sale in reality consisted of three seats, two on the larger and one on the smaller tract. From either tract the owner might lease one or more small plantations of a hundred acres.

SOURCE: Virginia Gazette (Williamsburg), February 5, 1767. Reprinted in Ulrich B. Phillips (ed.), Documentary History of American Industrial Society (Cleveland, Ohio, Arthur H. Clark, 1910), I, 245–246.

To Be Sold on Reasonable Terms

Three thousand acres of land, in King William county, two thousand of which lies on the river Mattapony, about eight miles above West Point, and about four miles from Clairbourne's ferry; there are two handsome seats on the said two thousand acres of land, the one on which the subscriber lives has a very fine large and genteel brick house, two story high, with four rooms above and four below, with a fireplace to each room, a large passage, four fine cellars, and cellar passage, the work, as well done as any in this colony, all convenient out-houses, a well accustomed mill, a large apple orchard of Hughes's and white apples, about fifty or sixty acres of very good marsh, a large garden newly paled in, the situation and prospect very pleasant, and a great plenty of fish and wild fowl. The other is also a fine and agreeable situation, with a good dwelling-house and out-houses, with peach and apple orchards. These lands are very good for tobacco, Indian corn, wheat, oats, &c. has several fine places for meadows, and is in general exceeding level and well timbered, and in very good order for cropping, with plenty of tobacco houses, barns, Negro quarters, &c. The other thousand acres of land lies on the same river (Mattapony) about two or three miles above West Point, is extremely level and well timbered, and has belonging to it one hundred and fifty or sixty acres of very fine marsh, so firm, dry, and hard, that carriages of great burthen go on it, and is of the greatest advantage to stocks of cattle, hogs, &c. where numbers may be raised with little trouble and expense, and a ready market for them. This land, as well as the other, is exceeding good, and produces fine tobacco, corn, wheat, oats, &c. has several places for meadow, great plenty of fish and fowl, is in good order for cropping, and has tobacco houses, quarters, and other convenient houses. Any person inclinable to purchase may be shown these lands, and know the terms, by applying to

THOMAS MOORE

N.B. Large stocks of cattle, hogs, &c. with several blooded mares and plow horses, may be bought with or without the land.—T.M.

12. Advent of the Land Companies

JUST how profitable speculation had become by mid-century is demonstrated by the advent of a new combination—the land company—which dwarfed the individual and the small partnership. The Ohio Company prefigures the combinations of affluent planters, British merchants, and members of Parliament who united into pressure groups for the purpose of carving out princely domains on the frontier just before the Revolution. The Ohio Company included such Virginia families as the Lees, the Fairfaxes, the Nelsons, and the Washingtons, all anxious to profit on an unprecedented scale by obtaining tracts beyond the dreams of single speculators. They joined to their group John Hanbury, a prominent London merchant heavily involved in the Virginia and Maryland tobacco trade. Hanbury himself presented the petition, which requested a grant extraordinary in two particulars. The grant was, for the time, unusual in size—half a million acres in all. Moreover, the company bypassed the machinery of the colonial land system to go directly to the crown for a grant that would be free of quit rents for ten years. In supporting their petition the company combined as many persuasive arguments as possible: expanding trade, increasing crown revenues, securing the back country for the British Empire, and the like. The effort shows the new direction in which entrepreneurs were guiding land operations as the colonial period drew to a close.

SOURCE: Public Record Office, CO 5: 1327 (Library of Congress Transcripts). Transcripts of Crown-copyright records in the Public Record Office appear by permission of the Controller of H.M. Stationery Office.

To the Kings most Excellent Majesty in Council. The humble Petition of John Hanbury of London Merchant in behalf of himself and of Thomas Lee Esqr. a member of Your Majestys Council and one of the Judges of the Supreme Court of Judicature in Your Majestys Colony of Virginia Thomas Nelson Esqr. also a member of Your Majestys Council in Virginia Colonel Cressup Colonel William Thornton William Nimmo Daniel Cressup John Carlisle Laurence Washington Augustus Washington George Fairfax Jacob Gyles Nathaniel Chapman and James Woodrop Esquires all of Your Majestys Colony of Virginia and others their Associates for Settling the Countrys upon the Ohio and extending the British Trade beyond the Mountains on the Western Confines of Virginia —Most humbly Sheweth

That by the Treaty of Lancaster and also by Deed bearing date the 2d day of July 1744 the Northern Indians by the Name of the Six Nations (who Claim all the Lands West of Virginia and also to and on the Waters of the Mississipi and the Lake by right of Conquest from several Nations of Indians who formerly inhabited that Country and have been Exterpated by the said Six Nations) did yield up and make over and for ever quit Claim to Your Majesty and Your Successors All their said Lands West of Virginia with all their Right thereto so far as Your Majesty should at any time thereafter be pleased to Extend the said Colony.

That most of the Nations of Indians West of the Mountains and upon the Lakes and the River Ohio have entered into an

Alliance with Your Majestys Subjects the Inhabitants of Virginia to send them British Goods and Manufactures as they inclined to Trade solely with Your Majestys Subjects.

That by laying hold of this Opportunity and improving this favourable Disposition of these Indians they may be for ever fixed in the British Interest and the prosperity and safety of the British Colonys be effectually Secured and which Your Petitioners are ready and willing to Undertake.

That Your Petitioners beg leave humbly to inform Your Majesty that the Lands to the West of the said Mountains are extreemely fertile the Climate very fine and healthy and the Waters of Mississipi and those of Potomac are only seperated by One small Ridge of Mountains easily passable by Land Carriage from thence to the West of the Mountains and to the Branch of the Ohio and the Lake Erie British Goods may be carried at little Expence and afforded reasonably to the Indians in those parts. In case the Lands to the West of the said Mountains were Setled and a Fort Erected in some proper place there for the protection and Encouragement of Your Petitioners and others Your Majestys Subjects in Adventuring their persons and fortunes in this Undertaking In which if Your Petitioners meet with that success they have the greatest reason to expect It will not only be made the best and strongest Frontier in America But will be the means of gaining a vast Addition and encrease to Your Majestys Subjects of that rich Branch of the Peltry and Furr Trade which Your Petitioners Propose by means of Settlement herein after mentioned to carry on with the Indians to the Westward of the said Mountains and on the said Lake and Rivers and will at the same time greatly promote the Consumption of Our own British Manufactures, enlarge Our Commerce, increase Our Shipping and Navigation and extend Your Majestys Empire in America and in a short space of time very considerably encrease Your Majestys Revenue of Quit Rents, as there is little room to doubt but that when this Settlement is once begun by Your Petitioners but that a great number of Foreign Protestants will be desirous of Settling in so Fertile and delightfull a Country under the just and Mild Administration of Your Majestys Government specially as they will be at little more Charge than the Transporting themselves from their Native Country—

That your Petitioners for these great and national Ends and purposes And in Order to improve and extend the British Trade amongst these Indians and to Settle these Countrys in so healthy and fine a Climate and which are Your Majestys undoubted Right have Entered into Partnership by the Name of the Ohio Company to Settle these Countrys to the West of the said Mountains and to carry on a Trade with the Indians in those parts and upon the said Lakes and Rivers But as effecting the same and more especially the Erecting a sufficient Fort and keeping a Garrison to protect the Infant Settlement will be attended with great Expence.

Your Petitioners who are the first Adventurers in this beneficial Undertaking which will be so advantageous to the Crown in point of Revenue, to the Nation in Point of Trade and to the British Colonys in point of Strength and Security most humbly pray that Your Majesty will be graciously pleased to encourage this their said Undertaking by giving Instructions to Your Governor of Virginia to Grant to Your Petitioners and such others as they shall admit as their Associates a Tract of Five hundred Thousand Acres of Land betwixt Romanettos and Buffalo's Creek on the South side of the River Aligane otherwise the Ohio and betwixt the two Creeks and the Yellow Creek on the North side of the said River or in such other parts to the West of the said Mountains as shall be adjudged most proper by Your Petitioners for that purpose and that two hundred Thousand Acres Part of the said Five hundred thousand Acres may be granted immediately without Rights on Condition of Your Petitioners Seating at their proper expence a hundred Familys upon the Land in Seven Years the Lands to be Granted free of Quit Rent for Ten Years on Condition of their Erecting a Fort and Maintaining a Garrison for protection of the Settlement for that time Your Petitioners paying the usual Quit Rent at the Expiration of the said Ten Years from the date of their Patent—and Your Petitioners further pray that Your Majesty will be graciously pleased to send Your said Governor a further Instruction that as soon as these two hundred thousand Acres are Settled and the Fort Erected That three hundred thousand Acres more residue of the said Five hundred Thousand Acres may be granted to Your Petitioners adjoining to the said Two hundred Thousand Acres of Land so first Granted with the like Exemptions and under the same Covenants and to give all such further and other Encouragements to Your Petitioners in this their so usefull and publick an Undertaking as to Your Majesty in Your great Wisdom shall seem meet.

And Your Petitioners will ever Pray.—
JOHN HANBURY

13. Protest Against Inequities

EVERY COLONIAL land system had some room for inequity. Surveyors and judges were not unmindful of the political leverage in the hands of wealthy squires who selected the best vacant lands for their estates. Some speculators entered into informal understandings with officials of the land systems that must have seemed close to conspiracy to defraud the common man of his rights. Occasionally a surveyor or a judge abused his position beyond the endurance of the community and brought down on himself the collective ire of the freemen. One such instance in Virginia finally reached the ears of the Board of Trade, when the neighbors of Major Thomas Swan severally preferred petitions to Governor Francis Nicholson protesting Swan's way of handling their request for surveys of vacant land. Whatever William Halleman's petition lacks in literary polish, it makes up in forthright presentation and sturdy determination to have justice done.

SOURCE: Public Record Office, CO 5: 1315 (Library of Congress Transcripts). Transcripts of Crown-copyright records in the Public Record Office appear by permission of H.M. Stationery Office.

To his Excelency fra Nicholason esqr. her Matys Lt. & Governor of Virginia. William Halleman most Humbly presenteth That on the 20th of November last your pitishener sent a setificate of Rits to Majr. Tho Swan desireing him at the very time that yr Excellency proclameation gave him permishon to take entryes to enter for your petishener a sartun parsell of land on the south side of the main black water swamp as in the said Entry is more full Exprest notwithstanding the said Swan hath uterly refused to make any entry for the said land for your petishoner but hath taken upon him to dispose of the same by way of entry to own [one] William May which your pitishoner Conseves to be beyond the power lodgged in him the surveyor to dispose of her Myties land soe by your pitishoner clamed withour your Excelensy advise and direction therein and most humbly pray your Excelency to give such orders and derecions therein for the releife of your Pitishener as to your great Wisdom shall sem met

Your most humble sarvent
WM HALLEMAN

december the 14th 1702

III

The Labor Base

THE MOST widely held misconception about the planting colonies concerns the prevalence of slaveholding. In the years immediately before the Revolution the slave population stood at its peak, both in proportion to total population of these colonies and in absolute numbers. Yet even for those years the simple model of masters and slaves describes only a part of the planting families. In the Chesapeake, oldest of the staple colonies, fewer than half of the families owned slaves on the eve of the Revolution; and an astonishingly large number of these families had three or fewer bondsmen. Turn back a hundred years to the last quarter of the seventeenth century, and you find that Negro slaves formed a small fraction of the population. The conclusion is inescapable: in the first century of the planting society the staggering labor of clearing, building, and cultivating was expended by free whites or by indentured servants, chiefly from Britain.

Planting families without bond labor have been equated with the yeomanry of England, and the image clashes with simple models of the plantation economy. Nevertheless, they formed easily half the population at the end of the colonial period, and in the decades before about 1720 they constituted an overwhelming majority. They were men of small estates living on family farms, and their labor accounted for the capital formation and production that brought the planting society to its fullest flower. Often illiterate and almost never given to writing, they left no literary memorials. When they are visible at all, it is through the eyes of unsympathetic witnesses. William Byrd viewed them with distaste. No one sang their praises. Travelers or commentators, when they notice the yeoman at all, speak of him in passing, usually with some reference to his rustic manners, his backward husbandry, or his drab surroundings. In all likelihood these small producers chafed under their condition and aspired to higher estate, but they were bound to the lower—except for those who had unusual qualities of foresight and drive.

The demand for labor—for extra hands—brought to the colonies, first from England and later from the Continent, thousands of servants, whose indentures or bonds could be purchased by planters. Commentators viewed the system of indentured servitude with varying degrees of approval, from Alsop's rhetorical enthusiasm to Jones's mild distaste. Doubtless few "colonists in bondage" truly enjoyed their terms of servitude, but unquestionably they helped solve the planters' need for labor and when free they became planters in their own right—at the bottom of the scale to be sure—thus adding to the productive labor force of the colonies.

The other source of bond labor was the Negro slave. The history of Negro slavery in the planting domain reaches back to 1619 when a Dutch trading vessel brought a cargo of black slaves to Virginia. In the words of one governor, planters loved Negroes as bondsmen for life. But high cost and problems of supply kept the number of slaves small throughout the seventeenth century. By various means the colonists encouraged importation of slaves around the turn of the century. In South Carolina the beginnings of rice culture made Negro slavery seem a necessity, and forty years later colonists in Georgia demanded the end of the prohibition on slaveholding.

Testimony on the productivity of slave labor is equivocal. The economics of the subject cannot be reduced to a mere statement of the number of barrels of rice or hogsheads of tobacco a prime fieldhand could produce. Slavery became institutionalized, with all the complications of nonproductive years and nonproductive uses of slave labor. It is striking that two thoughtful Virginians felt that slavery was undesirable; yet neither of them showed real concern about the morality of slavery. Their analyses assumed that chattel bondage had as just a place in the natural order as indentured servitude, which they did not question.

14. One View of Yeomen

THE FEW accounts of the small planter come from the pens of literate and sophisticated men who made no effort to conceal their distaste for this type. William Byrd's amusing comments give one view. But there is another perspective on the lowest economic stratum. These small producers were exceedingly numerous throughout the planting colonies, and in the mass they had both economic and political power. Each family brought only a small crop to market, but the sum total was great. Each of their votes counted in provincial elections exactly as much as each of those of their wealthier, and less numerous, neighbors. To be sure, their surroundings were dreary and their lives uneventful. But they had a kind of self-esteem that no grandee could overbear.

SOURCE: William Byrd, "A History of the Dividing Line," in John Spencer Bassett (ed.), The Writings of Colonel William Byrd of Westover in Virginia, Esquire. (New York: Doubleday, Page & Co., 1901), 44–45, 75–77.

[March 10, 1728] The Sabbath happen'd very opportunely to give some ease to our jaded People, who rested religiously from every work, but that of cooking the Kettle. We observed very few corn-fields in our Walks, and those very small, which seem'd the Stranger to us, because we could see no other Tokens of Husbandry or Improvement. But, upon further Inquiry, we were given to understand People only made Corn for themselves and not for their Stocks, which know very well how to get their own Living.

Both Cattle and Hogs ramble in the Neighbouring Marshes and Swamps, where they maintain themselves the whole Winter long, and are not fetch'd home till the Spring. Thus these Indolent Wretches, during one half of the Year, lose the Advantage of the Milk of their cattle, as well as their Dung, and many of the poor Creatures perish in the Mire, into the Bargain, by this ill Management.

Some, who pique themselves more upon industry than their Neighbours, will, now and then, in compliment to their Cattle, cut down a Tree whose Limbs are loaden with the Moss aforemention'd. The trouble wou'd be too great to Climb the Tree in order to gather this provender, but the Shortest way (which in this Country is always counted the best) is to fell it, just like the Lazy Indians, who do the same by such Trees as bear fruit, and so make one Harvest for all. By this bad Husbandry Milk is so scarce, in the Winter Season, that were a Big-belly'd Woman to long for it, She would lose her Longing. And, in truth, I believe this is often the Case, and at the same time a very good reason, why so many People in this Province are markt with a Custard Complexion.

The only Business here is raising of Hogs, which is managed with the last Trouble, and affords the Diet they are most fond of. The truth of it is, the Inhabitants of N. Carolina devour so much Swine's flesh, that it fills them full of gross Humours. For want too of a constant Supply of Salt, they are commonly obliged to eat it Fresh, and that begets the highest taint of Scurvy. Thus, whenever a Severe Cold happens to Constitutions thus Vitiated, tis apt to improve into the Yaws, called there very justly the country-distemper. This has all the Symptoms of the Pox, with this Aggravation, that no Preparation of Mercury will touch it. First it seizes the Throat, next the Palate, and lastly shews its spite to the poor Nose, of which tis apt in a small time treacherously to undermine the Foundation.

This Calamity is so common and familiar here, that it ceases to be a Scandal, and the disputes that happen about Beauty, the Noses have in some Companies much ado to carry it. Nay, tis said that once, after three good Pork years, a Motion had like to have been made in the House of Burgesses, that a Man with a Nose shou'd be incapable of holding any Place of Profit in the Province; which Extraordinary Motion could never have been intended without Some Hopes of a Majority. . . .

Surely there is no place in the world where the Inhabitants live with less Labour than in N. Carolina. It approaches nearer to the Description of Lubberland than any other, by the great felicity of the Climate, the easiness of raising provisions, and the Slothfulness of the People.

Indian Corn is of so great increase, that a little Pains will Subsist a very large Family with Bread, and then they may have meat without any pains at all, by the Help of the Low Grounds and the great Variety of Mast that grows on the High-land. The Men for their Parts, just like the Indians, impose all the Work upon the poor Women. They make their Wives rise out of their Beds early in the Morning, at the same time that they lye and Snore, till the Sun has run one third of his course, and disperst all the unwholesome Damps. Then, after Stretching and Yawning for Half an Hour, they light their Pipes, and, under the Protection of a cloud of Smoak, venture out into the open Air; tho' if it happens to be never so little cold, they quickly return Shivering into the Chimney corner. When the weather is mild, they stand leaning with both their arms upon the corn-field fence, and gravely consider whether they had best go and take a Small Heat at the Hough: but generally find reasons to put it off till another time.

Thus they loiter away their Lives, like Solomon's Sluggard, with their Arms across, and at the Winding up of the Year Scarcely have Bread to Eat.

To speak the Truth, tis a thorough Aversion to Labor that makes People file off to N. Carolina, where Plenty and a Warm Sun confirm them in their Disposition to Laziness for their whole Lives.

[March 26, 1728] Since we were like to be confin'd to this place, till the People returned out of the Dismal, twas agreed that our Chaplain might Safely take a turn to Edenton, to preach the Gospel to the Infidels there, and Christen their Children. He was accompany'd thither by Mr. Little, One of the Carolina Commissioners, who, to shew his regard for the Church, offer'd to treat Him on the Road with a Fricassee of Rum. They fry'd half a Dozen Rashers of very fat Bacon in a Pint of Rum, both which being disht up together, serv'd the Company at once for meat and Drink.

Most of the Rum they get in this Country comes from New England, and is so bad and unwholesome, that it is not improperly called "Kill-Devil." It is Distill'd there from forreign molosses, which if Skilfully manag'd, yields near Gallon for Gallon. Their molosses comes from the same country, and has the name of "Long Sugar" in Carolina, I suppose from the Ropiness of it, and Serves all the purposes of Sugar, both in their Eating and Drinking.

When they entertain their Friends bountifully, they fail not to set before them a Capacious Bowl of Bombo, so call'd from the Admiral of that name. This is a compound of Rum and Water in Equal parts, made palatable with the said long Sugar. As good Humour begins to flow, and the Bowl to Ebb, they take care to replenish it with Shear Rum, of which there always is a Reserve under the Table.

15. Two Commentators on Indentured Servants

INDENTURED servants provided the most readily available supply of labor in the early decades of the southern colonies. The indentures or bonds to serve for a term of years originated in various ways in the mother country; but once the servant arrived in the colonies, he was a salable commodity. Values of indentured servants varied according to length of term and capacity to work, for in the seventeenth century they were "hands." A fair estimate for a healthy servant with a five-year term of service would be somewhere between £10 and £18 sterling, considerably lower than the cost of a slave. Though a bondsman, the indentured servant had the benefit of laws prohibiting unduly harsh punishment and enjoining masters to provide adequate food and shelter. At the end of his period of servitude he was entitled to freedom dues, also specified by law or, as the expression went, by "the custom of the country."

Contemporaries appraising the system of indentured servitude give both friendly and hostile views. Both have validity. The human side exhibits the harshness and injustices, which come to light in court cases. From a different point of view indentured servitude appears an impersonal system supplying much-needed labor to planters and a start in a new life for the freed servant. Like so many other facets of the planting society, the institution of white servitude changed over the years. Planters demanded chiefly field labor in the seventeenth century. In the eighteenth, they put a premium on skills, both manual and intellectual. Early indentures were mainly English. After 1700, Germans and Scotch-Irish came in great numbers as servants.

SOURCES: George Alsop, A Character of the Province of Maryland (London, 1666), pp. 32–36, 38–39, 44. Reprinted in Clayton C. Hall, Narratives of Early Maryland, 1633–1684 (New York, Scribner's, 1910), 356–360. Hugh Jones, Present State of Virginia, 1724 (New York, Sabin's Reprint, 1865), 53, 54.

George Alsop

They whose abilities cannot extend to purchase their own transportation over into Mary-Land, (and surely he that cannot command so small a sum for so great a matter, his life must needs be mighty low and dejected) I say they may for the debarment of a four years sordid liberty, go over into this Province and there live plentiously well. And what's a four years Servitude to advantage a man all the remainder of his dayes, making his predecessors happy in his sufficient abilities, which he attained to partly by the restrainment of so small a time?

Now those that commit themselves unto the care of the Merchant to carry them over, they need not trouble themselves with any inquisitive search touching their Voyage; for there is such an honest care and provision made for them all the time they remain aboard the Ship, and are sailing over, that they want for nothing that is necessary and convenient.

The Merchant commonly before they go aboard the Ship, or set themselves in any forwardness for their Voyage, has Conditions of Agreements drawn between him and those that by a voluntary consent become his Servants, to serve him, his Heirs or Assigns, according as they in their primitive acquaintance have made their bargain, some two, some three, some four years; and whatever the master or Servant tyes himself up to here in England by Condition, the Laws of the Province will force a performance of when they come there: Yet here is this Priviledge in it when they arrive, If they dwell not with the Merchant they made their first agreement withall, they may choose whom they will serve their prefixed time with; and after their curiosity has pitcht on one whom they think fit for their turn, and that they may live well withall, the Merchant makes an Assignment of the Indenture over to him whom they of their free will have chosen to be their Master, in the same nature as we here in England (and no otherwise) turn over Covenant Servants or Apprentices from one Master to another. Then let those whose chaps are always breathing forth those filthy dregs of abusive exclamations, which are Lymbeckt from their sottish and preposterous brains, against this Country of Mary-Land, saying, That those which are transported over thither, are sold in open Market for Slaves, and draw in Carts like Horses; which is so damnable an untruth, that if they should search to the very Center of Hell, and enquire for a Lye of the most antient and damned stamp, I confidently believe they could not find one to parallel this: For know, That the Servants here in Mary-Land of all Colonies, distant or remote Plantations, have the least cause to complain, either for strictness of Servitude, want of Provisions, or need of Apparel: Five dayes and a half in the Summer weeks is the alotted time that they work in; and for two months, when the Sun predominates in the highest pitch of his heat, they claim an antient and customary Priviledge, to repose themselves three hours in the day within the house, and this is undeniably granted to them that work in the Fields.

In the Winter time, which lasteth three months (viz.) December, January, and February, they do little or no work or imployment, save cutting of wood to make good fires to sit by, unless their Ingenuity will prompt them to hunt the Deer, or Bear, or recreate themselves in Fowling, to slaughter the Swans, Geese, and Turkeys (which this Country affords in a most plentiful manner:) For every Servant has a Gun, Powder and Shot allowed him, to sport him withall on all Holidayes and leasurable times, if he be capable of using it, or be willing to learn. . . .

The Women that go over into this Province as Servants, have the best luck here as in any place of the world besides; for they are no sooner on shoar, but they are courted into a Copulative Matrimony, which some of them (for aught I know) had they not come to such a Market with their Virginity, might have kept it by them untill it had been mouldy, unless they had let it out by a yearly rent to some of the Inhabitants of Lewknors-lane, or made a Deed of Gift of it to Mother Coney, having only a poor stipend out of it, untill the Gallows or Hospital called them away. Men have not altogether so good luck as Women in this kind, or natural preferment, without they be good Rhetoricians, and well vers'd in the Art of perswasion, then (probably) they may ryvet themselves in the time of their Servitude into the private and reserved favour of their Mistress, if Age speak their Master deficient.

In short, touching the Servants of this Province they live well in the time of their service, and by their restrainment in that time, they are made capable of living much better when they come to be free; which in several other parts of the world I have observed, That after some servants have brought their indented and limited time to a just and legal period by Servitude, they have been much more incapable of supporting themselves from sinking into the Gulf of a slavish, poor, fettered, and intangled life, then all the fastness of their prefixed time did involve them in before. . . .

That which I have to say more in this business, is a hearty and desirous wish, that the several poor Tradesmen here in London that I know, and have borne an occular testimony of their want, might live so free from care as I did when I dwelt in the bonds of a four years Servitude in Mary-Land.

Hugh Jones

The Ships that transport these Things often call at Ireland to victual, and bring over frequently white Servants, which are of three Kinds. 1. Such as come upon certain Wages by Agreement for a certain Time. 2. Such as come bound by Indenture, commonly call'd Kids, who are usually to serve four or five Years; and 3. those Convicts or Felons that are transported, whose Room they had much rather have than their Company; for abundance of them do great Mischiefs, commit Robbery and Murder, and spoil Servants, that were before very good: But they frequently there meet with the End that they deserved at Home, though indeed some of them prove indifferent good. Their being sent thither to work as Slaves for Punishment, is but a mere Notion, for few of them ever lived so well and so easy before, especially if they are good for any thing. These are to serve seven and sometimes fourteen Years, and they and Servants by Indentures have an Allowance of Corn and Cloaths, when they are out of their Time, that they may be therewith supported, till they can be provided with Services, or otherwise settled. With these three Sorts of Servants are they supplied from England, Wales, Scotland and Ireland, among which they that have a Mind to it may serve their Time with Ease and Satisfaction to themselves and their Masters, especially if they fall into good Hands.

Except the last Sort, for the most Part who are loose Villains, made tame by Wild, and then enslaved by his Forward Namesake: To prevent too great a Stock of which Servants, and Negroes many attempts and Laws have been in vain made.

These if they forsake their Roguery together with the other Kids of the later Jonathan, when they are free, may work Day-Labour, or else rent a small Plantation for a Trifle almost; or else turn Overseers, if they are expert, industrious, and careful, or follow their Trade, if they have been brought up to any; especially Smiths, Carpenters, Taylors, Sawyers, Coopers, Bricklayers, etc. The Plenty of the Country and the good Wages given to Work-Folks occasion very few Poor, who are supported by the Parish, being such as are lame, sick or decrepit through Age, Distempers, Accidents, or some Infirmities; for which there is a numerous Family of poor Children the Vestry takes care to bind them out Apprentices, till they are able to maintain themselves by their own Labour; by which Means they are never tormented with Vagrant, and Vagabond Beggers, there being a Reward for taking up Runaways, that are at a small Distance from their Home; if they are not known or are without a Pass from their Master, and can give no good account of themselves, especially Negroes.

16. Problems of Obtaining Slaves

BY THE 1660's, when the Restoration in England opened the second wave of colonization which brought into existence the colonies south of the Chesapeake, Maryland had passed into a second generation and Virginia into a third. Planters in both colonies, hard-pressed for labor to clear and plant, had their own hands and those of indentured servants. Slaves were comparatively rare. The Royal African Company's monopoly of the slave trade kept prices beyond reach. Moreover, the company would not send its ships to the colonies without guaranteed sales. In 1664, Governor Charles Calvert alleged that he could not find even a hundred planters who could promise to take one slave a year:

I have endeavoured to see if I could find as many responsable men that would engage to take a 100 or 200 neigros every yeare from the Royall Company at that rate mentioned in your Lordships letter but I find wee are nott men of estates good enough to undertake such a buisnesse, but could wish wee were for wee are naturally inclin'd to love neigros if our purses would endure it.

Demand for Negro slaves set planters searching for expedients to stimulate importation. Merchant-planters like William Fitzhugh corresponded with New England slavers for small consignments. In the following document Fitzhugh is speaking of between fifteen and twenty-five slaves. Still planters connived with interlopers, who flouted the company monopoly and traded without license. In Maryland the assembly lent a hand by exempting provincially owned vessels from paying duties on slaves. Public and private efforts partially satisfied the demand for fieldhands and established Negro slavery on the Chesapeake as a permanent feature of the labor force.

SOURCES: William Fitzhugh to John Jackson, February 11, 1682/3 in Richard Beale Davis (ed.), William Fitzhugh and His Chesapeake World, 1676–1701 (Chapel Hill, N.C., University of North Carolina Press for the Virginia Historical Society, 1963), 127–128. "An Act to Encourage the Inhabitants," from the

Archives of Maryland, XXVI, 349–350. Partially printed in Elizabeth Donnan (ed.), Documents Illustrative of the History of the Slave Trade (Washington, D.C., 1930–1935), IV, 21. John Seymour to the Board of Trade, November 18, 1708, Public Record Office, CO 5: 716 (Library of Congress Transcripts). Partially reprinted in the Calendar of State Papers, Colonial: American and West Indies, 1708–1709, pp. 150–151; and in Donnan (ed.), ibid., IV, 21–23.

William Fitzhugh to John Jackson

MR. JACKSON

As to your Proposal about the bringing in Negros next fall, I have this to offer, & you may communicate the same to your owners & Employers, that I will deal with them for so many as shall amount to 50000 lb. Tobacco & cash which will be about 120 Hogsheads, under the Condition & at these ages and prices following, to say to give 3000 lb. Tobacco, for every Negro boy or girl, that shall be between the age of seven & eleven years old, to give 4000 lb. Tobacco for every youth or girle that shall be between the age of 11 & 15 & to give 5000 lb. Tobacco for every young man or woman that shall be above 15 years of age, & not exceed 24. the said Negroes to be delivered at my Landing, some time in September, next & I to have notice whether they will so agree some time in August next. And I do assure you & so you may acquaint them that upon your delivery & my receipt of the Negroes, according to the ages abovementioned, & that they be sound & healthfull at their Delivery. I will give such sufficient Caution for the payment of the Tobacco, accordingly, by the 20th. December then next following as shall be approved of. The ages of the Negros to be judged & determined by two or three such honest & reasonable men here, as your self shall nominate & appoint. The whole Sum of the Tobacco to be paid in the Compass of twenty miles perhaps not so remote. I am

Your W. F.

An Act to Encourage the Inhabitants of This Province to Adventure Their Shipps and Vessells More Freely Abroad to Import Rum, Sugar, Negroes, and Other Commoditys

Be it Enacted by the Queens most excellent Majesty by and with the Advice and Consent of her Majestys Governour Councill and Assembly of this Province and the Authority of the same that no Shipp or Vessell built in this Province whereof all the Owners shall be Actuall Residents of this province And that no Shipp or Vessell English or Plantation built purchas'd enjoy'd and held by Owners which are all Residents of this Province nor the Owners thereof shall be lyable . . . to pay the Duty of twenty shillings for every Negro imported mentiond in the aforesaid Act but from those Duties aforesaid And from the Duty of three pence per Tonn payable to the Governour of this Province for the time being shall be fully and Clearly exempted Any Former Act or Acts of Assembly to the Contrary notwithstanding.

And be it Enacted by the Authority aforesaid that such Owner or Owners of such Shipps or Vessells as aforesaid shall for entring and Clearing pay no more but half so much Fee to the Navall Officers and Collectors with whom they Enter and Clear as other Owners of other Shipps not belonging to the Inhabitants of this Province are lyable to pay Any former Act or Statute to the Contrary notwithstanding. . . .

John Seymour to the Board of Trade

I have pursuant to your Lordships' directions discurst many of the principall planters here, by whom I am inform'd that before the year 1698, this province has been supplyd by some small Quantitys of Negro's from Barbados and other her Majestys Islands and Plantations, as Jamaica and New England Seaven, eight, nine or ten in a Sloope, and sometymes larger Quantitys, and sometymes, tho very seldom, whole ship Loads of Slaves have been brought here directly from Affrica by Interlopers, or such as have had Lycenses, or otherwise traded there. At present the Trade seems to run high, there having been between six and seaven hundred Negro's imported hither this yeare 1708. And the Planters owne themselves obliged to the seperate Traders for these supplys having never had any from the Company, and now the price of Negro's begins to abate, as Wee suppose by reason of the plentifull Importation by the seperate Traders, so that 'tis the Opinion of most here, should the seperate Traders be totally excluded, the Company would take no better care to supply them with slaves, than they have formerly done, which would not only be a great Detriment to the planters, but also to her Majestys Revenue of so valuable Customes on Tobacco.

17. Productivity and Profits of Slaves

DEBATE on the economics of slavery has continued to the present and, like other big economic questions, is not easy to settle. Planters of the early eighteenth century were plagued by no doubts about the long run. They saw immediate possibilities for exploiting black labor, and they broke through the monopolistic controls on the trade. The first two decades of the century witnessed a transformation in the planting colonies from Maryland to South Carolina. A majority of the planting families still had no slaves, and fully half of the slaveholding planters owned three or fewer. But as never before slavery had won the day as a labor system enjoying economic and social sanctions which few disputed. The testimony of Splatt, Hunt, and Bradley to the Board of Trade leaves no doubt that, in their minds and in the minds of their relatives and customers in America, slavery was economically beneficial to the staple colonies.

SOURCE: Hearing before the Board of Trade, May 4, 1726, in *Journal of the Commissioners for Trade and Plantations, 1722–1728* (London, His Majesty's Stationery Office, 1928), 251–254. Reprinted here by permission of the Controller of Her Britannic Majesty's Stationery Office.

May 4, 1726, Post Meridiem

Present:—The Duke of Newcastle, Lord Viscount Townshend, Sir Robert Walpole, Mr. Chetwynd, Mr. Dominique, Mr. Pelham, Mr. Bladen, Mr. Ashe, Mr. Plummer.

Sir Robert Sutton and several other members of the Royal African Company, with Mr. Attorney General and Mr. Wills, their counsel, Mr. Humphry Morice and Mr. Richard Harris, with several other merchants of London in behalf of themselves and several other separate traders to Africa, as likewise Mr. Elton, Mr. Bootle, Mr. Brereton, Mr. Beacher and other gentlemen, who are concerned for the traders of Bristol and Liverpool, with Mr. Serjeant Darnell and Mr. Fazackerly their counsel, attending according to appointment. Mr. Beacher of Bristol read to their Lordships a paper containing his answer and observations upon the petition and representation of the Royal African Company, referred to this Board by His Grace the Duke of Newcastle's letter, mentioned in the Minutes of the 14th of the last month, which paper he left with the Board.

Mr. Fazackerly then proceeded in behalf of the separate traders from Bristol and Liverpool to Africa, and represented to their Lordships, that the said separate traders have an equal and natural right to trade to those parts. . . . Mr. Fazackerly particularized several branches of the Plantation trade, which depended upon it. Observing that ingrossing the African trade, would be in effect to ingross the Plantations, which he thought highly unreasonable, especially by a Company who, according to their own state of their affairs, seem to be in a broken condition, and therefore, as he thinks, they are not fit to be trusted with further priviledges. . . .

As to the number of negroes imported of late years into His Majesty's several Plantations, Mr. Humphry Morice acquainted their Lordships that there had not been time, since the Company's petition was communicated to the separate traders, for procuring certificates thereof.

Mr. Serjeant Darnell then called upon several witnesses present, who were respectively sworn and examined viz: Mr. Samuel Wragg, who informed their Lordships that he had been a trader to Carolina seventeen or eighteen years. That that country formerly had but very few negroes, but that now they employ near 40,000. That they now usually import 1,000 per annum, whereas they formerly imported none, and sometime 2 or 300. That the Company never supplied the Province with any on their own account, except by a particular contract with him, when they supplied him with 300 instead of 900. That the Province has been regularly supplied with what negroes they want by the separate traders. That the rice trade is increased from 1,500 to 25,000 barrels a year, and that the price is fallen from 45 shillings to 22 shillings per cwt. That the price of pitch and tar is likewise fallen from 50 shillings and £3 to 10 shillings or 11 shillings per barrel.

Mr. Splatt being likewise sworn, acquainted their Lordships, that he was lately come from Carolina, and that the Province was then very well supplied with negroes. That he never knew of any negroes brought into that country by the Company, excepting those contracted for with Mr. Wragg. That the Province annually takes about 1,000 per annum, and that they sell at about £30 or £35 sterling per head. That a negro can make £10 per annum clear profit to his master, and that he thinks the Colonies would be cheaper and better supplied by the separate traders than the company.

Mr. Perry, a Virginia merchant, being sworn, acquainted their Lordships, that by his accounts, that province is very plentifully supplied with negroes, and that there has been but very few of the Company's ships at Virginia since he has been concerned in trade, which is about three or four years.

Mr. Bradley being sworn, acquainted their Lordships, that he has been in the trade to Virginia above 20 years, and that the Province has been well supplied with negroes by the separate traders. That the labour of a negro produces about £15 annual duty to the Crown. That he believes negroes are cheaper now than they were formerly, but admits that there was formerly a duty of 5 per cent. laid on negroes, which made them dearer.

Mr. Hunt, a trader to Maryland, being sworn, acquainted their Lordships, that of late years there are annually imported into Maryland between 500 and 1,000 negroes. That the produce of a negro is about 4 hogsheads of tobacco per annum, and that the duty of 4 hogsheads is about £40 to £50. That the Province would take off more negroes, if they could get them, and that they would increase their trade. That Gambia, the Northern coast, and Angola, are the chief parts of Africa from whence Maryland is supplied. That he believes, if the trade was confined to a Company, negroes would be dearer, and the Province worse supplied. That the price of negroes had formerly been £30 or £40, but are now sold at £18, £20 and £25.

18. The Road to Wealth

South Carolina planters were least doubtful of the value of slavery to the economy, claiming that without Negroes rice production would be simply impossible. The author of American Husbandry supports the views of rice and indigo "millionaires," so called, with an elaborate calculation which shows how an initial investment of approximately fifty-five hundred pounds sterling could produce staggering profits. His planter is the true economic man, who holds himself to a modest scale of living and plows his profits back into additional slaves until after thirteen years his original 40 have increased to 556. By that time their com-

bined production gives the investor an annual income of twelve thousand pounds. In fact, investments never worked out in quite that way, and some planters came to disaster by overinvestment. Bankruptcies attest the widespread belief in such investment spirals.

Source: *American Husbandry* (London, 1775), I, 415–429. Text reprinted in Harry J. Carman (ed.), *American Husbandry* (New York, Columbia University Press, 1939), 292–303.

A Calculation Drawn from Actual Experience of the Expences, Produce, and Profit of a Considerable Plantation in This Province

[INITIAL INVESTMENT]

	£.	s.	d.
Freight and expences of six persons in one family from London to Charles Town, at 25	150	0	0
Freight of 10 tons, at 40s.	20	0	0
A couple of riding horses	40	0	0
Expences in searching for plantation	40	0	0
Patent fees of 10,000 acres	62	10	0
Building a house	200	0	0
——— offices, rice barns, etc.	700	0	0
——— tobacco house	20	0	0
——— saw-mill	500	0	0
Furniture	150	0	0
A canoe	50	0	0
Boats	30	0	0
Year's housekeeping	120	0	0
Implements of culture	200	0	0
20 horses at 5£	100	0	0
100 cows, at 30s.	150	0	0
Swine	20	0	0
Poultry	5	0	0
Wear and tear of implements	20	0	0

SUNDRY LABOUR EXCLUSIVE OF NEGROES

On cattle	15	0	0
100 acres of wheat at 20s.	100	0	0
40 acres of oats at 16s.	32	0	0

10 potatoes at 40s.	20	0	0			
Making hay	20	0	0			
Orchard and garden	15	0	0			
Sundries	30	0	0	232	0	0
40 negroes at 50£				2,000	0	0

EXPENCES ON DITTO

				£.	s.	d.
Overseer	1	0	0			
Cloth	1	0	0			
Sundry expences	0	10	0			
Province tax	0	3	0	86	0	0
				[sic]		

SEED

100 acres of wheat, at 8s.	40	0	0			
40 oats 8s.	16	0	0			
10 potatoes 8s.	4	0	0	60	0	0
Taxes; a quit-rent of 2s. per 100 shares				10	0	0
				4,965	10	0
Two year's interest at 5 per cent Interest				496	10	0
				5,462	10	0

[Here follows a tabulation of income and expenses for each of the twelve years following. With the above initial investment the planter goes into operation, investing his net profits in additional slaves every year, until by the thirteenth year he has 556 slaves and an annual income of approximately twelve thousand pounds.]

This profit is immense, and yet upon revision there do not seem any articles that are calculated too low. I am sensible that there are not any planters in South Carolina that lay up, or make an income of 12,000£ a year; but calculations of what may be done can take no cognizance of private conduct. There are some planters in this province who have more than 500 slaves; but very many causes may conspire to reduce their profit to a trifle, compared with what we see here: of 556 negroes only 40 were here supposed to be originally bought; all the rest were purchased annually by savings out of the preceding years products; but if instead of this the planter spends his income and borrows money to increase his stock of slaves, the profit at the end of the term will turn out very differently. The great profit here stated is entirely owing to an accumulation of profits for twelve years, the planter living upon £100 or £150 a year; but the event would prove very different if he takes at first a larger sum for his housekeeping; and if, instead of waiting the first twelve years patiently, in order afterwards to live more at his ease, and in almost any degree of affluence he pleases, if, instead of this, he frequents the taverns and concerts of Charles Town more than his plantation, any man may, without much sagacity, account for calculation turning out differently from real life. The only means of coming at useful truth in such cases as this, is to calculate what may be done—what such a business, under given circumstances, can produce: as to the caprices of individuals, they are beyond the power of calculation; but the profit here supposed will admit of great deductions in several articles which seem the lowest set in expence, and yet the remainder will turn out so considerable as to prove that planting in this country may be made the way to immense fortunes.

Now it must be apparent, at first sight, that no husbandry in Europe can equal this of Carolina; we have no agriculture in England—where larger fortunes are made by it than in any other country—that will pay any thing like this, owing to several circumstances which deserve attention. First, land is so plentiful in America, that the purchase of a very large estate costs but a trifle, and all the annual taxes paid afterwards for ten thousand acres, do not amount to what the window duty in England comes to on a moderate house; no land-tax, no poor's rate, no tythe. This plenty of land, which is at the same time so excellent, enables the planter to proportion his culture every year to the saving of the preceding, which is the grand circumstance in the increase of his fortune. . . . Secondly, the price of labour is incomparably cheaper in Carolina than in Britain: a negro costs 2£. 13s. per annum, to which if we add 2£. 10s. the interest of his prime cost, the total is only 5£. 3s. and as the common calculation is, that one English labourer does as much work as two negroes, a labourer to the planter costs 10£. 6s. a year, whereas to an English farmer he costs from 20£. to 25£. The difference is 125 per cent; this article therefore is very decisive in favour of the planter. Thirdly, we are to remember the peculiar circumstance of the prices of the planter's products and consumption: his crops, whether of indigo, tobacco, etc. are of a constant high value, the price rising, as it has done indeed for these fifty years; but his consumption of corn, meat, fruit, fowls, game, fish, etc. being chiefly the produce of his own plantation, stand him in little or nothing for his family. The common idea of the article game and fish is, that one Indian, or dextrous negroe, will, with his gun and netts, get as much game and fish as five families can eat; and the slaves support themselves in provisions, besides raising the staples mentioned above; but in Britain the servants kept in the house cost the farmers 12£. or 15£. a head in board, besides his own housekeeping being in the same articles as those he sells from his farm, so that he cannot in his sale have the advantage of high prices without being proportionably taxed in his consumption. This point in a large family is of great importance, and would, if calculated for a course of years, be found to amount to a very considerable sum. Besides this great superiority in respect of profit, the pleasing circumstance of being a considerable freeholder and living in a most plentiful, and even luxurious manner, is a point that has nothing among British farmers for opposition to it.

These three grand articles—plenty of good land free from taxes, cheapness of labour, and dearness of product sold, (together) with cheapness of that consumed—are, united, sufficient to explain the causes of a Carolina planter having such vastly superior opportunities of making a fortune than a British farmer can possibly enjoy.

19. Georgia Settlers Demand Slaves

GEORGIA settlers had no misgivings about either the economic or the social disadvantages of slavery. The trustees of Georgia had projected the colony as a land of opportunity for the poor and oppressed of England and the Continent. They made many rules to preserve their haven free from institutions and practices that had brought men into a distressed estate in Europe. Among these a provision prohibiting slavery met early opposition from the colonists. Within half a decade the first arrivals began petitioning for relaxation of the rule against slavery. Eleven years later the discouraged trustees removed the restriction.

Source: Petition of 117 inhabitants of Georgia to the Trustees, in *Collections of the Georgia Historical Society* (Savannah, Ga. Georgia Historical Society, 1842), II, 217–220. Partially reprinted in Donnan (ed.), *Documents Illustrative of the History of the Slave Trade*, IV, 590–591.

Savannah, December 9, 1738

To the Honorable the Trustees for Establishing the Colony of Georgia in America.

May it please your Honors: We whose names are underwritten, being all settlers, freeholders and inhabitants in the province of Georgia, and being sensible of the great pains and care exerted by you in endeavoring to settle this colony, since it has been under your protection and management, do unanimously join to lay before you, with the utmost regret, the following particulars. . . . Timber is the only thing we have here which we might export, and notwithstanding we are obliged to fall it in planting our land, yet we cannot manufacture it for a foreign market but at double the expense of other colonies; as for instance, the river of May, which is but twenty miles from us, with the allowance of negroes, load vessels with that commodity at one half the price of that we can do; and what should induce persons to bring ships here, when they can be loaded with one half the expense so near us; therefore the timber on the land is only a continual charge to the possessors of it, though of very great advantage in all the northern colonies, where negroes are allowed, and consequently, labor cheap. We do not in least doubt but that in time, silk and wine may be produced here, especially the former; but since the cultivation of the land with white servants only, cannot raise provisions for our families as before mentioned, therefore it is likewise impossible to carry on these manufactures according to the present constitution. It is very well known, that Carolina can raise every thing that this colony can, and they having their labor so much cheaper will always ruin our market, unless we are in some measure on a footing with them. . . . Your honors, we imagine, are not insensible of the numbers that have left this province, not being able to support themselves and families any longer. . . .

But we for our parts have entirely relied on and confided in your good intentions, believing you would redress any grievances that should appear; and now, by our long experience, from industry and continual application to improvement of land here, do find it impossible to pursue it, or even to subsist ourselves any longer, according to the present nature of the constitution; and likewise believing you will agree to those measures that are found from experience capable to make this colony succeed, and to promote which we have consumed our money, time and labor; we do, from a sincere regard to its welfare, and in duty both to you and ourselves, beg leave to lay before your immediate consideration, the two following chief causes of these our present misfortunes, and this deplorable state of the colony, and which, we are certain, if granted, would be an infallible remedy for both. . . .

The want of the use of negroes, with proper limitation; which, if granted, would both occasion great numbers of white people to come here, and also render us capable to subsist ourselves, by raising provisions upon our lands, until we could make some produce fit for export, in some measure to balance our importation. We are very sensible of the inconveniences and mischiefs that have already, and do daily arise from an unlimited use of negroes; but are as sensible that these may be prevented by a due limitation, such as so many to each white man, or so many to such a quantity of land, or in any other manner which your Honors shall think most proper.

20. William Byrd on Slavery

WILLIAM BYRD applauded the exclusion of slaves from Georgia. He was not concerned with the morality of slavery, but he was keenly aware of the consequences of a growing population of black labor. His letter to the Earl of Egmont, prominent trustee of the Georgia undertaking, is a classic expression of the eighteenth-century objections to Negro slavery: it degrades honest white labor, it impels slaveholders to cruelty, and it creates the danger of servile insurrection.

SOURCE: Letter of William Byrd to the Earl of Egmont, July 12, 1736, American Historical Review, I, 88–90. Reprinted in Donnan (ed.), Documents Illustrative of the History of the Slave Trade, IV, 131–132.

Virginia, July 12, 1736

Your Lordship's opinion concerning Rum and Negros is certainly very just, and your excludeing both of them from Your Colony of Georgia will be very happy. . . .

I wish my Lord we could be blesst with the same Prohibition. They import so many Negros hither, that I fear this Colony will some time of other be confirmed by the Name of New Guinea. I am sensible of many bad consequences of multiplying these Ethiopians amongst us. They blow up the pride, and ruin the Industry of our White People, who seing a Rank of poor Creatures below them, detest work for fear it should make them look like Slaves. Then that poverty which will ever attend upon Idleness, disposes them as much to pilfer as it dos the Portuguese, who account it much more like a Gentleman to steal, than to dirty their hands with Labour of any kind.

Another unhappy Effect of Many Negros is the necessity of being severe. Numbers make them insolent, and then foul means must do what fair will not. We have however nothing like the Inhumanity here that is practiced in the Islands, and God forbid we ever shoud. But these base Tempers require to be rid with a tort Rein, or they will apt to throw their Rider. Yet even this is terrible to a good naturd Man, who must submit to be either a Fool or a Fury. And this will be more our unhappy case, the more Negros are increast amongst us.

But these private mischeifs are nothing if compard to the publick danger. We have already at least 10,000 Men of these descendants of Ham fit to bear Arms, and their Numbers increase every day as well by birth as by Importation. And in case there should arise a Man of desperate courage amongst us, exasperated by a desperate fortune, he might with more advantage than Cataline kindle a Servile War. Such a man might be dreadfully mischeivous before any opposition could be formed against him, and tinge our Rivers as wide as they are with blood, besides the Calamity which would be brought upon us by such an Attempt, it would cost our Mother Country many a fair Million to make us as profitable as we are at present.

It were therefore worth the consideration of a British Parliament, My Lord, to put an end to this unchristian Traffick of makeing Merchandize of Our Fellow Creatures. At least the farther Importation of them in Our Colonys should be prohibited lest they prove as troublesome and dangerous everywhere, as they have been lately in Jamaica, where besides a vast expence of Mony, they have cost the lives of many of his Majesty's Subjects. We have mountains in Virginia too, to which they may retire as safely, and do as much mischeif as they do in Jamaica. All these matters duly considerd, I wonder the Legislature will Indulge a few ravenous Traders to the danger of the Publick safety, and such Traders as would freely sell their Fathers, their Elder Brothers, and even the Wives of their bosoms, if they could black their faces and get anything by them.

21. Peter Fontaine on the Baneful Hold of Slavery

No MORE concerned than Byrd with the ethics of chattel bondage, Peter Fontaine saw the ill consequences with a certain resignation. His tone approaches the apologetic: Virginians had no power to stop the traffic, and they had no adequate work force without slaves. Though he speaks of the "sin and curse" of slavery, he plainly has in mind undesirable consequences, not wrong inherent in the institution.

SOURCE: Ann Maury (ed.), Memoirs of a Hugenot Family, Translated and Compiled from the Original Autobiography of the Reverend James Fontaine (New York: G. P. Putnam, 1853), 348–353. Reprinted in part in Donnan (ed.), Documents Illustrative of the History of the Slave Trade, IV, 142–143, and Phillips (ed.), Documentary History of American Industrial Society, II, 29–30.

March 30, 1757

DEAR BROTHER MOSES:

Like Adam we are all apt to shift off the blame from ourselves and lay it upon others, how justly in our case you may judge. The negroes are enslaved by the negroes themselves before they are purchased by the masters of the ships who bring them here. It is to be sure at our choice whether we buy them or not, so this then is our crime, folly, or whatever you will please to call it. But, our

Assembly, foreseeing the ill consequences of importing such numbers amongst us, hath often attempted to lay a duty upon them which would amount to a prohibition, such as ten or twenty pounds a head, but no Governor dare pass such a law, having instructions to the contrary from the Board of Trade at home. By this means they are forced upon us, whether we will or will not. This plainly shows the African Company hath the advantage of the colonies, and may do as it pleases with the Ministry.

Indeed, since we have been exhausted of our little stock of cash by the war, the importation has stopped; our poverty then is our best security. There is no more picking for their ravenous jaws upon bare bones, but should we begin to thrive they will be at the same again. All our taxes are now laid upon slaves and on Shippers of tobacco, which they wink at while we are in danger of being torn from them, but we durst not do it in time of peace, it being looked upon as the highest presumption to lay any burden upon trade. This is our part of the grievance, but to live in Virginia without slaves is morally impossible. Before our troubles you could not hire a servant or slave for love or money, so that unless robust enough to cut wood, to go to mill, to work at the hoe, etc., you must starve, or board in some family where they both fleece and half starve you. There is no set price upon corn, wheat and provisions, so they take advantage of the nececessities of strangers, who are thus obliged to purchase some slaves and land. This of course draws us all into the original sin and curse of the country of purchasing slaves, and this is the reason we have no merchants, traders, or artificers of any sort but what become planters in a short time.

A common laborer, white or black, if you can be so much favored as to hire one, is a shilling sterling or fifteen pence currency per day; a bungling carpenter two shillings or two shillings six pence per day; besides diet and lodging. That is, for a lazy fellow to get wood and water, 19—16—3 current money per annum; add to this seven or eight pounds more and you have a slave for life.

IV

The Demands of Husbandry

ULTIMATELY production was the concern of planters in the southern colonies. The land system—distribution and terms of tenure—and the labor system—supply and employment of "hands"—came to bear on agricultural operations that fall under the general term "husbandry."

Agriculture of the planting domain has been judged harshly as wasteful, unprogressive, unimaginative. These value judgments, pronounced by contemporaries and later commentators, cannot be lightly dismissed. Still, before hastening to condemn, the student needs to understand the actual conditions of cultivation—just what the production of staples exacted from land and landlord. It is possible that planters made rational choices within the framework of their social values and economic imperatives.

From the beginning of staple production, southern agriculture was a commercial agriculture. The planter produced a cash crop for a market. Not only did he have to plant and cultivate, but he had to insure the marketability of his crop. In brief, he had to do some processing, to prepare the yield of his fields for transportation to a distant market, and to meet the demands of those commercial agents who conveyed his produce from barn to ultimate consumer. Tobacco had to be both cured and prized (packed), and indigo required even more exact processing, akin to manufacturing. The planter must have felt, as the seasons rolled by, more nearly like a prisoner of a system than like a free yeoman standing on his own acres, lord of all he surveyed and master within his small world.

In the first place, his cash crop made demands to which he could not remain deaf. None of the staples was an indigenous plant, inured to the climate and local pests of his province. True, certain types of tobacco and indigo were growing wild when settlers arrived, but these native species proved unsatisfactory commercially; and planters imported seed from the West Indies. An unseasonable frost could ruin a year's planting of tobacco or indigo. In time, producers settled into a rhythm of planting, tillage, and harvest—a slow pace measured by the annual calendar. As in agricultural communities everywhere, many planters were dominated by the spirit of routine. Doubtless the majority, particularly of the smaller producers, accepted without much question the pattern and its rationale, the conventional wisdom. Observers with more inquiring minds, natives and visitors alike, viewed the husbandry as unprogressive and unimaginative, and they said as much in their letters and treatises.

The anonymous author of *American Husbandry* summed up the agricultural practices and pronounced his judgments on shortcomings. Realizing that tobacco, rice, and indigo each required its own routine and skills, the author condemned what he felt to be waste, faulty land management, and mindless disregard of balance among possible crops. Although he is our most reliable and systematic witness on agricultural methods, his critique cannot be accepted without some reservations.

On the matter of soil mining, which distressed conservationists a century and a half later, two facts must be kept in mind. Colonial practices stemmed from a tradition made in England, a land of gentle, frequent rainfall and tough soils. In America, where the heavens crashed and emptied their contents in torrents on light forest mold of freshly cleared fields, tons of topsoil washed into the estuaries along the coast. The contour plowing of the twentieth century had no application for colonials, many of whom used only the mattock and hoe in cultivation. Moreover, deplorable as its results proved, soil mining—in the sense of cropping until fertility was depleted—was doubtless more economical in a period when land was cheap and labor scarce.

In the second place, experiment or deviation from established patterns could be expensive. Planters realized poignantly the disadvantages of one-crop agriculture, and throughout the colonial period their assemblies passed acts encouraging production of alternate commodities—hemp, flax, silk, wine; the statute books abound in such testimonials to the futility of political remedies. But most planters lived on what must have seemed to them a bare minimum, and few of these courted doubtful adventures. A handful of those who could afford the luxury of experimentation had moderate luck, and one heroine had a brilliant success. Eliza Lucas could afford the failures she experienced before she finally gave indigo to South Carolina as a second staple. In Maryland a similar venture in indigo paid off handsomely. We know just that and nothing more, except that indigo did not catch on in Lord Baltimore's palatinate and was not further cultivated there.

Once the great staples were established, a web of commercial arrangements and a system of labor grew up around them. All were integrated into an economy that provided a livelihood for the many and real fortune for a select few. Departure from approved ways exposed the planter to risks. Possible failure and consequent ridicule were penalties enough. But there was an even greater hindrance: he could not obtain credit to plant a crop that the neighborhood did not understand.

22. Cultivation of Tobacco

TOBACCO planters followed an artless pattern of planting, cultivation, and harvesting. Established in the earliest years of colonization, the routine required the simplest tools and easily acquired skills. Consequently tobacco culture lent itself equally well to family production by yeomen or to large-scale production on plantations worked by hands or slaves. In both cases, however, each stage of the uncomplicated tasks called for unremitting attention by the small planter or the overseer. In time, procedures settled into a routine that discouraged experiment and deviation from accepted ways. Thoughtful observers criticized some of the practices as having no basis in "rational principles." Yet a process of adaptation both to local geography and to world markets wrought slow changes. If the abundance of fresh land encouraged soil mining, the exigencies of marketing tobacco led some of the earliest legislation for regulating quality of the product.

SOURCE: American Husbandry, I, 222–248. Reprinted with notes by Carman (ed.), American Husbandry, 159–166, 176–177.

This plant [tobacco] is cultivated in all parts of North America, from Quebec to Carolina, and even the West Indies; but, except in Maryland, Virginia, and North Carolina, they plant no more than for private use, making it an object of such immense consequence. It was planted in large quantities by the Indians, when we first came to America, and its use from them brought into Europe; but what their method of culture was is now no longer known, as they plant none, but buy what they want of the English. Tobacco is raised from the seed, which is sown in spring upon a bed of rich mould; when about the height of four or five inches, the planter takes the opportunity of rainy weather to transplant them. The ground which is prepared to receive it, is, if it can be got, a rich black mould; fresh woodlands are best: sometimes it is so badly cleared from the stumps of trees, that they cannot give it any ploughings; but in old cultivated lands they plough it several times, and spread on it what manure they can raise. The negroes then hill it; that is, with hoes and shovels they form hillocks, which lie in the manner of Indian corn, only they are larger, and more carefully raked up; the hills are made in squares, from six to nine feet distance, according to the land; the richer it is, the further they are put asunder, as the plants grow higher and spread proportionally. The plants in about a month are a foot high, when they prune and top them; operations, in which they seem to be very wild, and to execute them upon no rational principles; experiments are much wanting on these points, for the planters never go out of the beaten road, but do just as their fathers did, resembling therein the British farmers their brethren. They prune off all the bottom leaves, leaving only seven or eight on a stalk, thinking that such as they leave will be the larger, which is contrary to nature in every instance throughout all vegetation. In six weeks more the tobacco is at its full growth, being then from four and a half to seven feet high: during all this time, the negroes are employed twice a week in pruning off the suckers, clearing the hillocks from weeds, and attending to the worms, which are a great enemy to the plant; when the tobacco changes its colour, turning brown, it is ripe and they then cut it down and lay it close in heaps in the field to sweat one night: the next day they are carried in bunches by the negroes to a building called the tobacco house, where every plant is hung up separate to dry, which takes a month or five weeks; this house excludes the rain, but is designed for the admission of as much air as possible. They are then laid close in heaps in the tobacco houses for a week or a fortnight to sweat again, after which it is sorted and packed up in hogsheads; all the operations after the plants are dried must be done in moist or wet weather, which prevents its crumbling to dust.

There are among many inferior distinctions of sorts, two [of which are] generally attended to, Oroonoko and sweet scented; the latter is of the finest flavour and most valued, growing chiefly in the lower parts of Virginia, viz. on James river and York river, and likewise on the Rappahannock and the south side of the Potomack: the Oroonoko is principally in use on Chesepeak [Chesapeake] bay, and the back settlements on all the rivers. It is strong and hot; the principal markets for it are Germany and the North.

. . .

One of the greatest advantages attending the culture of tobacco is the quick, easy, and certain method of sale. This was effected by the inspection law, which took place in Virginia in the year 1730, but not in Maryland until 1748. The planter, by virtue of this, may go to any place and sell his tobacco, without carrying a sample of it along with him, and the merchant may buy it, though lying a hundred miles, or at any distance from his store, and yet be morally sure both with respect to quantity and quality. For this purpose, upon all the rivers and bays of both provinces, at the distance of about twelve or fourteen miles from each other, are erected warehouses, to which all the tobacco in the country must be brought and there lodged, before the planters can offer it to sale; and inspectors are appointed to examine all the tobacco brought in, receive such as is good and merchantable, condemn and burn what appears damnified or insufficient. The greatest part of the tobacco is prized, or put up into hogsheads by the planters themselves, before it is carried to the warehouses. Each hogshead, by an act of assembly, must be 950 lb. neat or upwards; some of them weigh 14 cwt. and even 18 cwt. and the heavier they are the merchants like them the better; because four hogsheads, whatsoever their weight be, are esteemed a tun, and pay the same freight. The inspectors give notes of receipt for the tobacco, and the merchants take them in payment for their goods, passing current indeed over the whole colonies; a most admirable invention, which operates so greatly that in Virginia they have no paper currency.

The merchants generally purchase the tobacco in the country, by sending persons to open *stores* for them; that is, warehouses in which they lay in a great assortment of British commodities and manufactures; to these, as to shops, the planters resort, and supply themselves with what they want, paying, in inspection receipts, or taking on credit according to what will be given them; and as they are in general a very luxurious set of people, they buy too much upon credit; the consequence of which is, their getting in debt to the London merchants, who take mortgages on their plantations, ruinous enough, with the usury of eight per cent. But this is apparently the effect of their imprudence in living upon trust.

Respecting the product of tobacco, they know very little of it themselves by the acre, as they never calculate in that manner, and not many tobacco grounds were ever measured; all their ideas run in proportion per working hand. Some are hired labourers, but in general they are negroe slaves; and the product from the best information I have gained, varies from an hogshead and a half to three and an half per head. The hogshead used to be of the value of 5£. but of late years it is 8£. per head, according to the goodness of the lands and other circumstances. But [as for] the planters, none of them depend on tobacco alone, and this is more and more the case since corn has yielded a high price, and since their grounds have begun to be worn out. They all raise corn and provisions enough to support the family plantation, besides exporting considerable quantities; no wheat in the world exceeds in quality that of Virginia and Maryland. Lumber they also send largely to the West Indies. The whole culture of tobacco is over in the summer months; in the winter, the negroes are employed in sawing and butting timber, threshing corn, clearing new land, and preparing for tobacco; so that it is plain, they make a product per head, besides that of tobacco. . . .

There is no plant in the world that requires richer land, or more manure than tobacco; it will grow on poorer fields, but not to yield crops that are sufficiently profitable to pay the expenses of negroes, etc. The land they found to answer best is fresh woodlands, where many ages have formed a stratum of rich black mould. Such land will, after clearing, bear tobacco many years, without any change, prove more profitable to the planter than the power of dung can do on worse lands; this makes the tobacco planters more solicitous for new land than any other people in America, they wanting it much more. Many of them have very handsome houses, gardens, and improvements about them, which fixes them to one spot; but others, when they have exhausted their grounds, will sell them to new settlers for corn-fields, and move backwards with their negroes, cattle, and tools, to take up fresh land for tobacco; this is common, and will continue so as long as good land is to be had upon navigable rivers. . . .

A very considerable tract of land is necessary for a tobacco plantation; first, that the planter may have a sure prospect of increasing his culture on fresh land; secondly, that the lumber may be a winter employment for his slaves and afford casks for his crops. Thirdly, that he may be able to keep vast stocks of cattle for raising provisions in plenty, by ranging in the woods; and where the lands are not fresh, the necessity is yet greater, as they must yield much manure for replenishing the worn-out fields. This want of land is such, that they reckon a planter should have 50 acres of land for every working hand; with less than this they will find themselves distressed for want of room.

But I must observe that great improvements might be made in the culture of this crop; the attention of the planters is to keep their negroes employed on the plants and the small space that the hillocks occupy, being very apt to neglect the intervals; the expence of hoeing them is considerable, and consequently they are apt to be remiss in this work. Here they ought to substitute the horse-hoeing management, which would cost much less, and be an hundred times more effectual. The roots of the tobacco are powerful; they spread far beyond the hillocks, which ought to convince the planters that they should seed them there by good culture, but this is little considered. A few men once got into the use of a plough, invented in the back parts of Virginia, for opening a trench in the intervals, to kill weeds, loosen the earth, and carry the water of hasty rains off; but, from the carelessness of servants, the scheme came to nothing, though it promised better ideas in future. . . .

Before I quit these observations on this part of the husbandry of Virginia and Maryland, I should remark that to make a due profit on tobacco, a man should be able to begin with twenty slaves at least, because so many will pay for an overseer: none, or at least very few, can be kept without an overseer, and if fewer than twenty be the number, the expence of the overseer will be too high; for they are seldom to be gained under £25 a year, and generally from 30 to 50£. But it does not follow from hence, that settlers are precluded from these colonies who cannot buy twenty negroes; every day's experience tells us the contrary of this; the only difference is, that they begin in small; and either have no slaves at all, or no more than what they will submit to take care of themselves; in this case, they may begin with only one or two, and make a profit proportioned to that of the greater number, without the expence of an overseer. . . .

It is no slight benefit to be able to mix tobacco planting with common husbandry; this is as easily done as can be wished, and is indeed the practice of the greatest planters. A man may be a farmer for corn and provisions, and yet employ a few hands on tobacco, according as his land or manure will allow him. This makes a small business very profitable, and at the same time easy to be attained, nor is any thing more common throughout both Maryland and Virginia.

23. A Critique of Chesapeake Husbandry

MANY of the commentaries on agriculture in the planting colonies turn out in the end to be critiques of commercial agriculture. Compared with British farming, already in the eighteenth century stimulated by the progressives, American husbandry must have seemed mindless and wasteful. British farmers, however, produced for a different market—the growing urban communities. The assumption that staple producers ought to operate their plantations after British models underlies much of the criticism of American ways. Chesapeake planters do not pay enough attention to foodstuffs, they do not practice rotation, they have no regard for proper fencing, they mismanage their livestock, and in the management of woodlands they are sadly deficient. All of these observations are true enough. Visitor after visitor from Britain made the same remarks. But few of the critics seem to have grasped two essentials. Chesapeake planters raised a cash crop for a specialized market, and they rejoiced in rich, plentiful land, which they exploited for purposes of gain. Their object was neither the nice balance of the British farmstead nor the creation of a beautiful countryside. Unfortunately, in their pursuit of gain, planters were also establishing a tradition that left scars on the southern countryside.

SOURCE: American Husbandry, I, 262–277. Reprinted also in Carman (ed.), American Husbandry, 187–191, 197.

The wheat and other corn which is among these exports, are raised principally on old tobacco plantations that are worn out for that plant without the assistance of much manure. This is a point which deserves attention: exhaust the lands in these colonies as much as you will with tobacco, you will leave it in order for grain, which is a matter of great consequence to the settlers; since corn is there a very profitable article of culture, and upon the rich lands of this country will (even after tobacco) yield large crops with very little assistance from manure.

The usual course of the business has been the planters exhausting the land first with tobacco, and then retiring backwards with their negroes in quest of fresh land for tobacco, sell[ing] their old plantations to new comers who have not money enough to go largely into tobacco with negroes and therefore confine themselves

to common husbandry: and this is upon the whole very advantageous. Planters who meet with very rich fresh woodland, employ
themselves so eagerly on tobacco, as scarcely to raise corn enough
for their families, in which case their little neighbors are very useful
to them in selling it. This does not however seem to be good
management, as tobacco employs the negroes only in summer:
indeed, they may occupy the winter entirely in clearing fresh land.

Tobacco and hemp, I have already given as good an account of as
my intelligence will allow: but the common husbandry of these
provinces demands the same attention. Wheat they sow as we do
in England in October; about two bushels to an acre, which
produces seldom less than twenty-five; sometimes thirty-five and
forty. Rye they do not cultivate much, as their lands are in general
good enough to give them great crops of wheat. Barley produces
from twenty-five to forty bushels: oats from 30 to 60: pease from
10 to 60: Indian corn seldom less than 50 and sometimes 80.
Turneps and cabbages thrive in the greatest luxuriance, and produce crops far beyond any thing we know in Britain. Potatoes also,
with good management, yield, without any dung, crops much
greater than can in these islands be gained by the force of manur-
ing: yet are the farmers of these colonies most inexcusably negli-
gent in not giving these crops due justice, in properly preparing
their land, and keeping them during their growth free from weeds.
If the fertility of the soil and climate was well seconded by the
knowledge and industry of the planters, the crops would be much
greater than they are, and husbandry would prove the most profitable business in the known world. But the planters, who have the
power of being good cultivators of their fields, abandon them to
the overseers of their negroes, and pursue only their own pleasures
—and others, who may have more knowledge, have not the substance to make improvements: it is the same in Britain, and
probably in every other part of the world. The foregoing account of
the products of the crops of common husbandry is sufficient to
shew the immense profit which might be made by agriculture in
this country, if it was followed with understanding and spirit: for
want of these necessary ingredients, twice the land is run over to
produce that which half of it would be more than sufficient for,
under scientific management.

In the systems of crops generally pursued here, the farmers go
upon the bad ideas of their brethren to the northwards; they take
successive crops of corn, till the land will produce no more, then

they leave it fallow for some years, and serve fresh ground in the same manner: all the inconveniences which I have mentioned in preceding articles result from this, but the plenty of land seduces the planters to act thus contrary to their own interests. The summers in Virginia and Maryland being hotter than in Pennsylvania, this method must be still worse than there, because the land they leave in this manner fallow must be [left] the longer before it acquires a turf to support cattle: this shews the necessity, if the farmer would make the most of his grounds, of leaving the land in tolerable heart; and with the last crop of corn sowing grass seeds that are adapted to the climate. Good meadows are very scarce except where water can be thrown over them, a husbandry not practised near so much as it ought [to be].

In the management of their woods, they have shewn the same inattention to futurity with their neighbors; so that in the old settled parts of the provinces, they begin to fear a want of that most useful commodity, and would have felt it long ago, had they not such an immense inland navigation to supply them. The woods upon a tobacco plantation must be in great plenty for the winter employment of the slaves, or else the planter's profit will not equal that of his neighbors.

Their fences are extremely incomplete, and kept in very bad order: all their attention is to secure the tobacco-field, but the rest of the plantation is never in this respect kept in the order that it ought to be: this is another evil occassioned by plenty of land; they will grasp at more than they have money to cultivate, even upon the tobacco system, which requires plenty; and then they are forced to manage it in a slovenly manner.

Cattle might be made an article of great profit in these provinces: the planters are obliged, on account of manure, to keep great stock: but they are little attentive to make the most advantage of them, either in the raising manure, or in the management of the beasts themselves. The breed they think little of improving; and their treatment of their horses and oxen, for draft, is such as would move the ridicule of the smallest farmers in England. These are points which they mistakenly think of little importance, giving all their attention to the tobacco; but with better management these objects would prove so profitable as to shew that they demanded no less conduct than their principal crop. In the article of raising manure, particularly, they might make five times their present quantity, which would be attended with a corresponding increase of their staple in some of their fields; but for want of knowledge in this essential part of their business they lose much.

There are some improvements in the rural economy of these provinces which demand particular attention, for they would admit of more and greater profit than any of our other plantations. Under the article tobacco, I remarked several alterations which would render that culture much more beneficial; of which the effect of general good management, enabling them to keep more land under that staple, is an essential article, which would make a vast difference in the interest of Britain. No object in the American department is of such consequence; and this should induce the administration to take whatever measures that could be desired, in order to improve the agriculture of these provinces. Means might be invented which would introduce by degrees better ideas. . . .

On another occasion I remarked that the heat of the climate of Pennsylvania burnt up the grasses of the pastures, except the low tracts over which water was thrown; this is yet stronger with Virginia and Maryland, which are hotter than Pennsylvania; for this reason the culture of lucerne would, in these provinces, be attended with yet greater advantages: their tobacco and hemp demand far more manure than they can at present raise, no object therefore can be of greater importance than an increase of it. This is only to be brought about by keeping their cattle confined; if they were folded in yards, fed in the soiling way, on lucerne, they would raise greater quantities of dung than in any other method could be effected. This observation is also applicable to the winter food of cattle; the climate of these colonies is so mild that the cattle run out all winter; which, though an amazing advantage to the planter in many respects, is yet a preventive of raising manure, for it is the confinement alone of cattle which affords that. Upon this principle the planters here ought to attend to cabbages, turneps, potatoes, etc. as well as their brethren in the more northern settlements.

24. The Grand Staple of South Carolina

EARLY Carolina settlers tried both rice and indigo with indifferent success. During the first three decades, South Carolina planters produced some naval stores and such timber products as pipe staves for the West Indies. Their mainstay, however, was cattle raising, and by 1680 the area was on the road to becoming an important herding region. One observer asserted that an ox could be raised in Carolina with as little expense as a hen in England. A turning point came in the 1690's with the introduction of superior species of rice, followed by two decades of lively experimentation with planting methods. From the neighborhood of Charleston, rice culture expanded in both directions: to the Cape Fear region of North Carolina and later southward into Georgia. But the swamplands of South Carolina remained the staple-producing area par excellence. Continued experimentation with threshing and husking brought rice to the state described in the following account. By the time of the Revolution provincial planters were shipping over 100,000 barrels a year, each containing approximately 500 pounds.

SOURCE: *American Husbandry*, I, 391–397. Reprinted in Carman (ed.), *American Husbandry*, 275–279.

Rice is yet the grand staple production of South Carolina, and that for which the planters neglect the healthy, pleasant back country in order to live in the *Dismals* on the coast, for so the Americans justly call the swamps: rice can only be cultivated in land which lies so low as to admit of floating at pleasure, and all such lands in Carolina are necessarily swamps. The first business is to drain the swamp, in which work they have no particular methods deserving notice, or which are unknown in England. The moment they have got the water off they attack the trees, which in some swamps are very numerous; these they cut down at the root, leaving the stumps in the earth, and, oftentimes even the trunks and branches of the trees are left about the ground: some planters pile them up in heaps, and leave them to rot; others, more provident, cut them into lengths, and convert them into some sort of lumber. However they do not wait for the ground being cleared of them, but proceed to plant their rice among the stumps. In March, April, and May they plant; the negroes draw furrows eighteen inches asunder, and about three inches deep, in which the seeds are sown; a peck is sufficient for an acre of land: as soon as planted they let in the water to a certain depth, which is, during the season of its growth, repeated, and drawn off several times; but most of the growth is while the water is eight, nine, or ten inches deep on the land. The great object of the culture is to keep the land clean from weeds, which is absolutely necessary, and the worst weed is grass: if they would say a man is a bad manager, they do not observe such a person's plantation is not clean, or is weedy, but such a man is in the grass; intimating that he has not negroes enough to keep his rice free from grass. This is the only object till it is reaped, which is usually about the latter end of August or [the] beginning of September. Like wheat in England, they prefer cutting it while the straw is a little green, leaving it on the stubble to dry and wither two or three days in case the weather is favorable: after which they lay it up in barns or stacks, in the same manner as corn in Europe.

The next operation, as in other sorts of corn, is the threshing of it, after which it is winnowed, which was formerly a very tedious operation, but now much accelerated by the use of a windfan. When winnowed it is ground, to free the rice from the husk; this is done in wooden mills of about two feet diameter: it is then winnowed again, and put into a mortar large enough to hold half a bushel, in which it is beat with a pestle by negroes, to free it from its thick skin; this is a very laborious work. In order to free it from the flour and dust made by this pounding, it is sifted; and again through another sieve, called a market sieve, which separates the broken and small rice, after which it is put up in barrels, and is ready for market.

The reader must observe upon this account that the cultivation of it is dreadful: for if a work could be imagined peculiarly unwholesome and even fatal to health, it must be that of standing like the negroes, anckle and even mid-leg deep in water which floats an ouzy mud, and exposed all the while to a burning sun which makes the very air they breathe hotter than the human blood; these poor wretches are then in a furness of stinking putrid effluvia: a more horrible employment can hardly be imagined, not far short of digging in Potosi. We are told indeed that South Carolina breeds more negroes than she destroys, which is certainly a fact, as appears by the annual exportation of a few; but then let it not be imagined that it is in these properly denominated *dismals:* we are to remember that the proportion between the domestic and other negroes and planting ones, is as 30,000 to 40,000 when the total is 70,000; and we are further to remember, that many are employed on indigo where there are no rice swamps, and also in other branches of culture; all these with the 30,000, may increase greatly; but it does not from hence follow that those employed on rice do not decrease considerably, which is a certain fact, and it would be miraculous were it otherwise. It will therefore be no impropriety to determine that there must be a considerable expence in recruiting those negroes that are employed on rice and more considerable far than what attends others employed on tobacco, indigo, or indeed any plant not cultivated in a swamp.

As to the product of rice, it varies much, which is in proportion to the goodness of the swamp, and to the culture that is bestowed on it; the land it likes is the stiff, deep, miry mud on clay; the worst is the swamp with only a sandy bottom. Governor Glen observes that thirty slaves are a proper number for a plantation, and to be attended by one overseer. The common computation throughout the province is, communibus annis, that each working hand employed in a rice plantation, makes four barrels and a half of rice, each barrel weighing four or five hundred pounds weight neat; besides a sufficient quantity of provisions of all kinds for the slaves, horses, cattle, and poultry of the plantation for the year ensuing; the price 6s. 5d. per 100 lb. or from 1£. 5s. to 1£. 12s. per barrel; but since this gentleman wrote, the price has risen to 2£. and 4£. per barrel. We are told in an account written in 1710, that the product was from 30 to 60 bushels; suppose 40, and that a bushel weighed 65 lb.; at 450 lb. a barrel this would be 5 ¾ barrels to the acre; and at 2£. the amount would be 10£. 5s. . . .

But as this would by no means pay the planter for his other expences and his time, he makes a shift to save something in the articles of overseer and cloathing; but still the product from rice alone would be insufficient: the method in which they make it up is partly by lumber, as the slave will have time in the winter to thresh and dress more rice than he can plant in the summer; and consequently can spare it for sawing lumber. But yet rice would not answer were it not for other assistance; this is chiefly indigo. I before remarked that between the pine barrens and the swamps are dry slips of oak land, which is rich and good; on this they plant indigo, and to good profit, with this further advantage, that indigo requiring no winter work, the slaves may assist in manufacturing rice, and sawing lumber, etc.

25. Eliza Lucas Reintroduces Indigo

IN THE EARLY years of South Carolina, planters had experimented with indigo but had given up in the face of West Indian competition. Then, during the first decades of the eighteenth century; Jamaica turned from indigo to the more profitable production of sugar, so that English dyers had to depend on the French islands. About 1740 tensions with France threatened to cut off the prized "French Blue." In 1740, against this background, Eliza Lucas began her experiments with indigo and other West Indian commodities. Although she happened to be in the right place at the right time, her accomplishment was considerable, for her persistence in the face of failures succeeded in establishing indigo as a second staple in South Carolina. She savored the pleasures of both Charleston and country society, but she nonetheless rose at five o'clock in the morning to do the office work involved in managing three plantations.

SOURCES: Letter of Eliza Lucas to Mrs. Boddicott, May 2, 1740, in *Journal and Letters of Eliza Lucas* (Wormsloe, Ga., 1850), 6–7. Letter of Eliza Lucas to her father, 1743, in Harriott H. Ravenel, *Eliza Pinckney* (New York, Scribner's, 1896), 8–10.

Eliza Lucas to Mrs. Boddicott, May 2, 1740

DEAR MADAM,

I flatter myself it will be a satisfaction to you to hear I like this part of world as my lott has fallen here, which I really do. I prefer England to it tis true, but think Carolina greatly preferable to the West Indies, and was my Papa here I should be very happy. We have a very good acquaintance from whom we have received much friendship and Civility. Charles Town the principal one in this province is a polite agreeable place, the people live very Gentilie and very much in the English Taste. The Country is in general fertile and abounds with Venison and wild fowl. The Venison is much higher flavour'd than in England but 'tis seldom fatt.

My Papa and Mamas great indulgence to mee leaves it to mee to chuse our place of residence either in town or country, but I think it more prudent as well as most agreeable to my Mama and self to be in the Country during my father's absence. Wee are 17 mile by land, and 6 by water from Charles Town where wee have about 6 agreeable families around us with whom wee live in great harmony. I have a little library well furnished (for my Papa has left mee most of his books) in which I spend part of my time. My Musick and the Garden which I am very fond of take up the rest that is not imployed in business, of which my father has left mee a pretty good share, and indeed 'twas unavoidable, as my Mama's bad state of health prevents her going thro' any fatigue.

I have the business of 3 plantations to transact, which requires much writing and more business and fatigue of other sorts than you can imagine, but least you should imagine it too burthensome to a girl at my early time of life, give mee leave to assure you I think myself happy that I can be useful to so good a father. By rising very early I find I can go through with much business, but least you should think I shall be quite moaped with this way of life, I am to inform you there is two worthy Ladies in Charles Town, Mrs Pinckney and Mrs Cleland who are partial enough to mee to wish to have mee with them, and insist upon my making their houses my home when in Town, and press mee to relax a little much oftener than 'tis in my power to accept of their obliging intreaties, but I am sometimes with one or the other for three weeks or a monthe at a time, and then enjoy all the pleasures Charles Town affords. But nothing gives mee more than subscribing myself, Dear Madam

Your most affectionet and most obliged humble servant
ELIZA. LUCAS

Eliza Lucas to Her Father

HONORED SIR.

Never were letters more welcome than yours of February 19th and 20th, and March the 10th and 23rd, which came almost together, it was near 6 months since we had the pleasure of a line from you; our fears increased apace, and we dreaded some fatal accident befallen; but learning of your recovery from a dangerous Fitt of Illness has, more than equal'd, great as it was, our former anxiety. Nor shall we ever think ourselves sufficiently thankful to Almighty God, for the continuance of so great a blessing. . . .

The Cotton Guiney corn and most of the Ginger planted here was cutt off by a frost.

I wrote you in former letter we had a fine crop of Indigo Seed upon the ground and since informed you the frost took it before it was dry. I picked out the best of it and had it planted, but there is not more than a hundred bushes of it come up, which proves the more unlucky as you have sent a man to make it. I make no doubt Indigo will prove a very valuable commodity in time, if we could have the seed from the east Indies time enough to plant the latter end of March, that the seed might be dry enough to gather before our frost. I am sorry we lost this season we can do nothing towards it now but make the works ready for next year. The Lucern is yet

but dwindling, but Mr Hunt tells mee 'tis always so here the first
year. . . .

Mama tenders you her affections and polly joyns in duty with,
My Dear Papa

Your obedient and ever Devoted Daughter
E Lucas

26. Planting and Processing Indigo

South Carolina *planters enjoyed the luxury of a second, and highly
profitable, staple for approximately three decades before the Revolution
interrupted shipments to England. Those who grew indigo had both
handicaps and advantages. Their product commanded a lower price than
the best "French Blue"—at times no more than one third as much. Off-
setting the lower price, Carolina indigo enjoyed both a provincial bounty
and an English subsidy. Contemporaries estimated that indigo ranked
among the highest-yield products on capital invested; some thought
higher even than rice. Like rice production, indigo had its disagreeable
side: almost unendurable odors during the steeping process. Much more
than rice, production of an acceptable commodity for export depended
on skills and equipment not everyone possessed or could afford. Probably
the processing of harvested leaves was the weakest link in producing a
marketable dye. Efforts to raise quality to the standard set by the French
planters never succeeded. Nevertheless, exports rose to half a million
pounds and more a year in the decade prior to the Revolution. Even at
modest prices such shipments gave rise to a class of nouveaux riches
dubbed the "indigo millionaires."*

Source: *American Husbandry*, I, 400–406, 410–414. Reprinted in
Carman (ed.), *American Husbandry*, 281–290.

Indigo

There are three sorts of indigo cultivated in South Carolina—the
Hispaniola, the *Bahama*, which is a false Guatimala, and the
native; the two first are the most valuable, but the last is much
better adapted to the climate. The former is an annual plant, but
the wild sort, which is common in the country, is perennial; its
stalk dies every year, but it shoots up again next spring; the indigo
made from it is of as good quality as the other, the superiority of
that being owing to the superior fertility of the West Indies, and a

better climate for it. Dr. Mitchel reckons Carolina to have a great
inferiority to the West Indies in this article: his words are,

> Indigo thrives very indifferently either in the soil or the climate. In-
> digo is one of those rank weeds like tobacco, which not only exhaust
> the substance of the earth, but require the very best and richest
> lands, and such as have natural moisture in them; whereas the lands
> in Carolina are extremely poor and sandy, and have a barren dryness
> in them, which renders them very unfit to produce such a crop as
> this to any manner of advantage. This is planted by the French on
> the fresh woodlands of St. Domingo, which are too rich and moist
> even for sugar, and is intended to exhaust their luxuriant fertility, as
> we do with tobacco, in order to render them fit for that and other
> crops. They likewise cut it every six weeks, or eight times a year, and
> for two years together; whereas in Carolina it is cut but thrice; and
> as the land has not substance and moisture to make it shoot after
> cutting, and the summers are too short, the third cutting is but of
> little value, as even the second is in Virginia. Neither does the soil
> or climate seem to be fit to yield that rich juice which makes this
> dye in any plenty or perfection. The French and Spaniards make
> great quantities worth eight and ten shillings a pound, when the
> little we make in Carolina is not upon an average worth above two
> shillings, and a great deal has been sold for a shilling and less.

The proper soil for indigo is a rich, light, black mould, such as is
commonly found in the back country; but in the maritime part
they chuse oak land for it, not having the other; and as this is but
in small quantity, they are forced to cultivate their poor white
sands for indigo, which will not yield near the produce which all
cultivators of this commodity ought to be desirous of, and indeed
which will always be gained when proper land is employed for it.
The deficiency of common products appears from Governor Glen's
account, who asserts that 30 lb. an acre is all that is to be expected
in common, though good land will produce 80 [pounds].

Respecting this point of produce our accounts differ greatly, and
none yet in print are fully to be depended on; Mr. Glen's account
is that one acre of *good land* will produce 80 lb. and one slave may
manage two acres and upwards, and raise provisions besides, and
have all the winter months to saw lumber and be otherwise
employed: 80 lb. at 3s., the present price, is 12£. per acre; and 2½
acres at that rate amount to 30£. per slave, besides lumber, which is
very considerable: but I should observe, that there is much indigo
brought now from Carolina which sells in London for from 5s. to
8s. a pound, some even higher, though the chief part of the crop

may not yield more than 3s. or 4s.; this will alter the average price, but how much, is almost impossible to ascertain, as it depends on many unknown circumstances.

Before I quit this subject, I shall, in order to give the reader all the satisfaction possible, transcribe part of an account of the indigo culture, written in 1755, before the province had got so largely into the management of it as it has done since.

> Whoever plants indigo must be careful to have a good command of water in his reservoirs, which if in the center of his field, the better, to save time in bringing the plant when cut to the vats. We plant two kinds of land in Carolina, viz. high land and low land. The first is of the richest kind, overgrown with oak or hiccory, in which the plant will strike its roots very strait and deep. The second is either our river or inland swamps, where we plant rice, which lands are generally covered with huge oaks and cypresses; so that to gain a field of twenty acres in this country, as many noble trees must be felled and burnt as in England would bring many thousands sterling.
>
> This lowland is banked, ditched, trenched, and drained; but the soil must lie on a clay bottom, otherwise indigo will not thrive in it. In those lands the indigo roots spread horizontally, as in the high lands perpendicularly.

This idea of our author seems contradictory to the best accounts I have received, which confine the culture of indigo to hickory land and pine barren, as it requires a dry soil, though as fertile as possible, and consequently a swamp must be well *drained* indeed to be rendered proper for it: but what he says himself shews that the high land is the best for it, since all plants that strike a perpendicular root ought to be planted in a soil that will admit such roots shooting: a perpendicular root spreading horizontally proves clearly that the soil is improper; it meets with the wet retained by the clay, which prevents its running deeper. His situation within forty miles of Charles Town, prevented him, I suppose, from mentioning the deep black loams of the back country which are the only ones that will yield great crops of indigo. But to return,

> If the planter prefer the quality before the quantity of his indigo, he will be very careful to let his plants just blossom before he cuts; for the more young and tender the plant, the more beautiful will be the colour of the indigo, though it will not yield perhaps so much as if cut a week or two later; but what he loses one way he will gain another. On the contrary, if he lets his plants be overgrown, and

stand too long, he can never expect bright indigo. Indigo has a very disagreeable smell, while making and curing; and the fœces, when taken out of the steeper, if not immediately buried in the ground (for which it is excellent manure) breeds incredible swarms of flies.

The quality of indigo, when made, may be known by its brightness, closeness, and fine violet blue, inclining to copper. It is better by being kept some time, and ought to be light enough to swim on the water; the quicker and more it sinks, the worse its property. The very best and finest is of a fine lively blue, inclining to the violet; brilliant, of a fine shining colour when broke, and more beautiful within than without. A bushel of good indigo weighs about 50 or 55 pounds. The method for trial of its goodness is first to throw a cake into a glass of water, where will soon dissolve entirely if pure and well made, but if mixed with any foreign matter, the heterogeneous parts will sink. Secondly, another method is to burn it: good indigo entirely consumes away; but if adulterated, it will be discovered by the false mixtures remaining after the true indigo is consumed.

Our indigo making ceases with the summer. As soon as cold sets in, little or no fermentation can be excited. Double beating and labour is required; and in drying the indigo the cakes will break into powder. The first frosty night concludes our season. . . .

Besides rice and indigo, there are some other staples cultivated in Carolina, which though not of any great importance, yet demand a little attention. Cotton thrives well in the soil and climate, and though it is applied at present only to the home consumption of the province, yet it might certainly be extended so as to become a considerable article of exportation. Indigo and rice at present engross all their attention, not because they cannot raise other staples, but because these, while the demand is great, are more profitable. Cotton will hereafter be a valuable staple. Wine, silk, oil, hemp, and flax, are other products which in the back country may be cultivated in the greatest plenty; but this is not to be expected till the value of that healthy and fertile part of our southern colonies is better known and peopled.

It is an observation that demands much national attention that this very important colony should cultivate more staples than rice and indigo; it is of consequence that our colonies should not depend on one or two staples which are not of a permanent nature: indigo is the only article that ranks among the staples of South Carolina which is secure of a future sale, proportioned to the future increase of culture: I do not think that this is the case with rice, the sale of which depends very minutely on the plenty of corn in

Germany, the North, Spain, and Portugal; for in those countries is its principal sale; and the immense growth of the rice plantations in Carolina has of late years been much owing to a great failure in the corn crops of Europe, a failure which has been and is at present likely to prove of no slight advantage to this colony.

But silk, wine, oil, hemp, flax, etc. not forgetting tobacco, would, if well attended to in the back country, secure to this province those advantages which can only flow from the possession of various staples in common demand throughout the world; by which means, their profit would be greater than at present, and under the security of a much longer duration than ever will be found attendant on the exportation of rice.

Besides these articles, which are at present cultivated in large or small quantities (it is to be observed that every one of the products here mentioned are planted for private use, and in some in small quantities for sale), there are others which deserve mention; among these we find an exportation of the same fruits which are sent from Spain and Portugal, orenges, lemons, citrons, etc. pitch, tar, turpentine, rosin, naval timber, potash, sassafras, lumber, tallow, wax, leather, skins, etc. These articles which demand attention, and for which all endeavours should be tried to increase, since it is a number of staples upon which a flourishing colony depends for any permanency of prosperity: and this is the more necessary, as in proportion as the settlements extend, in such proportion does the benefit of lumber fall off; since the clearing of the woods pays the expence in lumber only in the maritime part of the province: now in plantations which are deprived of the advantage of lumber, there must accrue a certain loss, if a variety of staple be not introduced. Indigo and tobacco employ only the negroes the summer half of the year, and leave time sufficient for silk in the spring, an harvest in summer, and a vintage in autumn, besides the winter for other purposes, and completing the labour of other staples.

This object deserves the more attention, from the circumstance of the eagerness of the Carolina planters in the culture of their grand staples, rice and indigo, which is carried on to such a degree as to render them little solicitous about other objects. Herein they consult what we are to look for from all mankind—great attention to what they think their present interests and very little idea of futurity.This disposition which is so general among all people does very well for the present time and for present interests, but it will rarely, if ever, bring in those improvements, which in the introduction of new staples, become, in future, objects of the greatest importance. It is in such points as these that the attention of government is wanted, which can alone effect such material improvements by bringing people to an attention to other objects besides their immediate interests, by rewards and other encouragements.

The administration of our government has in these instances shewn too great an inattention to such important objects; our colonies have increased greatly in population and product, which has satisfied us, although the benefits received might have been greatly increased and been of such a nature as to promise a much longer and more secure duration than what they enjoy at present.

27. A Lady of Quality on American Husbandry

THE REACTION of *Janet Schaw to the scene in the planting colonies was total, and it was adverse. A native of Edinburgh, Scotland, she spent some weeks in the neighborhood of Wilmington, North Carolina, where her sharp eye took in an astonishing amount of detail. The unkempt countryside offended her sense of order and made her suspect the character of the people responsible for leaving last year's cornstalks standing in the fields and for constructing "zagly" fences. She found nothing to praise: neither implements nor methods. Though she understood how early settlers had acquired some of their practices, she could not comprehend the mindless continuation of them by their descendants.*

SOURCE: Evangeline W. Andrews (ed), *Journal of a Lady of Quality* (New Haven: Yale University Press, 1934), 162–164. Reprinted by permission of Yale University Press.

As I cannot produce my Authority, perhaps you may suspect I have none, but that it was coined for the present purpose, should you think so, I cannot help it, but should Gabriel himself assure the folks here that industry would render every thing better, they would as little believe him, as they would your humble servant. Truly the only parable they mind is that of the lily of the Valley, which they imitate as it toils not, neither does it spin, but whether their glory exceeds that of Solomon is another question, but certain it is they take things as they come without troubling themselves with improvements. I have as yet tasted none of their fruits, but am told that notwithstanding the vast advantages of climate, they are not equal in flavour to those at home in our gardens,—on walls which indeed they have no occasion for. Wherever you see the peach trees, you find hard by a group of plumbs so fit for stocks, that nature seems to have set them there on purpose. But her hints and the advice of those who know the advantages of it are equally unregarded. There are also many things that are fit for hedges, which would be a vast advantage, but these straggle wild thro' the field of woods, while every inclosure is made of a set of logs laid zagly close over each other.

On our arrival here the stalks of last year's crop still remained on the ground. At this I was greatly surprised, as the season was now so far advanced, I expected to have found the fields completely ploughed at least, if not sown and harrowed; but how much was my amazement increased to find that every instrument of husbandry was unknown here; not only all the various ploughs, but all the machinery used with such success at home, and that the only instrument used is a hoe, with which they at once till and plant the corn. To accomplish this a number of Negroes follow each other's tail the day long, and have a task assigned them, and it will take twenty at least to do as much work as two horses with a man and a boy would perform. Here the wheel-plough would answer finely, as the ground is quite flat, the soil light and not a stone to be met with in a thousand acres. A drill too might easily be constructed for sowing the seed, and a light harrow would close it in with surprising expedition. It is easy to observe however from whence this ridiculous method of theirs took its first necessary rise. When the new Settlers were obliged to sow corn for their immediate maintenance, before they were able to root out the trees, it is plain no other instrument but the hoe could be used amongst the roots of the trees, where it was to be planted, and they were obliged to do it all by hand labour. But thro' this indolence some of them have their plantations still pretty much encumbered in that way, yet to do justice to the better sort, that is not generally the case. Tho' it is all one as to the manner of dressing their fields, the same absurd method continuing every where. If horses were hard to come at or unfit for labour, that might be some excuse, but far is it otherwise. They have them in plenty, and strong animals they are and fit for the hardest labour.

28. An Understanding Observer of Primitive Husbandry

GOVERNOR ARTHUR DOBBS of North Carolina showed considerable understanding of the pioneering process and insight into the yeoman planter's psychology. Unlike Byrd, who saw only sloth and squalor, Dobbs saw industry and desire to make the most of difficult circumstances. The clearing and building that he described were far from tidy, and the husbandry he noted was both primitive and wasteful. But Dobbs did not set the yeoman against impossibly high standards. His comments to the Board of Trade resulted from an instruction to colonial governors directing them to vacate patents to land that was not brought to cultivation within a reasonable time. The instruction had a twofold aim: to prevent speculative holdings of large tracts of idle land, and to discourage bona fide planters from taking larger patents than they could cultivate. Dobbs argued that cultivation could be construed in more than one sense. He was willing to accept something rather crude as an earnest of enterprise to come, and he warned the board that local planters who made up the juries had much the same outlook.

SOURCE: Governor Arthur Dobbs to the Board of Trade, August 24, 1755, in *North Carolina Colonial Records* (Raleigh, 1887), V, 362–363.

The Instruction relative to cultivation I think cannot be put in execution with any prudence, and it is extremely difficult to know what true cultivation is, for different parts of the Province require different kinds if it be chiefly intended to clear the Land of Wood this they already do as far as it is advantageous for them, to have land to plant and sow for their consumption when they are at a distance from the Market; their method upon entering their Lands is to cut down, where they build their Loghouses, all the Trees fit for logs near their Houses, lest they fall upon them, as many are blown up by the rocks every season, and as many as will make rails to fence their corn field, the others within the Bounds of the field they bark for about 2 or 3 feet round the Tree, so that they die next year, and the Bark rots and falls off, and there is a forest of white dead Trees in the field, the anual burning of the woods has cleared all the dry grounds of underwood, so with one horse plow they pare of the upper swad of grass, and sow their Indian corn, etc. among these dead Trees, and use hows to earth and weed them, when plows can't do it sufficiently, in a few years these Trees rot, whilst they are taking in another field, and they proceed in the same manner. They then fell these dead Trees, and they break to pieces with the fall, and then they burn them, and all the black stumps of the Trees that are left 3 feet high remain in the field for many years before they decay, as many of these are red and black oaks and Hiccory, which won't split into rails, and are chiefly used as fire-wood, the bark being extremely good for tanning, tho' of little use here, but all extremely good for pot ash, the Hiccory I believe the best in the world, for its common ashes will blister like Spanish flies, and when put to it they use it as salt. It is rather a waste than improvement to loose all these Trees by being obliged to cut away more than is necessary to clear annually so many acres, and when they have cut down more than they can sow, and lay it down in grass, in 3 or 4 years it would be a young forest, and three times more expence to clear than old woods, for the small roots shoot up every year among their Corn, and if they are now howed away grow faster than the Corn, so that without keeping them down several years, they would grow up as close as in a nursery, besides on cutting away all the old Timber, they would soon want rails for their fences, and be at considerable expence in drawing rails for to repair them, as they soon rot, and often are burnt down, as they burn their woods notwithstanding their care to prevent it. These things considered and that the people are industrious and are desirous to cultivate as much as they can accomplish to turn to account, I think your Lordships will think it prudent to relax that Instruction, since no jury here would vacate the Lands that are occupied, the word cultivation being of so large a signification, as not often to determine what is or what is not cultivation, so that if the Patentee seats and occupies the Land, and pays his Majestie's Quit rents, I hope you will think that sufficient.

V

The Leaven of Enterprise

ALTHOUGH entrepreneurial activity was least familiar of the many aspects of the planting society, it was one of the most vital. Of course, clearing and cultivating the smallest tract of land required enterprise of the most persevering kind. But these labors have had their due: they were obvious and were commented upon. Planting, in the sense of producing staples, consumed the overwhelming proportion of hands and time—in a word, man-hours—in the southern colonies. And these man-hours devoted to planting produced the tangible goods—the tobacco, rice, and indigo—that were the cash crops of the area. But the web of arrangements for transporting, marketing, and financing the staples does not receive attention equal to its importance. In other words, the organization of commerce seems a paltry second fiddle in the ensemble. Yet the role of business, to bring a complicated matter to a single word, cannot be left out, even though its connotations do not seem quite harmonious with the stereotype of the planting order. For without business enterprise the southern colonies would have languished as little more than subsistence farming areas. And without the opportunities subsumed under the heading "enterprise," the chief avenue to personal wealth would have been eliminated.

The earliest business type to emerge in the staple colonies can hardly be distinguished from his fellows who tilled and harvested. Merchant-planter would be the most appropriate label to pin on him. By some means a planter acquired a petty stock of goods—textiles, hoes, and the like—which he sold, usually on credit, to his neighbors, marking the price down in his ledger. Thus was created a "book debt" for which the purchasers had to account. Such accounts were usually settled after the end of the planting season and most frequently in the cash crop of the debtor. The planter who "kept store" insensibly became a merchant, selling from an outbuilding on the premises and shipping the neighborhood produce, without ceasing his own agricultural operations. These he carried on with servants and, when he could afford them, Negro slaves. In almost every county a few men of this type appeared, most of them destined to small-scale business.

From modest beginnings a handful added new dimensions to their mercantile activities. They handled consignments of slaves, for example. In time, for some of them the merchant function became paramount, particularly as expanding cultivation increased commodity exports to a point where special skills and market contacts became essential to success. This was especially true of South Carolina, where an urban community like Charleston became a commercial center quite similar to northern seaport cities. Still, even Henry Laurens, who so much resembles his northern correspondents, held many acres and maintained his planting interests. Merchant-planters such as William Fitzhugh and William Byrd I lived at their countryseats, where their activities as merchants easily slip from sight behind the more attractive role of the great planter. Yet it would be fair to say that their wealth, which distinguished them from the more numerous small planters in their vicinity, came chiefly from nonplanting activities.

No simple model can encompass the variety among these great merchant-planters. They were individualists, strong of will, who worked out personal formulas for economic success. Many of them—perhaps most of them—began their ascent to affluence in country stores. Beyond that the formula varies. Some added land speculation to their interests; and for the shrewder heads, returns from this form of enterprise were handsome indeed. Others who acquired capital functioned as bankers for a community without banks: they dealt in exchange, and they extended credit in a country starved for capital. Still others found opportunities in one of the last pursuits associated with the planting colonies—manufacturing. Men of top wealth usually followed several of these gainful callings and occasionally all of them. They were in the fullest sense men of affairs.

It is striking that manufacturing yielded high returns on capital invested in several areas of the southern colonies. Unintentionally British statesmen made Carolina the largest producer of naval stores in the Empire. Bounties on naval stores were offered in the hope of developing a staple for New England, but exploiters of the southern pine forests, particularly in North Carolina, were the chief beneficiaries. Their tar, pitch, and turpentine entered Empire trade to compete as best they could with the Baltic products.

Easily the most profitable manufacture was iron. Both Virginia and Maryland had valuable deposits of ore situated near woodlands, where workmen made the charcoal used in smelting, and convenient to water transportation. Alexander Spotswood, William Byrd II, and the Washingtons took a lively interest in developing iron works in Virginia. Several companies operated in Maryland, most of them with English capital. One Maryland syndicate of five native capitalists established the Baltimore Iron Works, which proved in the end the biggest moneymaker of all. Each of the five partners subscribed £700 to commence operations. After three years the partners took respectable annual dividends but carefully plowed back into the business a substantial part of the profits. By the early 1760's each share was valued at £6,000. Such cases were exceptional to be sure, but their example was not lost on enterprising planters seeking opportunities for advancing their fortunes.

In fine, staple agriculture was the base of the planting economies of the southern seaboard. Planting pure and simple provided the market crop that supported households the length and breadth of the area. Most planters exemplified the truth of the aphorism "You can't get rich farming." The rewards of the highest order in wealth went to those who looked beyond their fields to the larger opportunities in commerce. They were planters, but they were also entrepreneurs.

29. A Virginian Begs for Trade Goods

ACQUIRING his initial stock of goods was only the first hurdle of the planter who yearned for the profits of commerce. No small producer had capital of his own, and few could command credit for even a modest inventory. All sorts of proposals and pleas crossed the Atlantic to British merchants, investors, and relatives. This semiliterate letter of Charles Rodes of New Kent County, Virginia, sounds the poignant note of a man once accustomed to better things. Rodes had come to Virginia some time before 1690 as an indentured servant—a slave for a time, he says. Now his own man and reformed to boot, he proposed a venture in merchandising to be underwritten by his cousin. He could urge few qualifications for business beyond the ties of kinship. Nor did he show much understanding of market conditions, besides the patent fact that King William's War had made trade goods scarce. The inventory of desirable goods that he submits illustrates local demand—everything except provisions. Whatever the response to his request, Charles Rodes did not move into the company of the great planter-merchants. He died a small landholder with a respectable personal estate.

SOURCE: Letter of Charles Rodes, New Kent County, Virginia, to Sir John Rodes of Barlborough, Derbyshire, November 9, 1693, in the Virginia Magazine of History and Biography, XXXIV, 362–364. Reprinted by permission of the editor of the Virginia Magazine of History and Biography.

Virginia, November 9, 1693

HONOURED SIR

After my humble service to your lordship, these are to acquaint you that I have sent too letters since I heard from you last which makes me not know what to wright; for I have had no answer from you nor your mother, but am doubtfull you are very indifferent whether you write to me or not. I have write to your mother conserning the proposall which shee and you write to me a bought in puting me into a way of trad which I should be bound to pray for you boath soe long as I live. Sir, have me in remembrance and forget not your owne kindred. I hope my cosen Anne will not forget me neither: Times is very hard in Virginia by Reason of the

warres; goods is extrodinary deare with us now; Tobacco may be
purchased for a small price; pray may [my] good Sir be not
bacward in speaking in my behalfe to your mother & I hope you
will not be backward your selfe toward me. You never gave me no
Account whether or no you ever Received any beaver skins or
Indian corne or noe, itt is Strange to me that you should bee so
unkind to your owne kindred. Tobacco may be purchased for a
penny per pound 25 Advance upon the goods; I hope you will send
me a venture this next year, for now is the time or never. I desire a
possitive Answer from you the next faule which is the time of the
ships coming to us for if you slip the oportuniti itt will be too yeare
be fore I can heare from you; goods suitable for our country is
everry thing all most but only provision. Nothing comes a miss. All
sorts of linen & wollen, shoes, and stockins Caster hatts & felt hatts,
soaps, nales knives sisers steel boxes, combes ivory & boane, gloves
for men & women, mens cloathes & womens gownes & pettecoats,
Reddy made Dimothys & blue linen, yarn, stockens, Thred, silk,
buttens, Pape foriting [paper for writing] Beds, blankets, ruggs,
anything for howse keeping, Pinn, brass or horn, or Ribbin the
most benefitiall of wollen cloath & linen cloath are these Carges,
serges & stripes frizes penestone & cotton cloath serges, verry little
broad cloath but what is.

Sir I hope you will not forgete me the next opportuniti which
present

Your humble servant & loveing kinsman
CHARLES RODES

[P.S.] I must confess its a greate troble to me to thing that there
should be so few of the Rodes left espeshally of the men kind &
that they should be so strange the one to another. Charity begins at
whome if you have any thing to spare itt sould be convenient to
think upon your owne kindred. I know verry well how strangers has
been looked upon by you and I that waited upon you & your Cosen
too should be no more regarded. I have not seen any of you this
seventeen yeare should be thus sleited; oh: Sir doe not forgete me.
Rather than I would come to be any troble or disgrace to you, I will
chuse to die upon the point of a sword. I am now a bought thirty
yeares of age & has gon through a greate dele of troble you may a
shure your selfe I shall be verry careful how I spend my time for
the futer. I am not so forgetfull but I shall ever Remember from

whome I came. I know our father was as much esteemed on as any belong to the family. Your farther loved him the best of all his cosens & was verry kind to us as long as hee lived, pore man, but I hope his soule is in heaven now; I am sensable the Rodes has all of them been extravagant to much. I remember all the transactions verry well and how things has been carreed ever since my father & your farther died. Your pore mother would a don well for me if there had not been too many constant beggars to troble her; you can not say that ever I have desired any thing of you since I left my native country for all. I weare a slave for a time. I was not cuzin you in the care with letters att every turne whilst I weare in that condition; for I know itt was my owne fault. Oh! Sir if I were to talke face to face with you would say that I have under gone more than all the Rodes that ever weare borne yete; but all wayes had a good heart for I scorned to be run down by aney one but this yeare the last winter I have been much afflicted with fevers & Ague blooding & sweetting which has brought my sperrits low & lower they will be if I heare not from you verry suddenly.

C.R.

30. Proposal for an Efficient Factorage

WILLIAM FITZHUGH negotiated from a position of strength. When in 1686 he wrote to Clayton and Richmond, Liverpool merchants, he was already a wealthy planter with a thousand-acre home place, large speculative holdings in wild land, twenty-nine slaves, a grist mill, and other valuable assets. Moreover, he had the acumen to understand how he and an English partner could reap maximum profits in two ways: by catching the early market and by efficient use of ships and crews. Fitzhugh's proposal for a factorage had a double appeal: he knew the market, and he had financial stability. The English merchant was essential to the tobacco trade: he furnished the credit, or a good part of it, and he dispatched the vessels for cargoes. Consequently, he risked a great deal in any venture. The minimum catalogue included bad debts, loitering ships, careless or incompetent masters, and uncertain return cargoes. Fitzhugh explicitly guaranteed a full return cargo, a loading in the shortest possible time, and the elimination of bad debts. Moreover, his personal service in arranging for return cargoes and in disposing of trade goods eliminated the merchant's need for a factor of his own in Virginia. Such a proposal only a planter of Fitzhugh's standing could make, and he was *able to exact his price. He would engage tobacco at 16s. 8d. per hundred pounds, or twopence per pound, a high figure in the 1680's. As a great planter, Fitzhugh could make the connection with an English merchant house a partnership, advantageous to himself as well as to the merchants.*

Source: Letter of William Fitzhugh to Thomas Clayton and Sylvester Richmond, Liverpool merchants, April 26, 1686, in Davis, *William Fitzhugh and His Chesapeake World*, 180–183. Reprinted by permission of the Virginia Historical Society.

April 26, 1686

Mr. Thos. Clayton

The Trade & Dealing that I have had with Mr. Greenhalgh this year, & by that means the Converse, Society, & acquaintance with Mr. Jno. Marshal is fully able, & I suppose will readily inform you, & whose persuasion & advice gives me the opportunity, & you the trouble, of this present Overture for a quick constant, & certain, & I believe advantageous trade, which in my apprehension you have not hitherto hit on. The offers I have to make are but of two sorts. The first for a quick and speedy Dutch Trade. The Second for a quick & sudden Trade, & Dispatch here, & a ready and full complyance to your whole Ships & Cargoe etc. As to the first which is the Dutch Trade, to have a Ship of 200 hogsheads burden here, the beginning of October, & to have her whole Loading ready by the 15th & on board by the 25th of the same month, that she might be dispatch'd out hence by the 27th at farthest, & by that means have the first & choice of the Crops here, & the first & best of the Dutch Market there. In which Design I myself would go a quarter, or rather than fail a third part, & engage to have my whole Loading ready by the 10th of October at farthest, but doubt your own remoteness, & the Indexterity of most of your own Factors in the Course of trading, you are now in, will not admit so ready a complyance, that Concern requires to be profitably carried on, shall be no more particular therein, but refer you to Mr. Marshal for a more ample account thereof.

As to the second, for a quick & sudden dispatch etc. I have this to offer, that at 16.8d. per Cent. I will engage to load a Ship of 200 hogsheads after this manner, that is, let her arrive any time by the 10th November, immediately upon her Arrival, after the 10th November aforesaid, I will give her Notes for one third of her

Loading, as soon as ever she has dispatch'd those Notes & got the Tobacco on board, I will then give her Notes for one third more of her Loading, & when she has dispatch'd them, I will then give her Notes for the remaining part of her full Loading, which beginning the 10th November, may be easily perfected & performed by the 28th of the same Month, & she ready to sail by the last of the same Month or beginning of December at farthest, Provided the Master be a diligent & Industrious man such a one as I can assure you Mr. Marshal is. And whatever Stay she makes for want of my Notes aforesaid, I will be bound to pay damage money per day to the full of these Ships Charge. The Conveniency of Tobacco & readiness of getting it on board, Mr. Marshall can pretty well inform you, & I must also tell you, that near one half thereof must come off my own Plantations, near a third more at one particular Rowling house or landing, & the whole remainder not above twenty miles distance, which in this Country is a very inconsiderable matter. The 200 hogsheads at 460 per hogshead, which will certainly be the smallest weight of forward Tobacco will amount to 92000 lb. Tobacco which at 16.8d. per Cent comes to £776.13.4 half of which money I would have deposited in such hands as I shall appoint, & the other half in goods sortable for this Country Cargoe, the money there deposited, I covet not the disposal of, nor the goods hither sent the possession of, till I have first answer'd my Contract per the Delivery of Notes for good Tobacco. Thus I have shortly touched at the Trade proposed, & if you doubt in any thing, I refer you to Mr. Marshal, with whom I have more amply discoursed thereof, & who is fully able to inform you, of my capacity and ability for performance, & the conveniency that will be in it. By this way of Trade, your Shop has no stay, your men a full employment, your goods a certain Sale, your Shop a certain Loading, your selves but one half the risque by reason one half of the money is left in England no fear of bad or slow Debts, no doubtfull careless or giddy Factors to overthrow the voyage & reckoning the charge of the Ships stay, upon the Course of Trade you are now in, & the bad debts left, the same quantity of Tobacco must needs stand you in a great deal more money, with all the hazards & disadvantages aforesaid.

What is before said for the forward Ships arrival & dispatch in November, I have the same to propose in the same Circumstances & under the same Conditions for the said ship or some other of the same burden, arriving here by the 10th of February, which may likewise be as suddenly dispatch'd, but the weights of the hogsheads round, cannot be expected so great as the first Ships, yet may & I believe will hold out 420 per hogshead which will amount to 84000 lb. Tobacco at 16.8d. per Cent is 700£, which money I would have likewise ordered as the former, half there deposited, & half in sortable goods as before, which latter Ship will be dispatch'd before most if not all your Ships, that come hither under the course of Trade you are now in. By this means one Ship will readily & easily perform two voyages in one year, the Seamen kept in full employment, & consequently deserve their wages, the Master busily & constantly employ'd & the Ship according to the intent of her building in a continuall Run, & as above all things in certainty, & what loytering time is made, (provided the Master be diligent and dextrous) at my charge, which I believe well weighed & considered, will deliver Tobacco in England at cheaper rates than it is now purchased, by those that make the cheapest Purchases. If this Method & proposal be acceptable, then care must be taken, to give me for the first year timely & speedy notice, either per the last September or the beginning of October at farthest, of the acceptance & continuance for at least three years, provided we live so long, but mortality must separate, because the Contract is personal. Now the Directions that I have to propose for your methods to take therein to give Mr. Hayward Notary publick near the Exchange London, notice thereof who will give me a speedy & sudden account of it, also to pay the money for the first and second Ship into his hands, or else to take such care that shall be to his satisfaction for the payment thereof, together with such Caution for the same as he shall approve of, after notice of the same from him, I shall be ready then to make my full complyance in Tobacco as aforesaid.

And for the goods sort then, as if you were to send a Cargoe to purchase your Loading there, (with this Caution that it well bought & with ready money) which is this way advantageous that in case of my mortality it may suitably fit you towards your Loading, according to your present Course of Trading, & will most properly suit me for my second Ship's loading & such sortable goods in your second Ship, will suitably prepare me for my Summers Market, & your next forward Ships punctual & ready complyance. To Mr. Nicholas Hayward I refer the security & receiving the money

payable in England as Aforesaid, & therefore expect the application & complyance first to be made to him, who will by the first opportunity & timely enough give notice thereof, to make preparation accordingly, for that reason do expect to receive my first letters from you sub Cover of his, & upon reception of them, shall take care to be provided pursuant thereunto And whereas I have set the sums of money according to the weights of Tobacco I guess at it, if the weights of the hogsheads fall short bulking may make up the complement, or if it overdoes your matter, order must be large enough, to make an allowance. Also as to the set times of 10th November & 10th February, for the giving the first Notes, I have set them down because of certainty, & as boundaries to the proceedings, but if the Ship arrives before either of the Times, immediately upon her Arrival she may keep going, & if I have sufficient Tobacco ready by me, she may get her Dispatch, but if for want of Seasons or Receipts, I should not have Tobacco to make complyance, I may then have as much time given me afterwards, before I pay damage money, as I gave them employment by my notes, before the prefixed time aforesaid. Also if the Ship by contrary winds or bad weather stay longer before her Arrival than the times prefix'd, I do not expect the exactness, of three times for the Delivery of Notes, but they may have Notes for the whole or the half, according to the time of her Stay immediately upon her Arrival. Now my Intentions being to make a full complyance of 400 hogsheads at the time, & under the penaltys, in the manner & method before mentioned, for the money & goods there expressed, if I have been defective in any thing that may relate to your interest, provided the main intention be kept good, upon notice thereof, I shall be ready to supply that defect or if I have been deficient in any particular relating to my own Interests, the main being kept whole, I expect the same Measure, for every particular perhaps may not occur to my memory, in a bargain of this weight & nature, but in the general, if you approve I will make a full & sure complyance, which is the needfull at present from
>   Worthy Gent: Your W.F.

31. Mercantile Connections of the Planter-Merchant

BEFORE the end of the seventeenth century, planters of the Chesapeake had developed a trade network strikingly similar to the New England pattern. The bilateral commerce with England—tobacco exports and commodity imports—was dominant; but traffic with the West Indies, the Madeiras, and the Iberian ports provided outlets for cereals and lumber and a source of supply for wine, sugar, and molasses. Chesapeake merchants carried on their business through overseas correspondents—usually, like John Thomas, merchants themselves who were not above shipping back goods of something less than first quality. William Byrd I complained strongly about short measure, inferior quality, and high prices. Not all the fault lay at the correspondent's door. Principal and correspondent alike stood at the mercy of ships and crews. Captains and crews packed goods into small holds with turnscrews, which damaged even tobacco and worked ruin on molasses and wine. Sailors, too, discovered all the tricks of pilfering petty amounts of almost every commodity carried by the light ships that were the rule in all the trades. Somehow the Byrds and the Fitzhughs managed to avoid open ruptures with correspondents, who were after all essential to the business in corn, wheat, flour, and pipe staves. While these trades to the Madeiras and the West Indies did not match the traffic in tobacco, still in good years they gave the planter-merchant a sale for commodities produced locally but not wanted in England. They also brought him welcome exchange and goods that he could mark up 100 per cent for retail sale.

SOURCE: Letters of William Byrd I, in The Virginia Magazine of History and Biography, XXV, 133, 361–362. Reprinted by permission of the editor of the Virginia Magazine of History and Biography.

Letter to Sadlier and Thomas, Merchants in Barbados,
Virginia, October 18, 1686

GENTLEMEN
Yours per Jacob Green & Wynne came safe to hand with what goods you sent. The white sugar very bad. I bought better here at 19s. & 6d. per cwt. The Limejuice was not worth one farthing, all the rest of the goods very dear, as all others affirme that had goods

from Barbados at that time. I doubt not but you will hear of itt largely from others. Our designe was to have sent the ship immediately backe to you with corne, pipe staves, etc. but the sickness of Wyn & all his men hath occasioned a long stay, & I fear lost his market. However I desire hee may be immediately dispatch'd from Barbados, least hee allso loose his Voyage to Maderas. His wheat is now all ready, & wee designe shall bee at one place ere his returne. I desire you to send mee the goods underwritten, but pray lett the rum mellasses & sugar bee all in Barrells, which are much fitter for sale here than great caskes. You will receive herewith from mee 12 hogsheads of corne 8 Barrells of flower & about 2500 pipe staves, what they will come to I know not. I beg pardon now, my family being very sicke with the Small Pox but hope to have oppertunity to write more largely hereby. If not, have desired Capt. Randolph to take my bills of Ladeing.

The negros proved well, but two of them have the Small Pox which was brought into my family by Negro's I received from Gambo; not else at present but with best respects take leave. Gentlemen,

Your Humble Servant
WM. BYRD

I desire these following Goods to bee sent on my particular Account. Vizt

1200 Gallons Rum
3000 S Muscavado Sugar
1 Barrell of white, about 2 s. lett it bee better then last year
2 Tun of Mellasses
1 Caske Limejuice, 2 lb. Ginger

Letter to John Thomas & Company in Barbados,
Virginia, February 20, 1688

GENTLEMEN

I beg pardon that I have not written to you ere this, my abode being so remote from shipping I rarely hear of any bound for your parts. The goods by the Effingham & Wyn I received; though very much damage by the last by reason of bad Caske. All the goods (especially the Melasses) thought by all extravagantly dear, the Caske very bad & small. Scarce one had above 25 Gallons in itt 8 of those to a tun is very hard. Others within a moneth of that had in great Caske 320 Gallons to the tun att the same price; though Small Caske are most convenient here for sale, yet no man would loose above 1/3 for that conveniency & those Small Sugar Caske with the other paid as much fraight as if they had been as big again; I find all persons here extreamly dissatisfyed with your proceedings. If Wynne had as he promised sold the Madera Wine for 4 or 5£ per pipe wee had all been well satisfyed, for wee should have been certain of our Losse, which now wee cannot guesse att. When the last was left, you were pleased to write, that you have 10 or 12£ per pipe. Though I thinke none of us clear'd what it cost at first in Madera's with the Freight, Now it was worth nothing, with you & if you had sent itt hither, wee doubt not, but wee could have doubled what you allowed us for the last, without the Charges upon itt. I have given Messrs Perry & Lane an Account of the bills Wynne charged on my Account & doubt not but they are allowed: I find it impossible for us to continue our Trade to your parts, otherways then by ready mony or bill of Exchange. Wynne is gone before Xmas for England if hee arrive safe I have left my part to Messrs Perry & Lane to send him hither again by Barbados or what else they may judge most convenient or the Least Losse, times being so unsettled wee know not what to resolve. God send all for the best. I hope when you have disposed of the Wine, you will send us an Account, that I may see in what state my particular is, & satisfy if I remain debtor on the Ballance I am, Gentlemen,

Your most Humble Servant
W.B.

Letter to Messrs Perry and Lane in London per My Lord Effingham, Virginia, February 28, 1688

GENTLEMEN

This serves onely to cover the inclosed bills of Exchange & acquaint you that his Excellency my Lord Effingham (by whom this comes) now goeing for England, I have charged bills of Exchange on you payable to his Lordship for 607£ 04 s. which I desire you to pay Accordingly and place to my Account as Auditor, allso to give mee Creditt for all the bills I send you on the said Account & not mix them with my private concernes. I hope to write more att Large by Captain Morgan who I expect will sail

herewith. Therefore with best respects now take leave I am,
Gentlemen,

Your Humble Servant
WB

32. Proof of Book Debts

COMMERCE and planting in the southern colonies rested on a tissue of debt. The planter-merchant transacted little business on a cash-and-carry basis. His customers among the smaller producers bought their necessities during the year, and he credited them on his ledger for each purchase against a settlement at the end of the season. These "book debts" were the subject of much legislation, of repeated acts designed to clear up misunderstandings of older laws or to eliminate abuses as they appeared. For many transactions the only record was the merchant's account book, and the only witnesses were the buyer and the seller. A Virginia law required merchants to have customers initial these entries or make their marks if illiterate, as a way of validating accounts. But no amount of legislation corrected every possible abuse or forestalled all disputes. So huge was this fabric of debt, and so essential was it to the exchange of goods and services, that every colony evolved a system for settling book debts. The North Carolina statute of 1756 has the features common to most colonial arrangements. This law provided for the manner of proving book debts, the time limits for bringing suit, and maximum sums collectable. Substantial debts were always secured by mortgages, bonds, and the like, but book debts were unsecured. Hence the importance attaching to legislation for proving such debt, which in total amounted to perhaps a third of all provincial indebtedness.

SOURCE: Act of 1756, Chap. IV, *The State Records of North Carolina*, XXIII, 440–442.

An Act for Ascertaining the Method of Proving Book Debts

I. Whereas Doubts have arisen upon construction of the Law now in Force, prescribing the Manner of proving Book Debts: For Prevention whereof for the future,

II. Be it Enacted, by the Governor, Council, and Assembly, and by the Authority of the same That in Any Action of Debt, or upon the Case, which hath been or shall be brought, where the Plaintiff hath declared, or shall declare upon an Emissit, Indebitatas Assumpsit, Quantum Valebant, or Quantum Meruit, for Goods, Wares, and Merchandises, by him sold and delivered, or for work done and performed, shall file his account with his Declaration; and upon the Trial of the Issue, or executing a Writ of Enquiry of Damages in such Action, shall declare upon his Corporal Oath, or solemn Affirmation (as the case may be) that the matter in Dispute is a Book Account, and that he hath no means to prove the Delivery of such Articles as he shall then propose to prove by his own Oath, or any of them, but by his Book and in that case, such Book shall and may be given in Evidence, if he shall make out, by his own Oath or Affirmation, that such Book doth contain a true Account of all the Dealings, or the last Settlement of Accounts between them, and that all the Articles therein contained, and by him so proved, were bona fide delivered, and that he hath given the Defendant all just Credits; and such Book, and Oath or Affirmation, shall be admitted and received as good evidence in any Court of Law, for the several Articles so proved to be delivered within Two Years before the said Action brought, but not for any Article of a longer standing; And where the Person who delivered such Goods, Wares, or Merchandises, or performed such Work and Labour, shall die, his Executors or Administrators may give his Book in Evidence, upon his or their making Oath, or Affirmation, that they verily believe the Account as there charged is Just and true, and that there are no Witnesses to his or their Knowledge, capable of proving the Delivery of the several Articles as he shall propose to prove by the said Book, and Oath or Affirmation, and that he found the Book so stated, and doth not know of any other or further Credit to be given than what is there mentioned; and such Book, and Oath or Affirmation, shall be admitted and received as Evidence for any Articles delivered within the time aforesaid.

III. But whereas it may be inconvenient and hazardous, by reason of bad Weather or Accidents, to carry Books of Accounts, great distances to Court, when a Copy of the Account, proved in the same Manner as by this Law, the Book is to be proved, may satisfy the Defendant as fully; Be it therefore Enacted, by the Authority aforesaid, That a Copy from the Book of Accounts proved in Manner hereinbefore directed, shall and may be given in Evidence in any such Action as aforesaid, and shall be as available as if such Book had been produced, unless the Defendant, or his

Attorney, shall give notice to the Plaintiff, or his Attorney, at the joining of the Issue, that he will require the Book to be produced at Trial; and in that Case, no such Copy shall be admitted, or received as Evidence.

IV. Provided nevertheless, That the Defendant shall be at Liberty to content the Plaintiff's Evidence, and oppose the same by other legal Evidence; and where the Defendant shall be an Executor or Administrator, his Testator or Intestate's Book, shall and may be given in Evidence against the Plaintiff's Book, where the Plaintiff is an Executor or Administrator, for such Articles as shall be proved in Manner aforesaid.

V. Provided also, That no Book of Accounts, although the same may be proved by Witness or Witnesses, shall be admitted or received as Evidence in any Action for Goods, Wares, or Merchandises delivered, or for Work done, above Five Years before the said Action brought; except in case of Persons being out of the Government, or where the Account shall be settled and signed by the Parties.

VI. Provided nevertheless, That no Plaintiff shall be at liberty to prove by his Book, and Oath or Affirmation as aforesaid, on the Trial of any such Action as aforementioned, any Article or Articles, the amount whereof shall exceed the Sum of Thirty Pounds, Proclamation Money.

VII. And for preventing a Multiplicity of Law suits, Be it further Enacted, by the Authority aforesaid, That in all cases where there are, or shall be mutual Debts subsisting between the Plaintiff and Defendant, or if either party sue, or be sued, as Executor or Administrator, where there are mutual Debts subsisting between the Testator or Intestate, and either Party, one Debt may be set against the other, either by being pleaded in Bar, or given in Evidence, on the General Issue on Notice given of the Particular Sum intended to be set off, and on what Account the same is due notwithstanding such Debts shall or may be deemed in Law to be of a different Nature; but if either Debt arose by Reason of a Penalty, the Sum intended to be set off shall be pleaded in Bar, setting forth what is justly due on either side; any Law, Usage, or Custom, to the contrary, in any wise notwithstanding.

VIII. And be it further Enacted by the Authority aforesaid, That one Act of Assembly made in the Thirteenth Year of his present Majesty's Reign, intituled an Act prescribing the Method of proving Book Debts, shall be and is hereby repealed.

33. Services of a Pioneer Merchant

EARLY Georgia produced no staples that matched tobacco, rice and indigo, but once slavery became legal, it adopted all three. After very few years rice and indigo moved to the fore, while tobacco languished in the face of Chesapeake competition. The business interests of Thomas Rasberry illustrate the accommodation of merchants to trade possibilities in the rapidly developing area of Georgia. He came to Savannah in 1751 or 1752, when traffic in rice and indigo could scarcely have kept him afloat. His early prosperity depended on his cultivation of the frontier trade, particularly the Swiss and the Germans, who sent him wax, butter, hides, corn, flour, and even some beaver. These products came down the river on barges and are carefully accounted for in his ledgers and letters, even to a half-bushel of corn paid to someone for blowing the horn as the boat progressed toward Savannah. Rasberry had the usual book debts; but by 1758, when his letter books begin, his business was maturing into more sophisticated dealings, with payments in bills of exchange after the manner of the adjacent Charleston trade orbit. His letters contain a wealth of detail on the kind of services merchants performed for their customers: keeping an eye on their overseers, settling their financial obligations, as well as supplying special articles they required. Like many prosperous merchants, Rasberry became a public man. He held several minor offices before his election to the Commons House of Assembly in 1758, a post he held until his death in 1762.

SOURCE: Letters of Thomas Rasberry, in the Georgia Historical Quarterly, XLI, 53, 161, 265, 391–392, 394.

Letter to John Smith, Planter,
March 8, 1759

SIR

Your new Overseer came to me two Days agoe and Desired me to inform you that he intends to quit your Plantation about the 20th of this Month as the Place is not at all agreeable to him and as he says doth not Answer his Expectation of it. I disired him to Consult Mr Bryan before he resolved on leaving your Service as I apprehended he was under some contract with you for a Time certain and also urged the Damage you might probably Sustain by his leaving the Plantation before you could procure an Overseer but he yet seemed to be Determined to return to Carolina as soon as possible.

Mr Bryan is now absent from his Plantation but as soon as he returns he shall be acquainted herewith.

As we could not get possibly a Boat to carry your Rice to Beaufort Mr Russell & I thought it proper to offer it to Mr MacKenzie of your Town who is Loading a Vessell for the W. Indies on Condition of its being replaced in Charles Town which he excepted. The Barrels were very light & he has returned 5 of them again on account of there Quality which is really very bad Rice tho I apprehend he may have taken some on Board of the same Quality unperceived.

Letter to William Thomson, English Merchant, May 24, 1759

SIR

By this Opportunity of our mutual Friend Mr Grey Elliott I hand you the 1st. of 4 setts of Bills [of] Exchange on your City amounting to one hundred three Pounds & three Shillings Sterling which I make no Doubt will be duly honour'd and passed to my Credit Vizt

	£.	s.	d.
John M Bolzius first Bill to me on Reverend Thomas Broughton dated 28th Ulto	3	3	0
John M Bolzius first Bill to me on Reverend Thomas Broughton 2d Instant	50	0	0
Govr. Ellis's first Bill on John Ellis to Francis Harris 2d Instant	30	0	0
Jos. Ottolenghe's first Bill to me on Reverend Mr Browhton 11th Instant	20	0	0
	103	3	0

The Gun Powder you shipt me in per the Harrietta is extremely bad, and am afraid will not sell at any rate. Some that you sent me per the Venus Cecil was of like Quality and am of Opinion that Mr Norman has imposed on you by putting up either Decayed Powder or such that is not proporly made as the grain of it is immediately reduced to a fine Flour by rubbing it in the Hands. I am Sir

Your very Humble Servant
T R

PS. to the above

As Mr. Elliott will be with you (I hope) in Time for chartering the Vessell I wrote you about the 3d Instant, and in which he is partly concerned I make no doubt but your joint Consultation's may tend to our mutual Advantage in this Affair.

Letter to William Elliott, Planter,
September 14, 1759

SIR

Your Negro Cato brings you agreeable to your order of yesterday's date 2 doz. extraordinary rice hooks at 8/0 per doz & 50 Gun Flints bought of Graham's & Mossman.

Your Negro being very impatient to be gone permitts me only to tell you that whatever your overseer may want for the Future I shall very readily (if I may not have those articles myself) procure them if to be had in this Town so that you'l please to direct Mr. H. Hueguenin to me for what ever he may have occasion for which shall be supplyed on the most reasonable Terms.

By Sir, Your most Obedient
T R

Letter to John and Ulrick Tobler, Merchants,
November 19, 1759

GENTLEMEN

The first Parcel of Beaver was extreemly foul & bad. I got Mr Nunes (who then bought Beaver) to look at it who said he would not give above 2/0 per lb. for it, upon which I sent it to Charles town where you see it sold for 31/0 that money but a little lost in weight. After I had sold all the Bacon 2 pieces of it prov'd quite bad & rotten & was return'd me again by the Buyer. I therefore gave them 2 pieces to some poor People here as it was impossible to offer it for sale again & I would advise you for the future if you send Bacon or Hams down to send them as early in the Winter as possible because People your way are so sparing of salt that the first warm weather greatly effects the Meat. Butter would be more saleable in smaller Kegs which should be Tarred before fill'd & the tares mark'd on the heads. Flour also would do much better in Barrells near the size & shape of the N York & Philadelphia flour Barrels. They should not exced 190 or 200 lb. at most. One of the 2 beef hides per Mr Rae's Boat was so much worm eaten that it was hardly worth any thing. I dont know yet what Mr. Haner will allow for it. There was a good Number of other Hides I believe came down in the said Boat. I have not yet put down the Almanacks because I sent a parcel of them to Medway & have not yet an Account of them. I have likewise omitted the Articles come down now. The Butter is all sold at 3 d. & hope soon to sell the Flour. The Cash I receiv'd for the Corn I have given you Credit for: 62 bushels Corn at 2/0 [equal] £6–4–0. ½ bushel was given for blowing the horn. The skins will be look'd over tomorrow & plac'd to your Credit with the Butter, Wax, & beef Hides, & the Flour when sold. I have not yet seen the Indico open'd because Mr Holmes hurries to be gone. Tomorrow I shall look at it & give you my opinion of it per next opportunity & am Sir

Your most obedient Servant

Letter to Mrs. Elizabeth Butler, Planter's Wife, December 18, 1759

MADAM

Mr. Butler has doubtless acquainted you that he made me an offer of 80 or 100 Barrels Rice in Case I could answer a Demand that Mr Yonge was to settle with him & as I find I can readily accomodate that matter with said Mr Yonge, if its agreeable to you. You'l Please to draw on me for the Amount. I should be glad to know whether I can depend on the above Quantity of 80 or 100 barrels Rice & when it would suit you to deliver it for which the Market Price of Charles Town is to be given at the Time of Delivery

I am Madam your humble Servant
THOMAS RASBERRY

Mr. Hueguenin brings you a fine rice Scieve cost 7/0. Theres no Flour come in since Mr. Butler Sail'd.

34. Activities of a Merchant Prince

CHARLESTON, the only city in the planting domain, has special interest as the focus of commerce in the southern wing of the colonies and as the seat of an extraordinary group of merchant princes, including during the eighteenth century such figures as Gabriel Manigault, Andrew Rutledge, and Christopher Gadsden. Among them, Henry Laurens, son of a prosperous saddler, rose to particular prominence and riches in the true Huguenot tradition of his ancestors. Like William Byrd II of Virginia earlier in the century, Laurens had training in a London counting-house. His service of three years, 1744–1747, with James Crokatt seemed at one time to be leading toward a junior parnership in the firm; but a misunderstanding sent Laurens back to Charleston, where he became a partner of George Austin. Over the following fourteen years the firm of Austin & Laurens became one of the largest in Charleston. Their trade network included the entire Atlantic community. In Great Britain they dealt with correspondents in London, Liverpool, Bristol, and Glasgow; in the West Indies, with correspondents in Jamaica, Barbados, St. Christopher's, and Guadeloupe; in North America, with correspondents in Boston, New York, and Philadelphia; in the Iberian countries, with merchants in Lisbon, Oporto, and Madrid. They also carried on business with houses in Havana and Rotterdam. Mercantile activity of this magnitude required quasi-diplomatic contacts which took the form of firm letters noting ship sailings, exchange rates, prices of staples, prospects in the slave market, and the like. Such information was essential to large-scale business and particularly to the slave trade, which was of special concern to Laurens but which was, as he explains, subject to many disappointments.

SOURCE: *South Carolina Historical and Genealogical Magazine,* XXVIII, 150–152, 158–159, 163–165. Reprinted by permission of the South Carolina Historical Society.

Letter of Henry Laurens to James Crokatt, London,
July 10, 1747

I wrote you the 24th ultimo per the Europa Capt. Wright 1st Copy of which is per Contra to which referr, since arriv'd the Friendship Capt. Swetnam from London, but am without any your favours. Since my last I have purchased about £370 Sterling in Bills of Exchange most of which I shall now remitt to Sundry Persons &

as I imagine all said Bills will be duly paid gives me a Prospect of Paying for my Cargo per the Neptune in due time, and encourages me to write for another small Cargo the Particular Orders you have Inclosed, & I must beg the favour of your care to get them ship'd. You will observe I have wrote for few Winter Goods as I imagine 'tis now full late, & I desire all the Woolens I have order'd may be Omitted in case you have not opportunity to ship them in a Vessel which you are pretty sure will sail from England Clear, by the 1st November—'tis my desire they may be ship'd in the first Vessel for this Port after receipt of this, and I must further desire to Leave it wholly to your judgement whether to ship said Goods or not on my Account, as 'tis possible there may about that time be a prospect of a sudden peace which I apprehend will make great alteration in our Trade here. Per the Inclos'd orders you may observe I have sent Copys to severals as are there noted but have desir'd them all to follow your Instructions in Respect to getting the same ready for shipping. By this Conveyance I shall remitt five Bills of Exchange, James McKay on P. Fury, Esquire all dated 26th June, 1747 Payable to Hector Berenger De Beaufaine or order & by him Properly endorsed to the Persons remitted to. Vizt, One to Rogers & Dyson £20; one to Samuel Wilson & Son £35; one to Samuel Fouchett & Co. £40; one to Pomeroy & Streatfeate £55; one to Handley & Palmer £30—in all £180 Sterling. If said Bills are duly paid, please to get Receipts on my Account for the Several Sums. I have wrote each of them in case said Bills should not be paid to advise with you about returning them, in which case be so kind as to do the best you can for my Interest. I now enclose you three first Bills of said McKay on said Fury all of the same date (26th June 1747) two of them payable to said Beaufain or order for Sixty Pounds & Fifty Pounds Sterling. The Order payable to Lieutenant Colonel Alexander Heron or Order for Fifty Pounds Sterling all Endors'd Payable to you, value of me, said Bills amounting to £160 Sterling. Please to receive and pass to the credit of my account & in case of non Payment do the needful for my Interest. . . . I am ashamed to be thus troublesome to you without Power to make it worth your while, however, that won't always be the case, as I hope the coming Crop to ship considerably in the Produce of this Province, when I expect to make you amends.

I shall by every opportunity make what remittances I can &

doubt not to put you fully in cash to pay for what is now unpaid of my late Cargo before it becomes due which I hope you'll please to do if any accident or disappointment should possibly prevent my making you sufficient remittances in time. I have presum'd thus far upon the Encouragement you were pleas'd to give me when I left London to which I hope you'll be pleas'd to impute this freedom. At present we have a good Prospect of large Crops of Indigo & tolerable Crop of Rice. This day arriv'd from Antigua the Planter, Capt. Lavers, the Alexander, Capt. Powel, & the —— Capt. Mc-Neal, all belonging to Bristol & are come to seek freight. What will be done with them I can't tell as here is at present neither Rice nor Naval Stores at Markett. Capt. Lavers says that on the 4th instant he din'd on board the Adventure, Capt. Hamar, at sea with Sundry Ships under his Convoy, 3 or 4 of them for this Port, so we are hourly expecting their arrival. If I am to be concerned in the Loading any of them (which you best know) please to make insurance as you may think sufficient to Secure my Interest. Rice is now at 40/0 per 100. Pitch 50/0 per barrel. Tarr 40/0 per barrel. Turpentine 10/0 per 100. Deer skins 15/6. Exchange 750 per cent. Below is a list of the Ships now ready to sail under Convoy of the Aldborough, man-of-war, Capt. Innes, & if the wind permits will sail tomorrow morning. The George, Capt. Elms & Neptune, Capt. Bellegarde, well here but just beginning to load. I send you our latest Gazette per this Bearer. I beg leave to repeat my offers of Service, & Compliments to all your good family & am

Very respectfully, Sir,
Your humble Servant

Ships ready to sail from Charles Town to be Convoy'd off the Coast by the Aldboro, man-of-war

Betsey	Capt. Conachy	for Leith
Landale		for ditto
Concord	Capt. Young	for London
Brown		for ditto
Ann	Capt. Pearson	for ditto
Dragon	Capt. Sherbourn	for London
Endeavour	Capt. Purvis	for Lisbon
Magdalane	Capt. McKenzie	for Leith

Firm Letter of Austin & Laurens to James Cowles, Bristol, July 4, 1755

SIR

After confirming the foregoing copy of our last per Capt. White, we must acknowledge the receipt of your favour of the 10th May of the Live Oak, are glad to see Capt. Copithorn was arriv'd safe with you & that you had so good a prospect of the State of the Skins by him but you would find them upon opening only so so, the thinest parcel we have ship'd you for many a day but the best we were able to get. By what we hear from our Neighbors of the prices their untrim'd Skins have sold for (viz) when trim'd ones sold for 3/3 & now 3/2 when the trim'd sell at 3/5 which is but 3 d. difference we think we are loosers by trimming many sorts of Skins particularly the Winter Cherokees from which we generally crop 16 to 18 percent. Be pleased to look into this, and give us your opinion whether to go on or to desist. The Skins we have now bought are at 13/6 each. One of our neighbors topd that price upon us when we had in a manner agreed for 13/0. We think the two Casks of Indigo at Col. Hyrne's are well sold. We hope you have got off the others before this as our expectations of a large Crop the present Year within all probability give a Damp to the Market as soon as it shall reach you.

If the White Plains shall continue so dear as they were last Year the fewer come 'twill be the more agreeable, tho' if a War should take place it must be an advantage to have such staple articles out before they are clogd with so high an Insurance as we may reasonably expect. We are as attentive as possible to get you all the Skins we can but 'tis not in our power to obtain a quarter part so many as we could wish for. Patrick Brown who was at the head of the Company that consign to Mr. Rock was buried the night before last. The rest of the Company we are told are about to separate, which will very probably carry the bulk of the Creek Trade to Georgia, as none of our People who have abilitys to carry on that Trade think it worth the Trouble & Risque. This late Company two or three of them was always in the Nation to make the most of their Affairs & by it they must have made money which is not to be done by sending People abroad to trade for you unless better men could be found for the purpose than are at present.

Firm Letter of Austin & Laurens to Wells, Wharton & Doran,
St. Christopher's, May 27, 1755

Your kind favour of the 28th December now before us did not reach us till 14th March, from which time we have had no opportunity of replying to it. We are sorry Capt. Raite in the Earl of Radnor brought down so sickly a cargo that you could not Venture to Stop her at so low a limit as £21 per head. From this we conclude that she must have made the Gentlemen concern'd but a bad Voyage; are glad She did not come here as a Sickly Cargo from Callabar at that Season of the Year especially would have mov'd very heavily & very probably have been order'd a long Quarantine; had they been healthy & in good flesh we shou'd have been glad to have seen her as there never was a better opening for a Cargo of Calabar Slaves than in the Months of October & November last owing to a Number of Small Indigo Planters finding a ready Sale for their Crops at 32/0 to 35/0 per lb. which brought them in such large Sums they were all mad for more Negroes, & gave for very ordinary Calabar Men £250 Cash. Our Imports this Year hitherto have been very Small, none yet Sold but a few small Parcels from Barbadoes and a little Cargo of about 70 in a Sloop of Rhode Island, Capt. Godfrey, from Gambia. A few of the fine Men sold so high as £280 or £40 Sterling but our People will not Currently give that Price. They seem very content to give £260 for Men & a large Number would this day sell at that rate. We have two from Africa now under Quarantine on Account of the Small Pox, one of them a Sloop of New York, Griffith Master, with about 40 Slaves from Gambia, the other the Matilda of Bristol from Calabar with 190. These we apprehend cant be sold this Month or two. Many more Vessels are expected, but if a Warr with France should take place which we seem to be at the Eve of we presume most of them will stop in the West Indies. Such an Event would give a sudden check to the Rice Planters but not at all to those who go upon Indigo, so that we judge we may have vend for about half the Number in time of Warr that we have in Peace, say from 12 to 1500 per Annum. We are sorry Capt. Darbyshire's Tender brought no more than 60 Slaves as our Good Friend Mr. Knight promis'd himself 100 by her, but Mr. Furnell advises us from Jamaica that he made a great sale of Darbyshire's Cargo, sold about 350 Slaves at upwards of £46 per head that money which we think must make up for the deficiency of the other. We were empower'd to order down here 100 of the Prime Men out of Darbyshire's Cargo, but did not chuse to do it, being of Opinion we could not for those Slaves exceed the Prices at Jamaica. Our People like the Gambia & Windward coast full as well or the Angola Men such as are large.

The Contracts we enter into for Slaves is to load the Ship with Produce when it can be had, to pay coast Commission & Half Wages, to remit the remainder as Payments shall grow due; which makes that Business sufficiently heavey in this Country for in our small Business where we would not out of Choice receive above 700 Slaves per Annum we are often in advance more than £10,000 Sterling. We have hitherto always Balanc'd our Accounts by the Month of March succeeding the Sale, but 'tis not to be done without a large advance of Money. Indeed for this we have an Interest of 8 percent. We have for 4 or 5 years past had so great a Plenty of Bills that we have been at very little loss at any time to Gratify our Friends with a Remittance therein.

We are extremely oblig'd to you for the enquiry you made of Capt. Corruthers relating to the Emperor, Capt. Gwin. We are in hopes from the Information he gave you that the Ship was arriv'd at Milimba but are willing to hope that some other parts of his account were eronious, for if he had 200 Slaves on board when the Jesse came away 'tis high time he was arriv'd in Some part of America which we can't learn he is; if it be true that he wou'd not be able to purchase more than 350 Slaves shou'd he bring them all in Well we shall make a most tatter'd Voyage, as the cost of her Cargo and outsett was upwards of £7100 Sterling. The African trade is more liable to such Accidents than any other we know of so it highly concerns such as become adventurers in that branch to fortify themselves against every disappointment that the trade is Incident to; the Captain is infatuated to that Ship which we think a good deal too large for the times at present but we don't care to give him the Mortification of Withdrawing our Concern.

Tho our Crops last year were large the Country is become well drain'd of its Produce. A little Rice Remains in some hands. The price of it 40 per hundredweight. The Produce of your Islands is a mighty dull poor Sale & as far as we are able to judge no signs of growing better soon unless a sudden Warr shou'd make an alteration in the present System. We have too many Tradeing Men here in proportion to the business of the Country which we believe is pretty much the case in all other the British settlements. We can only assure you that if you think at any time it may be in our Power to serve you we shall with great chearfullness attempt it being with great respect & Esteem Gentlemen

Your most Obedient Servants

35. A Quest for Industry

HOUSEHOLD manufacturing is familiar to students of the planting society. Some of the largest planters prided themselves on their self-sufficiency in everything but the luxuries. Not so well known are the industrial enterprises that ranged from relatively simple production such as cooperage to complex and costly establishments like an ironworks. Of all these, the manufacture of iron returned the largest dividends on invested capital when ideal conditions could be found, as they were in a few areas of the Chesapeake. In the year after five Maryland partners had formed the Baltimore Company, William Byrd II set out to learn the mysteries of iron production. He visited the three largest works in Virginia, including the concern in which the Washingtons had a part and the more famous furnaces of Alexander Spotswood. His informants freely gave him both information and demonstrations, which he recorded in a sprightly narrative which has become a classic. Informants told Byrd about capital costs, about the necessity of locating works adjacent to water transportation and charcoal supply, and enough about the techniques of constructing and operating furnaces to make him an authority on iron production in Virginia. Although Byrd never developed an ironworks of his own, he left a clear picture of this profitable branch of Chesapeake manufacturing.

SOURCE: "A Progress to the Mines in the Year 1732," in Bassett (ed.), The Writings of Colonel William Byrd of Westover in Virginia, Esquire, 343–346, 348–363, 370–372, 374–378.

I found Mr. Chiswell a sensible, well-bred man and very frank in communicating his knowledge in the mystery of making iron, wherein he has had long experience. I told him I was come to spy the land and inform myself of the expense of carrying on an ironwork with effect; that I sought my instruction from him, who understood the whole mystery, having gained full experience in every part of it, only I was very sorry he had bought that experience so dear. He answered that he would with great sincerity let me into the little knowledge he had, and so we immediately entered upon the business.

He assured me the first step I was to take was to acquaint myself fully with the quantity and quality of my ore. For that reason I ought to keep a good pickax man at work a whole year to search if there be a sufficient quantity, without which it would be a very rash undertaking. That I should also have a skillful person to try the richness of the ore. Nor is it great advantage to have it exceeding rich, because then it will yield brittle iron, which is not valuable. But the way to have it tough is to mix poor ore and rich together, which makes the poorer sort extremely necessary for the production of the best iron. Then he showed me a sample of the richest ore they have in England, which yields a full moiety of iron. It was of a pale red color, smooth and greasy, and not exceedingly heavy; but it produced so brittle a metal that they were obliged to melt a poorer ore along with it.

He told me, after I was certain my ore was good and plentiful enough, my next inquiry ought to be how far it lies from a stream proper to build a furnace upon, and again what distance that furnace will be from water carriage; because the charge of carting a great way is very heavy and eats out a great part of the profit. That this was the misfortune of the mines of Fredericksville, where they were obliged to cart the ore a mile to the furnace, and after 'twas run into iron to carry that twenty-four miles over an uneven road to Rappahannock River, about a mile below Fredericksburg, to a plantation the company rented of Colonel Page. If I were satisfied with the situation, I was in the next place to consider whether I had woodland enough near the furnace to supply it with charcoal, whereof it would require a prodigious quantity. That the properest wood for that purpose was that of oily kind, such as pine, walnut, hickory, oak, and in short all that yields cones, nuts, or acorns. That two miles square of wood would supply a moderate furnace, that so what you fell first may have time to grow to a proper bigness (which must be four inches over) by that time the rest is cut down.

He told me farther than 120 slaves, including women, were necessary to carry on all the business of an ironwork, and the more Virginians amongst them the better; though in that number he comprehended carters, colliers, and those that planted the corn.

That if there should be much carting, it would require 1,600 barrels of corn yearly to support the people and the cattle employed; nor does even that quantity suffice at Fredericksville.

That if all these circumstances should happily concur, and you could procure honest colliers and firemen, which will be difficult to do, you may easily run eight hundred tons of sow iron a year. The whole charge of freight, custom, commission, and other expenses in England, will not exceed 30s. a ton, and 'twill commonly sell for £6, and then the clear profit will amount to £4 10s. So that allowing the 10s. for accidents, you may reasonably expect a clear profit of £4, which being multiplied by eight hundred, will amount to £3,200 a year, to pay you for your land and Negroes. But then it behooved me to be fully informed of the whole matter myself, to avoid being imposed upon; and if any offered to put tricks upon me, to punish them as they deserve. . . .

After saying some very civil things to Mrs. Chiswell for my handsome entertainment, I mounted my horse and Mr. Chiswell his phaeton, in order to go to the mines at Fredericksville. We could converse very little by the way, by reason of our different *voitures*. The road was very straight and level the whole journey, which was twenty-five miles, the last ten whereof I rode in the chair and my friend on my horse, to ease ourselves by that variety of motion. . . .

We arrived here about two o'clock, and Mr. Chiswell had been so provident as to bring a cold venison pasty with which we appeased our appetites without the impatience of waiting. When our tongues were at leisure for discourse, my friend told me there was one Mr. Harrison in England who is so universal a dealer in all sorts of iron that he could govern the market just as he pleased. That it was by his artful management that our iron from the plantations sold for less than that made in England, though it was generally reckoned much better. That ours would hardly fetch £6 a ton, when theirs fetched seven or eight, purely to serve that man's interest. Then he explained the several charges upon our sow iron after it was put on board the ships. That in the first place it paid 7s. 6d. a ton for freight, being just so much clear gain to the ships, which carry it as ballast or wedge it in among the hogsheads. When it gets home, it pays 3s. 9d. custom. These articles together make no more than 11s 3d, and yet the merchants, by their great skill in multiplying charges, swell the account up to near 30s. a ton by that time it gets out of their hands, and they are continually adding more and more, as they serve in our accounts of tobacco. . . .

After dinner we took a walk to the furnace, which is elegantly built of brick, though the hearth be of firestone. There we saw the founder, Mr. Derham,who is paid 4s. for every ton of sow iron that he runs, which is a shilling cheaper than the last workman had. This operator looked a little melancholy because he had nothing to do, the furnace having been cold ever since May for want of corn to support the cattle. This was, however, no neglect of Mr. Chiswell, because all the persons he had contracted with had basely disappointed him. But, having received a small supply, they intended to blow very soon. With that view they began to heat the furnace, which is six weeks before it comes to that intense heat required to run the metal in perfection. Nevertheless, they commonly begin to blow when the fire has been kindled a week or ten days.

Close by the furnace stood a very spacious house full of charcoal, holding at least 400 loads, which will be burnt out in three months. The company has contracted with Mr. Harry Willis to fall the wood, and then maul it and cut it into pieces of four feet in length and bring it to the pits where it is to be coaled. All this he has undertaken to do for 2s. a cord, which must be four foot broad, four foot high, and eight foot long. Being thus carried to the pits, the collier has contracted to coal it for 5s. a load, consisting of 160 bushels. The fire in the furnace is blown by two mighty pair of bellows that cost £100 each, and these bellows are moved by a great wheel of twenty-six foot diameter. The wheel again is carried round by a small stream of water, conveyed about 350 yards overland in a trough, from a pond made by a wooden dam. But there is great want of water in a dry season, which makes the furnace often blow out, to the great prejudice of the works. Having thus filled my head with all these particulars, we returned to the house, where, after talking of Colonel Spotswood and his stratagems to shake off his partners and secure all his mines to himself, I retired to a homely lodging which, like a homespun mistress, had been more tolerable if it had been sweet.

Over our tea, Mr. Chiswell told me the expense which the company had been already at amounted to near £12,000; but then the land, Negroes, and cattle were all included in that charge. However, the money began now to come in, they having run 1200 tons of iron, and all their heavy disbursements were over. Only they were still forced to buy great quantities of corn, because they had not strength of their own to make it. That they had not more than eight Negroes, and few of those Virginia born. That they need forty Negroes more to carry on all the business with their own force. They have 15,000 acres of land, though little of it rich except in iron, and of that they have a great quantity. . . .

After breaking our fast we took a walk to the principal mine, about a mile from the furnace, where they had sunk in some places about fifteen or twenty feet deep. The operator, Mr. Gordon, raised the ore, for which he was to have by contract 1s. 6d. per cartload of twenty-six hundredweight. This man was obliged to hire all the laborers he wanted for this work of the company, after the rate of 25s. a month, and for all that was able to clear £40 a year for himself.

We saw here several large heaps of ore of two sorts, one of rich, and the other spongy and poor, which they melted together to make the metal more tough. The way of raising the ore was by blowing it up, which operation I saw here from beginning to end. They first drilled a hole in the mine, either upright or sloping, as the grain of it required. This hole they cleansed with a rag fastened to the end of an iron with a worm at the end of it. Then they put in a cartridge of powder containing about three ounces and at the same time a reed full of fuse that reached to the powder. Then they rammed dry clay or soft stone very hard into the hole, and lastly they fired the fuse with a paper that had been dipped in a solution of saltpeter and dried, which burning slow and sure, gave leisure to the engineer to retire to a proper distance before the explosion. This in the miner's language is called "making a blast," which will loosen several hundredweight of ore at once; and afterwards the laborers easily separate it with pickaxes and carry it away in baskets up to the heap.

At our return we saw near the furnace large heaps of mine with charcoal mixed with it, a stratum of each alternately, beginning first with a layer of charcoal at the bottom. To this they put fire, which in a little time spreads through the whole heap and calcines the ore, which afterwards easily crumbles into small pieces fit for the furnace. Then was likewise a mighty quantity of limestone brought from Bristol by way of ballast, at 2s. 6d. a ton, which they are at the trouble to cart hither from Rappahannock River, but contrive to do it when the carts return from carrying of iron. They put this into the furnace with the iron ore, in the proportion of one ton of stone to ten of ore, with design to absorb the sulphur out of the iron, which would otherwise make it brittle. And if that be the use of it, oyster shells would certainly do as well as limestone, being altogether as strong an alkali, if not stronger. Nor can their being taken out of salt water be any objection, because 'tis pretty certain the West India limestone, which is throne up by the sea, is even better than that imported from Bristol. But the founders who never tried either of these will by no means be persuaded to go out of their way, though the reason of the thing be never so evident.

I observed the richer sort of mine, being of a dark color mixed with rust, was laid in a heap by itself, and so was the poor, which was of a liver or brick color. The sow iron is in the figure of a half round, about two feet and a half long, weighing sixty or seventy pounds, whereof three thousandweight make a cartload drawn by eight oxen, which are commonly shod to save their hoofs in those stony ways. When the furnace blows, it runs about twenty tons of iron a week. The founders find it very hot work to tend the furnace, especially in summer, and are obliged to spend no small part of their earnings in strong drink to recruit their spirits.

Besides the founder, the collier, and miner, who are paid in proportion to their work, the company have several other officers upon wages: a stocktaker, who weighs and measures everything, a clerk, who keeps an account of all receipts and disbursements; a smith to shoe their cattle and keep all their ironwork in repair; a wheelwright, cartwright, carpenter, and several carters. The wages of all these persons amount to £100 a year; so that including Mr. Chiswell's salary they disburse £200 per annum in standing wages. The provisions, too, are a heavy article, which their plantations don't yet produce in a sufficient quantity, though they are at the charge of a general overseer. But while corn is so short with them, there can be no great increase of stock of any kind.

Having now pretty well exhausted the subject of sow iron, I asked my friend some questions about bar iron. He told me we had as yet no forge erected in Virginia, though we had four furnaces. But there was a very good one set up at the head of the bay in Maryland, which made exceeding good work. He let me know that the duty in England upon bar iron was 24s. a ton, and that it sold there from £10 to £16 a ton. This would pay the charge of forging abundantly, but he doubted the parliament of England would soon forbid us that improvement, lest after that we should go farther and manufacture our bars into all sorts of ironware, as they already do in New England and Pennsylvania. Nay, he questioned whether we should be suffered to cast any iron, which they can do themselves at their furnaces.

Thus ended our conversation, and I thanked my friend for being so free in communicating everything to me. Then, after tipping a pistole to the clerk, to drink prosperity to the mines with all the workmen, I accepted the kind offer of going part of my journey in the phaeton. . . .

[Here Byrd describes his journey to Spotswood's Germanna.]

After breakfast the Colonel and I left the ladies to their domestic affairs and took a turn in the garden, which has nothing beautiful but three terrace walks that fall in slopes one below another. I let him understand that besides the pleasure of paying him a visit I came to be instructed by so great a master in the mystery of making iron, wherein he had led the way and was the Tubal-cain of Virginia. He corrected me a little there by assuring me he was not only the first in this country but the first in North America who had erected a regular furnace. That they ran altogether upon bloomeries in New England and Pennsylvania till his example had made them attempt greater works. But in this last colony, they have so few ships to carry their iron to Great Britain that they must be content to make it only for their own use, and must be obliged to manufacture it when they have done. That he hoped he had done the country very great service by setting so good an example. That the four furnaces now at work in Virginia circulated a great sum of money for provisions and all other necessaries in the adjacent counties. That they took off a great number of hands from planting tobacco and employed them in works that produced a large sum of money in England to the persons concerned, whereby the country is so much the richer. That they are besides a considerable advantage to Great Britain, because it lessens the quantity of bar iron imported from Spain, Holland, Sweden, Denmark, and Muscovy, which use to be no less than twenty thousand tons yearly, though at the same time no sow iron is imported thither from any country but only from the plantations. For most of this bar iron they do not only pay silver, but our friends in the Baltic are so nice they even expect to be paid all in crown pieces. On the contrary, all the iron they receive from the plantations, they pay for it in their own manufactures and send for it in their own shipping.

Then I inquired after his own mines, and hoped, as he was the first that engaged in this great undertaking, that he had brought them to the most perfection. He told me he had iron in several parts of his great tract of land, consisting of 45,000 acres. But that the mine he was at work upon was thirteen miles below Germanna. That his ore (which was very rich) he raised a mile from his furnace and was obliged to cart the iron, when it was made, fifteen miles to Massaponax, a plantation he had upon Rappahanock River; but the road was exceeding good, gently declining all the way, and had no more than one hill to go up in the whole journey. For this reason his loaded carts went it in a day without difficulty.

He said it was true his works were of the oldest standing; but that his long absence in England, and the wretched management of Mr. Graeme, whom he had entrusted with his affairs, had put him back very much. That, what with neglect and severity, above eighty of his slaves were lost while he was in England, and most of his cattle starved. That his furnace stood still great part of the time, and all his plantations ran to ruin. That, indeed, he was rightly served for committing his affairs to the care of a mathematician, whose thoughts were always among the stars. That nevertheless, since his return he had applied himself to rectify his steward's mistakes and bring his business again into order. That now he had contrived to do everything with his own people, except raising the mine and running the iron, by which he had contracted his expense very much. Nay, he believed that by his directions he could bring sensible Negroes to perform those parts of the work tolerably well.

But at the same time he gave me to understand that his furnace had done no great feats lately, because he had been taken up in building an air furnace at Massaponax, which he had now brought to perfection and should be thereby able to furnish the whole country with all sorts of cast iron as cheap and as good as ever came from England. I told him he must do one thing more to have a full vent for those commodities: he must keep a shallop running into all the rivers, to carry his wares home to people's own doors. And if he would do that I would set a good example and take off a whole ton of them. . . .

Then the Colonel and I took another turn in the garden to

discourse farther on the subject of iron. He was very frank in communicating all his dear-bought experience to me and told me very civilly he would not only let me into the whole secret but would make a journey to James River and give me his faithful opinion of all my conveniences. For his part, he wished there were many more ironworks in the country, provided the parties concerned would preserve a constant harmony among themselves and meet and consult frequently what might be for their common advantage. By this they might be better able to mannage the workmen and reduce their wages to what was just and reasonable. After this frank speech he began to explain the whole charge of an ironwork. He said there ought at least to be an hundred Negroes employed in it, and those upon good land would make corn and raise provisions enough to support themselves and the cattle and do every other part of the business. That the furnace might be built for £700 and made ready to go to work, if I went the nearest way to do it, especially since, coming after so many, I might correct their errors and avoid their miscarriages. That if I had ore and wood enough and a convenient stream of water to set the furnace upon, having neither too much nor too little water, I might undertake the affair with a full assurance of success, provided the distance of carting be not too great, which is exceedingly burdensome. That there must be abundance of wheel carriages shod with iron and several teams of oxen provided to transport the wood that is to be coaled, and afterwards the coal and ore to the furnace, and last of all the sow iron to the nearest water carriage, and carry back limestone and other necessaries from thence to the works; and a sloop also would be useful to carry the iron on board the ships, the masters not being always in the humor to fetch it.

Then he enumerated the people that were to be hired, viz.: a founder, a mine-raiser, a collier, a stocktaker, a clerk, a smith, a carpenter, a wheelright, and several carters. That these altogether will be a standing charge of about £500 a year. That the amount of freight, custom, commission, and other charges in England, comes to 27s. a ton. But that the merchants yearly find out means to inflame the account with new articles, as they do in those of tobacco. That, upon the whole matter, the expenses here and in England may be computed modestly at £3 a ton. And the rest that the iron sells for will be clear gain, to pay for the land and Negroes, which 'tis to be hoped will be £3 more for every ton that is sent over. As this account agreed pretty near with that which Mr. Chiswell had given me, I set it down (notwithstanding it may seem a repetition of the same thing) to prove that both these gentlemen were sincere in their representations. . . .

We drove over a fine road to the mines, which lie thirteen measured miles from Germanna, each mile being marked distinctly upon the trees. The Colonel has a great deal of land in his mine tract exceedingly barren, and the growth of trees upon it is hardly big enough for coaling. However, the treasure underground makes amends and renders it worthy to be his lady's jointure.

We light[ed] at the mines, which are a mile nearer to Germanna than the furnace. They raise abundance of ore there, great part of which is very rich. We saw his engineer blow it up after the following manner. He drilled a hole about eighteen inches deep, humoring the situation of the mine. When he had dried it with a rag fastened to a worm, he charged it with a cartridge containing four ounces of powder, including the priming. Then he rammed the hole up with soft stone to the very mouth; after that he pierced through all with an iron called a primer, which is taper[ed] and ends in a sharp point. Into the hole the primer makes the priming is put, which he fired by a paper moistened with a solution of saltpeter. And this burns leisurely enough, it seems, to give time for the persons concerned to retreat out of harm's way. All the land hereabouts seems paved with iron ore; so that there seems to be enough to feed a furnace for many ages.

From hence we proceeded to the furnace, which is built of rough stone, having been the first of that kind erected in the country. It had not blown for several moons, the Colonel having taken off great part of his people to carry on his air furnace at Massaponax. Here the wheel that carried the bellows was no more than twenty feet [in] diameter but was an overshot wheel that went with little water. This was necessary here, because water is something scarce, notwithstanding 'tis supplied by two streams, one of which is conveyed 1,900 feet through wooden pipes and the other sixty.

The name of the founder employed at present is one Godfrey of the kingdom of Ireland, whose wages are 3s. 6d. per ton for all the iron he runs and his provisions. This man told me that the best wood for coaling is red oak. He complained that the Colonel starves his works out of whimsicalness and frugality, endeavoring to do everything with his own people, and at the same time taking them off upon every vagary that comes into his head. Here the coal carts discharge their load at folding doors, made at the bottom, which is sooner done and shatters the coal less. They carry no more than 110 bushels. The Colonel advised me by all means to have the coal made on the same side the river with the furnace, not only to avoid the charge of boating and bags, but likewise to avoid breaking of the coals and making them less fit for use. . . .

Not far from [Fredericksburg] are England's Iron Mines, called so from the chief manager of them, though the land belongs to Mr. Washington. These mines are two miles from the furnace, and Mr. Washington raises the ore, and carts it thither, for 20s. the ton of iron that it yields. The furnace is built on a run, which discharges its waters into [the] Potomac. And when the iron is cast, they cart it about six miles to a landing on that river. Beside Mr. Washington and Mr. England, there are several other persons in England concerned in these works. Matters are very well managed there, and no expense is spared to make them profitable, which is not the case in the works I have already mentioned. Mr. England can neither write nor read, but without those helps is so well skilled in ironworks that he don't only carry on his furnace but has likewise the chief management of the works at Principia, at the head of the bay, where they have also erected a forge and make very good bar iron. . . .

[Byrd continues to Colonel Spotswood's furnace at Massaponax.]

The Colonel received us with open arms and carried us directly to his air furnace, which is a very ingenious and profitable contrivance. The use of it is to melt his sow iron in order to cast it into sundry utensils, such as backs for chimneys, andirons, fenders, plates for hearths, pots, mortars, rollers for gardeners, skillets, boxes for cartwheels; and many other things, which, one with another, can be afforded at 20s. a ton and delivered at people's own homes, and, being cast from the sow iron, are much better than those which come from England, which are cast immediately from the ore for the most part.

Mr. Flowry is the artist that directed the building of this ingenious structure, which is contrived after this manner. There is an opening about a foot square for the fresh air to pass through from without. This leads up to an iron grate that holds about half a bushel of charcoal and is about six feet higher than the opening. When the fire is kindled, it rarefies the air in such a manner as to make a very strong draft from without. About two foot above the grate is a hole [that] leads into a kind of oven, the floor of which is laid shelving toward the mouth. In the middle of this oven, on one side, is another hole that leads into the funnel of a chimney, about forty feet high. The smoke mounts up this way, drawing the flame after it with so much force that in less than an hour it melts the sows of iron that are thrust toward the upper end of the oven. As the metal melts, it runs toward the mouth into a hollow place, out of which the potter lades it in iron ladles, in order to pour it into the several molds just by. The mouth of the oven is stopped close with a movable stone shutter, which he removes as soon as he perceives through the peepholes that the iron is melted. The inside of the oven is lined with soft bricks made of Sturbridge or Windsor clay, because no other will endure the intense heat of the fire. And over the floor of the oven they strew sand taken from the land and not from the waterside. This sand will melt the second heat here, but that which they use in England will bear the fire four or five times. The potter is obliged to plaster over his ladles with the same sand moistened, to save them from melting. Here are two of these air furnaces in one room, so that in case one wants repair the other may work, they being exactly of the same structure.

The chimneys and other outside work of this building are of free stone, raised near a mile off on the Colonel's own land, and were built by his servant, whose name is Kerby, a very complete workman. This man disdains to do anything of rough work, even where neat is not required, lest anyone might say hereafter Kerby did it. The potter was so complaisant as to show me the whole process, for which I paid him and the other workmen my respects in the most agreeable way.

There was a great deal of ingenuity in the framing of the molds wherein they cast the several utensils, but without breaking them to pieces I found there was no being let into that secret. The flakes of iron that fall at the mouth of the oven are called geets, which are melted over again.

The Colonel told me in my ear that Mr. Robert Cary in England was concerned with him, both in this and his other ironworks, not only to help support the charge but also to make friends to the undertaking at home. His Honor has settled his cousin, Mr. Graeme, here as postmaster, with a salary of £60 a year to reward him for having ruined his estate while he was absent. Just by the air furnace stands a very substantial wharf, close to which any vessel may ride in safety.

36. Forest Industry in the Planting Colonies

NAVAL stores had become a staple in the Carolinas after 1705, when Parliament provided bounty payments for tar, pitch, turpentine, and other products useful to the British navy and merchant marine. In the middle 1730's the Carolinas shipped nearly 20,000 barrels of pitch and tar a year, most of it from North Carolina. Parliament had meanwhile cut bounties almost in half (Act of 2 George II, ch. 35). Even so, export of naval stores was important in the Carolina balance of payments. Without alluding to shortcomings, John Brickell described the primitive processes in producing pitch, tar, and turpentine. Governor Gabriel Johnston tried to explain why planters marketed an inferior product, and recommended corrective measures. Naval stores returned smaller profits than iron, but capital investment was negligible. Consequently the industry was open to a larger number of planters throughout the southern colonies. Both Maryland and Virginia shipped sizable quantities of naval stores, but the Carolinas predominated. Carolina products never overcame the prejudices of British experts, who insisted that American tar and pitch were "hot" and burned the ropes. Yet production reached high levels. North Carolina had outstripped South Carolina by the middle 1730's. Altogether, in the years before 1776, North Carolina shipped seven tenths of all American tar, one fifth of all American pitch, and over one half of all American turpentine used in Britain.

SOURCES: John Brickell, The Natural History of North Carolina; with an account of the trade, manners, and customs of the Christian and Indian Inhabitants (Dublin: printed for the author, 1737), 265–267. Letter of Governor Gabriel Johnston to the Board of Trade, December 12, 1734, Colonial Records of North Carolina, IV, 5–7.

John Brickell

It will not be improper, in this place, to give an account how the Turpentine, Tar, Pitch, and Rosin are made, being all the produce of one Tree, and a very good Stable Commodity in these parts. The Planters make their Servants or Negroes cut large Cavities on each side of the Pitch-Pine Tree (which they term Boxing of the Tree) wherein the Turpentine runs, and the Negroes with Ladles take it out and put it into Barrels: These Trees continue thus running most commonly for three Years, and then decay, but in process of time fall to the Ground, which is what they call Light-wood, of which their Pitch and Tar is made. (viz.)

The Planters at certain Seasons of the Year, and especially in Winter, make their Negroes gather great quantities of this Light-wood, which they split about the thickness of the small of a Man's Leg, and two or three Feet in length; when they have got a sufficient quantity of it in readiness, they set their Kilns on some rising Ground or Earth thrown up for that purpose, in the center whereof they make a hollow place, from whence they draw a Funnel some distance from the Kiln. Then they take the Light-wood which they pile up with the ends of each, placed slanting towards the center of the Kiln, which is generally made taper from the Ground, afterwards they cover it very secure with Clay, Earth, or Sods, to keep in the Flames, after this is done they set it on fire at the Top, the Weather permitting, which must be neither too dry nor too wet. By this means the Tar runs into the center, and from thence into the Funnel, where they attend Night and Day (with Ladles to put it into Barrels prepared for that purpose) till the Kiln is quite burnt out, which is generally in eight and forty hours or less, according to the dimensions of the Kiln. It sometimes happens through ill management, and especially in too dry Weather that these Kilns are blown up as if a train of Gun-powder had been laid under them by which Accident their Negroes have been very much burnt or scalded. The Planters generally know very near what quantity of Tar each of their Kilns will produce, according to their dimensions, for which reason they are always provided with a sufficient Number of Barrels for that end.

The Pitch is made of the Tar, which is done in the following manner. They have large Furnaces made in several parts, and more now than ever, by reason of a late act of Parliament made in the Reign of his present Majesty, which obliges every Person or Persons that burn Tar-kilns in his Majesties dominions in America to make half of the first running into Tar, and the other half into Pitch, the penalty being a forfeture of the whole. With this second running they fill their furnaces, and so place a fire underneath it till such time as it begins to boyl, then they set on fire and burn it to the consistence of Pitch.

The Rosin is very scarce in these parts, few giving themselves the trouble; but when made, it is done after the following manner, viz.

Take Turpentine, as much as you think proper, put it into an Alembick or a Copper Vesica, with four times its weight of fair Water, and distill it, which will produce a thin and clear Oil like Water, and at the bottom of the Vessel will remain the Rosin. The Indians never make either Pitch, Tar or Turpentine, ranging and hunting continually through the Woods, being all the Industry they are given to, except they plant some small quantity of Indian Corn or Maiz, and dress their Deer-Skins, being as well satisfied with this way of living as any among us, who by his Industry has acquired immense Treasure.

Governor Gabriel Johnston to the Board of Trade, December 12, 1734

My Lords,
    Your orders to Mr. Burrington of May last relating to the Naval Stores and the other Products of the Continent of America came to my hands But a few days ago. And though I have some reason to be afraid that my answer may come too late to fall under your Lordships Consideration before you make your report to the House of Peers, yet I take this affair to be of so great consequence to his Majesties Colonies in America that I cannot forbear informing your Lordships of what I have observed since my arrival here.
    There is more pitch and tarr made in the two Carolinas than in all the other Provinces on the Continent and rather more in this than in South Carolina but their two commodities (tarr especially) bear so low a price in London (1000 pound Barrels scarce clearing 20s. sterlin) that I find the Planters are generally resolved to make no more. I beleive that it is principally owing to their own conduct that the tarr of this Country is of so small a value for in order to make a larger Quantity they make so large and violent fires in their kilns as forces all the coarce juices of the lightwood along with the tarr which gives it so hot a Quality that masters of Ships have observed it frequently burns their ropes which makes them very shy of meddling with it. Now if by a gentle fire they would attempt to make nothing but cool tarr though the Quantity would fall short by one-third yet in Quality they all agree it would equal East Country Tarr if not exceed it, for their Materials for this Manufacture are excellent and in great plenty. But as the loss of one third of

a kiln would fall very heavy upon them they cant pretend to set about this Method unless the Crown will be so good as to allow them the old Bounty of 10s. per Barrel. If your Lordships approve of this I humbly propose that the Planter in person be obliged to attend the kilns and see that it is cool drawn and to make Oath before the Governor that it is so with heavy penalties in case of fraudes etc. . . .

As the ship by which I send this sails to-morrow I shall defer to send your Lordships an account of the state in which I found this Country upon my arrival here, till next opportunity I am

Your Lordships most obedient and most humble servant

GABRIEL JOHNSTON

37. The Great Planter as Businessman

GREAT planters were few, not more than one out of twenty planting families in the Chesapeake and an even smaller proportion farther south. Nearly all arrived at their high level of material wealth with the assistance of one form of nonplanting enterprise or another. But as their invest-ment in slaves and land increased, so did their commitment to planting. Often the second generation, gently raised, lacked something of the zest their fathers had shown for enterprise, and were swallowed up in the measured routine of planting. Nevertheless, large-scale planting itself was a business, calling for the same foresight, ability to manage sub-ordinates, and knowledge of techniques as any other business. The largest planters nearly always held several plantations and allocated production among them to achieve almost complete self-sufficiency in consumption. Since beyond a certain point they could not carry on all the routines by means of overseers alone, they retained managers or stewards to co-ordinate operations. Richard Corbin's instructions to his manager pre-scribe standards of managerial duty and call for annual reports on the state of each plantation just as the head of a business exacts an account-ing from his subordinates.

SOURCE: Instructions given by Richard Corbin, Esq., to his agent, Mr. James Semple, for the management of his plantations in Vir-ginia, January 1, 1759, in Phillips (ed.), Documentary History of American Industrial Society, I, 109–112. Reprinted by permission of the publishers, The Arthur H. Clark Company.

January 1, 1759

MR. JAMES SEMPLE:

As it will be necessary to say something to you and to suggest to you my thoughts upon the business you have undertaken, I shall endeavor to be particular & circumstantial.

1st. The care of negroes is the first thing to be recommended that you give me timely notice of their wants that they may be provided with all Necessarys: The Breeding wenches more particularly you must Instruct the Overseers to be Kind and Indulgent to, and not force them when with Child upon any service or hardship that will be injurious to them & that they have every necessary when in that condition that is needful for them, and the children to be well looked after and to give them every Spring & Fall the Jerusalem Oak seed for a week together & that none of them suffer in time of sickness for want of proper care.

Observe a prudent and watchful conduct over the overseers that they attend their business with diligence, keep the negroes in good order, and enforce obedience by the example of their own industry, which is a more effectual method in every respect of succeeding and making good crops than Hurry & Severity; The ways of industry are constant and regular, not to be in a hurry at one time and do nothing at another, but to be always usefully and steadily employed. A man who carries on business in this manner will be prepared for every incident that happens. He will see what work may be proper at the distance of some time and be gradually & leisurely providing for it, by this foresight he will never be in confusion himself and his business instead of a labor will be a pleasure to him.

2nd. Next to the care of negroes is the care of stock & supposing the necessary care taken, I shall only here mention the use to be made of them for the improvement of the Tobacco Grounds, Let them be constantly and regularly penned. Let the size of the Pens be 1000 Tobacco Hills for 100 Cattle, and so in proportion for a Greater or less Quantity, and the Pens moved once a week. By this practise steadily pursued a convenient quantity of land may be provided at Moss's neck without clearing, and as I intend this seat of land to be a settlement for one of my sons, I would be very sparing of the woods, and that piece of woods that lies on the left hand of the Ferry Road must not be cut down on any account. A proper use of the cattle will answer every purpose of making Tobacco without the disturbance too commonly made of the Timber land & as you will see this Estate once a Fortnight, you may easily discover if they have been neglectful of Pening the Cattle and moving the Cowpens.

Take an exact account of all the Negroes & Stocks at each Plantation and send to me; & Tho once a year may be sufficient to take this account yet it will be advisable to see them once a month at least; as such an Inspection will fix more closely the overseers' attentions to these points. As complaints have been made by the negroes in respect to their provision of Corn, I must desire you to put that matter under such a Regulation as your own Prudence will dictate to you; The allowance to be Sure is Plentiful and they ought to have their Belly full but care must be taken with this Plenty that no waste is Committed; You must let Hampton know that the care of the Negroes' corn, sending it to mill, always to be provided with meal that every one may have enough & that regularly and at stated times, this is a duty as much incumbent upon him as any other. As the corn at Moss's neck is always ready money it will not be advisable to be at much Expense in raising Hogs: the shattered corn will probably be enough for this purpose. When I receive your account of the spare corn At Moss's Neck and Richland which I hope will be from King and Queen Court, I shall give orders to Col. Tucker to send for it.

Let me be acquainted with every incident that happens & Let me have timely notice of everything that is wanted, that it may be provided. To employ the Fall & Winter well is the foundation of a successful Crop in the Summer: You will therefore Animate the overseers to great diligence that their work may be in proper forwardness and not have that to do in the Spring that ought to be done in the Winter: there is Business sufficient for every Season of the year and to prevent the work of one Season from interfering with the work of Another depends upon the care of the overseer.

The time of sowing Tobacco seed, the order the Plant Patch ought to be in, & the use of the Wheat Straw I have not touched upon, it being too obvious to be overlooked.

Supposing the Corn new laid & the Tobacco ripe for Housing: To cut the Corn Tops and gather the blades in proper time is included under the care of Cattle, their Preservation in the Winter depending upon Good Fodder. I shall therefore confine myself to Tobacco. Tobacco hogsheads should always be provided the 1st week in September; every morning of the month is fit for striking & stripping; every morning therefore of this month they should strike as much Tobacco as they can strip whilst the Dew is upon the Ground, and what they strip in the morning must be stemmed in the Evening: this method Constantly practised, the Tobacco will be all prised before Christmas, weigh well, and at least one hogshead in Ten gained by finishing the Tobacco thus early. You shall never want either for my advice or assistance. These Instructions will hold good for Poplar Neck & Portobacco & perhaps Spotsylvania too.

I now send my two Carpenters Mack & Abram to Mosses Neck to build a good barn, mend up the Quarters & get as many staves and heading as will be sufficient for next years Tobacco hogshead. I expect they will compleat the whole that is necessary upon that Estate by the last of March. . . .

38. Pure Commercial Agriculture

THE USUAL economy of the plantation unit maintained a balance between the cash crop and production for subsistence. Commercial planting in its purest form was not unknown, however, especially in the sugar colonies of the West Indies, where food, lumber, livestock, and other necessities were imported, and to a lesser degree in the Carolina rice country. The "St. Domingo scheme" is an example of purely commercial cropping and an instance of experimentation in growing indigo in the tobacco country. Two young merchants hatched the idea. Kensey Johns, Jr. was the son of a Quaker merchant on the Patuxent River in Maryland, who did most of the outdoor work of collecting cargoes for his father's house. Brian Philpot, Jr., scion of the London merchant house of Philpot & Co., was in Maryland learning the tobacco business in the field. Their project made a neat profit for them, but they did not plant again.

SOURCE: Letters of Brian Philpot, Jr. to Kensey Johns, Jr., dated December 2, 1756 and August 28, 1757, Kensey Johns Papers (Maryland Hall of Records, Annapolis).

Letter of December 2, 1756

DEAR KENSEY

If Mr. Stewart wont give more than the £100 for the family & girl, that he has got, he must then have them at that. Please to send up Jack when you send up your hand for the Indigo Scheme. I have been with Mr. Johns upon the land, and he has pitch'd upon a place, just by Saytre Quarter, on your land, which he says Nature has design'd for the very purpose, and makes not the least doubt of it's answering to all our advantages, and I think we had better put three hands apiece, then baulk the design. The following is a calculation what the out set will be, but you must contrive to write to Col. Hunter, or get Mr. Galloway amongst his Virginia acquaintance, to procure us a bushell of right French Indigo seed, for it must be that sort, and we must get it by 1st March. I think we can saw the plank on the land for the vatts. Mr. Johns agrees if we put 5 hands he is to have 1/4, if 6 hands 1/5 so I think we better put the six hands, for should he not succeed in this, it will be helping toward making a plantation. The corn, pork, axes, hoes etc. I can procure. . . . I had liked to forget, Mr. Middleton can get his Father Mr. Sutten to get the seed for us in Virginia.

DR. ST. DOMINGO SCHEME	CURRENCY			PER CONTRA CR.
	£.	s.	d.	
To meat for 6 hands	9	0	0	By 6 hands makes 600
To corn for ditto	9	0	0	weight of indigo—
To axes for ditto	3	0	0	deduct ⅕ for Mr.
To hoes for ditto	1	4	0	Johns 120 [lbs.]
To matox for ditto	2	5	0	leaves 480 for us
To Quarter Building	5	0	0	
To Indigo House	15	0	0	
To plank etc. & making vatts	20	0	0	
To boxes for Indigo	1	10	0	[480 lbs.] at 5/0 ster-
To sundry items	5	0	0	ling per lb. 120–0–0
To Mr. Johns maintainance	10	0	0	
	80	19	0	
To put in our pockets	117	1	0	[120–0–0 sterling] at
	198	0	0	165 per cent. ex-
				change in currency
				198–0–0

N.B. The Kings Bounty pays Fraight & Commision

I am with usuall Compliments yours most affectionately,
BRIAN PHILPOT JUNR.

Letter of August 28, 1757

DEAR KENSEY

I left Joppa yesterday morning, after having been there three days waiting for the sloop, when I gave her 30 hogsheads Tobacco, which with 10 she had on board makes exactly 40 hogsheads & that will be all, and I expect she will sail this morning for the ship with them. I shall be down with you the last of the week. Pray tell the Doctor I depend upon his money to make payment to Mr. Nickolson & also that Note I had of Franks, you must contrive for me. Our Indigo is making & I am going to see what is done this very morning, in order that I may be able to give you the best account in my power & am with love [to] Sister & Children, Dear Kensey,

Your most loving brother
BRIAN PHILPOT JUNR.

VI

The Capital Base

ONE of the few statements that can be made with any degree of certainty about capital in the planting colonies is that it was crucial. The subject is more difficult to treat than any other factor of production because it is entangled in so many unanswered questions. None of these questions is in fact unanswerable, but answers do not come easily. Source materials are both refractory and bulky. Unfortunately they are frequently full of gaps as well. Moreover the broad generalizer finds that conditions vary from place to place, even within a colony, not to mention variations among the provinces themselves. Finally the subject is intrinsically difficult, for— as Robert Morris once pointed out—funds and money are of "too spiritual a nature" to be controlled by "the rude hands of laws and man-made rules."

Nevertheless some observations on the role of capital are relatively safe to make. First, capital was scarce and always in demand. It would be no exaggeration to say that the colonies felt the pangs of chronic capital starvation. Planting, merchandising, manufacturing, land speculation—all required some initial investment, and all demanded further doses of capital for expansion. Entrepreneurs were always eager for more.

The chief sources of capital were two in number: British capital seeking returns from investment in colonial enterprises of all sorts; and native American capital, increasingly important as the eighteenth century progressed. In certain areas—notably the sugar islands of the West Indies—British capital was dominant. There the returns on invested capital ran so high that planters could frequently retire to England after a few years to live an easy, sometimes an ostentatiously luxurious, life. Like the nabobs from India, the "sugar interest" formed a kind of club, which protected the special privileges of the fraternity. By contrast the mainland colonies offered no bonanzas, no instant returns from investment. The

146

consequences were important. Nearly all continental planters and entrepreneurs looked forward to a lifetime of slower accumulation, the work of their own hands and minds which required their presence and effectively ruled out absentee ownership. A few toyed with the fancy of retiring to the good life "back home," but all save a handful remained where they had risen to competence during their lifetimes. By the beginning of the eighteenth century many successful men could speak of themselves as "country-born" and they said it with pride. Their active lives in business were connected with the development of native capitalism.

A simple model most easily discloses the role of native capitalists in the planting colonies. The economies of these colonies were textbook cases of the "pioneer economy." In broad outline the pioneer economy is characterized by a basic movement essential to its well-being and growth: namely, commodity exports, particularly of a staple, and capital imports. Almost like the reciprocal drive of an engine, this basic movement in and out sets up within the country a secondary circular motion: high investment rate, full employment (in spite of immigration and a high birth rate), rising prices, and profit inflation.

Within this system a few men had the wit to perceive and to lay hold of opportunities. They were the entrepreneurs who made money in land speculation, mercantile activities, manufactures, and in moneylending. Some of the wealthiest were described by contemporaries simply as "traders"—for instance, Richard Bennett of Maryland. In the early years of the eighteenth century Bennett and others like him extended small credit to borrowers, and, as resources increased, larger credit. On their ledgers they entered the book debts, and in their portfolios they collected the bonds, notes of hand, and mortgages—in short the commercial paper, in the nomenclature of a later age. All these could be pledged as security when the occasion arose, or sold outright if need be. Thus was woven an immense web of debt.

The owners of this debt were the native capitalists. Even in the early part of the century, when Governor Calvert underscored the difficulties of carrying on commercial agriculture without paper money as a circulating medium, the trading element had somehow managed to refine a system of private credit arrangements that made possible the exchange of goods. Accounts of estate settlements show how well merchants and traders wrought. Later the issuance of paper money changed nothing essential, but merely added flexibility to a somewhat awkward, though still workable, system. The native capitalist rode upward on a growth factor of a magnitude suggested by the increase in population, the rising level of staple exports, and the steady process of capital formation.

To the question, then, of who owned the planting colonies, the answer must be: the colonists themselves. Of course some owed debts to British merchant houses, but the sum total of these is dwarfed by the bulk of local debt owned by wealthy and moderately well-to-do colonists themselves. And the debts to Britain must be counterbalanced with sterling of American planter-merchants in the hands of British merchants. The balance of payments problem has not yet been unraveled by students of our economic history, but a picture of American planters uniformly bound by indebtedness to British merchant houses would be hopelessly inaccurate. Perhaps it might be a fair approximation in the present state of our knowledge to describe the colonies as approaching autonomous economies within an Atlantic community knit together by strands of trade essential to the prosperity of all.

No manageable selection of documents can give the comprehensive picture of early American capitalism that students desire and deserve. Had contemporaries been commentators given to reflective analysis and to the production of informative essays, we might be in better case today. But the shrewdest heads concentrated on the workaday tasks of carrying on business, not on dispassionate analysis. The source materials they left us are by-products of their activities rather than scholarly model-making. We must, therefore, re-create the reality from such fragments as probate records, legislation against usury, and bits of bookkeeping which brought properties under control. These show us something quite different from a somnolent colonialism, drugged by the twin evils of outside domination that saps initiative, and of internal inertia that results from servile labor.

39. Governor Calvert on Money and Politics

BENEDICT LEONARD CALVERT, younger brother of the Lord Proprietor, came to Maryland as governor after study at Oxford and brief experience in international trade. He hoped to write a history of Maryland and studied the sources with considerable insight. Unfortunately the duties of office robbed him of leisure to write, but he did leave behind as testimony to his understanding of the province and its problems a twenty-three-page letter to his brother. Calvert accurately described the differences in footing of the planter and the merchant, and in part he discerned why merchants had an advantage. He strongly advocated paper money as a circulating medium to lift the "dead palsie on the publick" which he felt resulted from the lack of currency. But political disagreements had prevented passage of a paper-money bill at a recent session of the assembly, and now Calvert feared the payment of quit rents to the Lord Proprietor was about to become an issue in politics during these times of dear money. The governor sincerely desired to ease "the planter's lay," but not at the expense of the proprietary income from quit rents. These rents—some years previously commuted to an export duty on tobacco—took many thousands of pounds sterling out of Maryland every year and had an adverse effect on the provincial balance of payments. Calvert may not have perceived this effect, or if he did, he may have chosen to ignore it. But at bottom here was the reason that quit rents were involved in politics quite as much as paper money.

SOURCE: Letter of Benedict Leonard Calvert to Charles, Lord Baltimore, dated Annapolis, Maryland, October 26, 1729, Archives of Maryland, XXV, 601–610.

DEAR BROTHER,

By Captain Russell in August last, I wrote you and gave you some account of our Assembly Proceedings in the preceding month, and sent you also the printed votes of the session. I now send you the Journall of the Upper House, the perusall whereof, with the printed votes, will sufficiently inform you of the particular matters therin debated, with the mode and circumstances of their final issue. . . .

You will find a Bill for the Emission of a Paper Currency passed the Lower House, long debated and much amended in the Upper House, and at last, upon the amendments proposed, rejected by the Lower House. It were needless as well as tedious, to trouble you with the grounds or reasons for those amendments insisted on by the Upper House and rejected by the Lower; since it would of necessity lead me into the detail of the country affairs in generall, as well in relation to the publick as to the private interests therof, in various matters of trade and property, the which not being necessary for the present I shall omit. . . .

Money, or somewhat to answer its current effects in trade, is certainly much wanted here; we may barter between one another our staple tobacco, but to carry on and inlarge our trade abroad & to invite artificers, shipwrights, etc. to settle amongst us, another species of currency in payments seems very desirable; New York, Pennsylvania etc. are vastly improved in foreign trade, as well as home manufactures, by a paper currency; it is that, in lieu of specifick coin, which seems to give life, expedition, and ease to trade and commerce. This has drawn them into comminities or towns. They are daily growing more and more populous, and are supposed to increase as proportionably in credit and riches.

In Virginia and Maryland, the case is much otherwise. Tobacco, as our staple, is our all, and indeed leaves no room for anything else. It requires the attendance of all our hands, and exacts their utmost labour, the whole year round. It requires us to abhorr communitys or townships, since a planter cannot carry on his affairs without considerable elbow room within his plantation. When all is done, and our tobacco sent home, it is perchance the most uncertain commodity that comes to markett, and the management of it there is of such a nature and method that it seems to be, of all other, most lyable and subject to frauds in prejudice to the poor planters. Tobacco merchants, who deal in consignments, get great estates, run no risque, and labour only with the pen. The planter can scarce get a living, runs all the risques attendant upon trade, both as to his Negroes and tobacco, and must work in variety of labour. I write not this in malicious envy to the merchants nor do I wish them less success in business but I heartily wish the planters lay was better.

When our tobacco then is sold at home whatever is the produce of it returns not to us in money, but is either converted into apparell, tools or other conveniences of life, or else remains there, as it were dead to us, for where the staple of a country upon foreign sale yields no return of money to circulate in such a country the want of such circulation must leave it almost inanimate. It is like a dead palsie on the publick, since it can never exert its members or faculties in the pursuit of trade and commerce. An increasing country and growing people as this is, and a staple, at best uncertain, but of late visibly declining in value, as tobacco is, incited the people here to look about and enlarge their foundation in trade, to the which money or some currency, which may answer the same uses, is necessary, and the expedient to such end is a paper currency as proposed in the Act. I herewith send you a copy of the said Bill as it came up from the Lower House. . . .

I shall now trouble you with a word or two, upon the general situation of affairs in government that I may receive your advices and instructions in the fullest manner; and I think by taking a view of the relation the people bear to you and you to them, in the points of interest, I shall best explain myself to you. You are the Proprietary of the soil and as such the people from time to time owe you and may be compelled to pay you rents and fines. You and they have for some years past compounded for their value an other way. [Namely, by taking in lieu of the rents the proceeds of a duty of two shillings per hogshead on all exported tobacco.]

The people grow jealous that you have too good a bargain. You on the other side have been I believe informed that the amount of your rent roll exceeds vastly the equivalent you accept of. I must deal so candidly as to give my opinion that their seems error in computation on both sides. It is certain that people could no ways so easily, so insensibly pay their rents as by this method now they are in. The poor and orphans scarce bear any share in the present payments. The husbandmen from the produce in stock and tillage pay nothing, which is a great incouragement to husbandry, so necessary and beneficial to a young country. In short the traders who purchase tobacco bear the greatest share from the shoulders of the planter. And yet it is as nothing to such trader. For as Mr. Bennett, a great and knowing trader here, observes the trader gets as much for his goods as he can in tobacco, having allways the whip hand of the planters necessitys for cloaths and tools, and when people are aiming at getting such advances on their goods, as from 100 to 200 per cent, the value of 2 s. per hogshead is scarce calculated or even thought of. Thus in generall is the composition easy and almost insensible to the people. . . .

I hope Dear Brother you will favourably accept this rough

draught of your publick affairs; of your private interest you will I suppose hear from others. My weaknesses I doubt are many, but yet sure I am, they cannot outnumber my affections to your service. For I am most sincerely and entirely devoted to you as becometh Dearest Brother

Your Most Affectionate Brother and Most Obliged Servant
BENEDICT LEONARD CALVERT

40. The Tissue of Debt

AN OFFICIAL and exact accounting of a property owner's estate was made at the time of his death. Appraisers viewed his assets and set them down in minute detail in an inventory that was entered in the court records. The executor then settled the estate by paying all claims and dividing the remainder among the heirs. Executors reported on their settlement in the form of an account, also an official record duly entered on the books. From these records it is possible to reconstruct a picture of debtor-creditor relations and to determine the financial position of a planter at the time of his death. Three accounts reproduced here from among the many thousands recorded in the Commissary General's (probate) office show a spectrum of estates: small, medium, and large.

Henry Clarvoe of Prince George's County had an inventory of £ 70. 7 s. 6 d. in currency plus some debts due him and some small amounts of produce, all of which brought his gross assets to £ 98. 5 s. 8 d. He owed eighteen debts in all: the largest was to the Scottish tobacco firm, John Glassford & Company, and the rest were to local persons, including the merchant Stephen West. Altogether his debts, when paid by his widow and executrix, ate up nearly half his assets, leaving a net estate of £ 50. 6 s. 2 d. for his heirs.

Anthony Joye, a planter with an inventory more than twice as large, ended his days a bankrupt, as appeared when six debts, all owed to Richard Bennett, an Eastern Shore capitalist, were paid. When assets in the inventory were insufficient to meet claims against the estate, the executor customarily sold an amount of real property to cover the deficit.

Richard Harrison, wealthy Quaker merchant-planter of Calvert County, had not only a large inventory, but sterling balances totaling £ 1,952 0 s. 6¼ d. in the hands of four British merchants: Gilbert Higginson, John Hyde, Jonathan Scarth, and Joseph Jackson, all of whom were large importers of the Chesapeake staple.

SOURCE: Accounting for the estate of Henry Clarvoe, Prince George's County, 1763, Accounts, Liber 50, folios 122–124; accounting for the estate of Anthony Joye, Queen Anne's County, September 8, 1715, Inventories and Accounts, Liber 36C, folio 123; accounting for the estate of Richard Harrison, Calvert County, May 17, 1720, Accounts, Liber 3, folios 11–14 (Maryland Hall of Records, Annapolis).

The Account of Sarah Clarvoe
Executrix of the Last Will and Testament of Henry Clarvoe

	£.	s.	d.
This accountant chargeth herself with the inventory of the deceased's estate as the same was appraised and returned to the prerogative office and there duly recorded amounting	70	7	6
With current money due to the deceased from Elizabeth Hardy and received by this accountant	20	0	0
With current money due to the deceased from Thomas Edelin and received by this accountant	0	7	0
With current money due to the deceased from John Thompson and received by this accountant	1	7	0
With current money due to the deceased from Charles Perry and received by this accountant	0	7	6
With six barrells of corn at 12/6 per barrel	3	15	0
With 250 lbs. tobacco at 16/8 per cent	2	1	8
Amount of the debit of this account	98	5	8

	£.	s.	d.
And this accountant craves an allowance for the following payments and disbursements:			
Of funeral charges allowed per account	2	0	1
Of £5–15–8 sterling due from the deceased to John Glassford & Company per account proved and paid to James Marshall their factor as per account appears. At 68 per cent is in currency	8	10	9
Of 365 pounds tobacco due to John Glassford and paid to James Marshall as per account proved and receipt appears at 16/8 per cent	3	1	0
Of current due from the deceased to John Glassford and paid to James Marshall as per account proved and receipt appears	8	11	10

	£.	s.	d.
Of current money due from the deceased to Stephen West as per account proved and paid as per receipt appears	6	14	4½
Of current money due from the deceased to Winnefred Lanham as per account proved and paid as per receipt appears	3	3	0
Of current money due from the deceased to Thomas Lanham, Sr. per account proved and paid as per receipt appears	2	18	0
Of current money due from the deceased to Robert Davis per account proved and paid as per receipt appears	1	5	0
Of current money due from the deceased to Elizabeth Kelly per account proved and paid as per receipt appears	1	0	2½
Of current money due from the deceased to Ann Philips per account proved and paid as per receipt appears	1	0	0
Of current money due from the deceased to Arnold Burgess per account proved and paid as per receipt appears	1	0	0
Of current money due from the deceased to John Davidson per account proved and paid as per receipt appears		19	7
Of current money due from the deceased to Enoch Magruder per account proved and paid as per receipt appears	0	17	0
Of current money due from the deceased to John Haggarty per account proved and paid as per receipt appears	0	15	9
Of current money due from the deceased to Edward Blacklock per account proved and paid as per receipt appears	0	12	6
Of current money due from the deceased to Alexander Burrell per account proved and paid as per receipt appears	0	9	3
Of current money due from the deceased to Robert Todd per account proved and paid as per receipt appears	0	7	6

	£.	s.	d.
Of current money due from the deceased to Hanson and Middleton per account proved and paid as per receipt appears	0	4	10
Of current money due from the deceased to Henry Hardy per account proved and paid as per receipt appears	0	2	6
Of commission at 10 per cent on paying away £43–12–3 allowed this accountant	4	7	3
All of payments and disbursements	47	19	6
Balance to be applied as directed by the Testators will	50	6	2

This a final account

Prince George's County, ss

On the 2d day of August 1763 came Sarah Clarvoe executrix as before mentioned and made oath on the Holy Evangelists of Almighty God that the above account is just and true as it stands stated and the same after due examination is passed by

G. SCOTT, Deputy Commissary
Prince George's County

The Account of Renatus Smith, Administrator of All & Singular the Goods & Chattles of Anthony Joye

	£.	s.	d.
This accountant chargeth himself with an inventory thereof taken & exhibited into the Commissary's office amounting to	233	8	1
And humbly prays allowance for the following payments & disbursements since made (viz.)			
Of cash paid Richard Bennett, Esq. as per a bond and receipt appear	78	18	3
Of cash paid Richard Bennett, Esq. more as per bond and receipt appear	61	1	9
Of 15,785 lbs. tobacco paid Richard Bennett, Esq. as per bond & receipt appear and interest at 1 d. per lb.	65	15	5
Of 3658 lbs. tobacco paid Richard Bennett, Esq. as per bond & receipt appear & interest at 1 d. per lb.	15	4	0

	£.	s.	d.
Of 13,787 lbs. tobacco paid to Richard Bennett, Esq. as per bond & receipt appear & interest at 1 d. per lb.	55	18	11
Of 16,780 lbs. of tobacco paid to Richard Bennett, Esq. as per bond & receipt & interest thereon at 1 d. per lb.	69	18	4
Of cash to be paid for drawing & stating this account	0	4	0
	347	10	6
Of salary for paying £ 347–10–6 at 10 percent	34	15	0
	382	5	6

September 8th, 1715

Then came Mr. Renatus Smith administrator above said and made oath upon the Holy Evangelists of Almighty God that the above account is just & true.

WILLIAM BLADEN
Commissary General

The Account of Samuel Harrison of Anne Arundel County, Executor of the Last Will and Testament of Richard Harrison

		£.	s.	d.
This accountant charges himself with the amount of an inventory of the deceased's estate returned by him into the prerogative office amounting to		3222	16	3¼
And with a list of debts [in currency] also returned into the same office amounting to		67	4	10
And [debts] in sterling to £ 231–18–1½ which in currency is		309	4	2
And with cash received of John Seriviner		0	4	4
And with more [cash] received of Mark Ord		1	12	0
And with money sterling received from Gilbert Higginson	60	14	3	
And with money sterling received from John Hyde	944	19	5	

	£.	s.	d.
And with money sterling received from Jonathan Scarth	583	13	5
And with money sterling received from Joseph Jackson	362	13	5¼
	1952	0	6¼
Which 1952–0–6¼ in current money of Maryland is	2602	14	0¼
	6203	15	7½

And this accountant humbly craves allowance for the following payment and disbursements by him made out of the said deceased's estate, viz.

Of cash due from the deceased to George Simmons and paid by this accountant as per account proved and receipt appears 8 12 0

Of cash due from the deceased to John Perry and paid by this accountant as per account proved and receipt appears 5 5 10

Of cash due from the deceased to Doctor William Lock and paid by this accountant as per account proved and receipt appears 1 5 8

Of tobacco due from the deceased to the sherriff of Anne Arundel County for levys and rents of land and paid by this accountant as per account and receipt appears 3776

Of tobacco due from the deceased to Calvert County sheriff for levys and paid by this accountant as per account and receipt appears 1612

£.   s.   d.

Of commissary general and deputy commissary fees due on account of the deceased's estate
and paid by this accountant as
per account and receipt appears   1970
Of tobacco due from the deceased
to William Harry and paid by
this accountant as per account
and receipt appears   264
Of tobacco due from the deceased
to Charles Carroll for fees in
the land office and paid by this
accountant as per account and
receipt appears   408
                                   ____
                                   8030
Of the above 8030 lbs. tobacco at
10/6 percent is   42   2   11
Of a legacy of £ 10–0–0 in goods
at first cost distributed among
the poor of the neighborhood
according to the deceased's will   13   6   8
                                             ___ ___ ___
Of sallary at 10 percent for £ 70–   70   13   1
13–1   7   1   3
                                             ___ ___ ___
                                             77   14   4

Of a negro boy called Jo delivered
unto Sarah Lane for her son
Harrison Lane being a legacy
given by the deceased and ap-
praised at   15   0   0
Of a negro boy called Jeffry de-
livered unto Sarah Lane for her
son Harrison Lane being a
legacy given by the deceased
and appraised at   20   0   0
Of a legacy paid by this accoun-
tant to Sarah Lane being so
much left her by the deceased
in his will as per receipt appears 50   0 0

	£.	s.	d.
Of a legacy paid by this account to Elizabeth Bond being so much left her by the deceased in his will as per receipt appears	5	0	0
Of a legacy paid by this accountant to' Richard Jones being so much left him by the deceased in his will as per receipt appears	3	0	0
Of a legacy paid by this accountant to Elizabeth Chew being so much left her by the deceased in his will as per receipt appears	50	0	0
Of a legacy paid by this accountant to William Richardson being so much left him by the deceased in his will as per receipt appears	3	0	0
Of a legacy paid by this accountant to the people called Quakers being so much left them by the deceased in his will as per receipt appears	20	0	0
Of a legacy paid by this accountant to Samuel Chew & to Mary the wife of the said Samuel being so much left them by the deceased in his will as per receipt appears	50	0	0
Of cash due from the deceased to Phillip Smith and paid by this accountant as per account current & this accountant's test appears	5	7	0
Of cash due from the deceased to Solloman Brickhead an account of a bill of exchange drawn by the deceased but not protested			

	£.	s.	d.
till after his death and since paid by this accountant as per receipt and Capt. Hyde's account current appears	10	0	0
Of cash due from the deceased to George Henderson and paid by this accountant as per account current & this accountant's test appears	26	11	0
Of cash due from the deceased to Doctor Fisher and paid by this accountant as per account current & this accountant's test appears	10	0	0
Of cash due from the deceased to Doctor Hepburn and paid by this accountant as per account current & this accountant's test appears	9	6	6

	£.	s.	d.	£.	s.	d.
[Sterling]	242	4	6			
Which in currency is				322	19	4
Of sallary at 10 percent for £322–19-4				32	5	11
Of about 108 lbs. tobacco for commissary general fees to be paid Thomas Bordley, Esq., on this account at 10/6 percent				0	10	9
Of cash for drawing and stating this account				0	15	0
Of sallary [for two preceeding items] at 10 percent for 1–5–9				0	2	7
				469	7	11

Memorandum: The accountant declares that Abraham Brickhead's bond contained in the list of sheriff's debts amounted to 18–15-9 he is satisfied is not nor was at the time of the testator's decease due to the estate he having made inquiry into the consideration of passing the same when he was in England.

May the 17th 1720. The aforementioned Mr. Samuel Harrison being one of the people called Quakers, makes his solemn affirmation that the aforegoing account is just and true which after due examination is past save in respect to that article of ten pounds prime cost in goods to the poor which is left subject to the objections or exceptions of the proper officers for the poor of the parish wherein Herring Creek is included.

THOMAS BORDLEY
Commissary General

Memorandum: The residuary legatus being of age the ballance need not be transmitted.

41. Control of Interest Rates

CONTROL of interest rates in the eighteenth century had twofold sanction. Ancient teaching against usury running back to medieval times had not entirely disappeared. A stronger justification, mercantilist doctrine, called for regulation of the economy in many particulars, including wages, interest rates, tolls, and the like. The era of unfettered capitalism lay in the future. Legislatures in all the planting colonies passed acts restricting interest rates, and the standard, almost universal ceiling was 6 per cent per year. The expression of the law ran about as follows: A shall not take more than six pounds for the forbearance of one hundred pounds lent to B. This restrictive rate on direct loans tended to turn investment capital to productive enterprise, which promised greater returns, and away from what might have become a kind of rudimentary money market. The question arises why the merchant-planter capitalists lent "money at interest" at all, when they could realize far greater returns in other ways. This question must be answered by reference to case studies (see documents 42 and 43).

SOURCE: Act of 1741, chap. XI, *State Records of North Carolina,* XXIII, 169.

An Act for Restraining the Taking of Excessive Usury

I. Forasmuch as the settling of interest at a reasonable rate will greatly tend to the advancement of trade, and improvement of lands, by good husbandry, with many other considerable advantages to this province; and whereas divers persons of late have taken great and excessive sums for the loan of money, goods, and merchandizes, to the great discouragement of industry, in the husbandry, trade, and commerce of this province:

II. We pray that it may be enacted, and be it enacted, by his Excellency Gabriel Johnston, Esq., Governor, by and with the advice and consent of his Majesty's Council, and General Assembly of this province, and it is hereby enacted, by the authority of the same, that no person or persons whatsoever, from and after the first day of May, which shall be in the year of our Lord One Thousand Seven Hundred and Forty One, upon any contract, to be made after the said first day of May, shall, directly or indirectly, take for loan of any monies, wares, merchandizes, or commodities whatsoever, above the value of six pounds, by way of discount or interest, for the forbearancy of one hundred pounds, for one year, and so after that rate for a greater or lesser sum, or for a longer or shorter time; and that all bonds, contracts and assurances whatsoever, made after the time aforesaid, for the payment of any principal or money to be lent, or covenanted to be performed upon or for any usury, whereupon or whereby there shall be reserved or taken above the rate of six pounds in the hundred, as aforesaid, shall be utterly void: and that all and every person or persons whatsoever, which, after the time aforesaid, upon any contract to be made after the said first day of May, shall take, accept and receive, by way or means, of any corrupt bargain, loan, exchange, shift, or interest, of any monies, wares, merchandizes, or other thing or things whatsoever, or by any deceitful way or means, or by any discount, covin, device, or deceitful conveyance, for the forbearing or giving day of payment, for one whole Year, of or for their money or other thing, above the sum of six pounds for the forbearing of one hundred pounds for a year, and so after that rate for a greater or lesser sum, or for longer or shorter time, shall forfeit and lose, for every such offence, the double value of the monies, wares, merchandizes and other things so lent, bargained, exchanged, or shifted; the one moiety of all which forfeitures, to be to our Sovereign Lord the King, his heirs and successors, for and towards the support of this government, and the contingent Charges thereof, and the other moiety to him or them that will sue for the same, by action of debt, bill, plaint, or information, in any court of record within this province; wherein no essoign, protection or wager of law, shall be allowed or admitted of.

42. Planter-Capitalists:
The Case of Richard Bennett

THE DEATH of Richard Bennett in 1749 brought to a close a remarkable career. For fifty years, the first half of the eighteenth century, Bennett had figured in land dealing, commerce, and the host of activities that earned him the several appellations of "squire," "the greatest trader in the province," and "the richest man on the continent." Bennett's only literary memorials are a will, far too long to print, and two notices from the Maryland Gazette. These notices sum up his career without exaggeration. His will did in fact make handsome bequests: he gave over 12,000 acres of plantations with slaves and equipment to twenty cousins and one godson. Most revealing of all is the schedule, annexed to his will, of poor debtors whom he excused from payment: the list includes 178 names. All these bequests and benefactions touched only a fraction of his estate, which devolved largely on his cousin, Edward Lloyd. Planter-merchants of Bennett's stripe can easily escape notice. He held no public office of consequence; he left no collection of letters, no diary, no account books. Yet such prosaic documents as land records and court proceedings·show his incessant activities. He paid quit rents on thirty-four plantations totaling 14,000 acres in Queen Anne's County and on twenty-six tracts comprising 13,000 acres in Talbot County. These were but a part of his landholdings. The county and provincial court proceedings show him collecting thousands of debts from a few pounds up to a thousand pounds in the fifty years of his activity as a trader.

SOURCE: Maryland Gazette, Wednesday, October 19, 1749 and Wednesday, November 8, 1749.

October 19, 1749

On the Eleventh Instand Died, as his Seat on Wye River in Queen Anne's County, Richard Bennett, Esq., in the Eighty-third Year of his Age, generally lamented by all that knew him. As his great fortune enabled him to do much good, so (happily for many) his Inclination was equal to his Ability to relieve the indigent and distressed, which he did very liberally, without regarding of what Party, Religion or Country they were. As he was the greatest Trader in this Province, so great Numbers fell in his Debt, and a more merciful Creditor could not be, having never deprived the

Widows or Orphans of his Debtors of a Support; and when what the Debtors left was not sufficient for that purpose, frequently supply'd the deficiency. His long Experience and great Knowledge in Business, as well as his known Candor and generosity, occasion'd many to apply to him for Advice and Assistance, and none were ever disappointed of what was in his Power, and several were by his means extricated out of great Difficulties. He was always solicitous to prevent Differences among his Neighbors and to reconcile such as he could not prevent. In short, nothing gave him so much pleasure as doing humane and benevolent Actions; and it may be truly Affirm'd that by his Death the poor and needy have lost their greatest Friend and Benefactor.

November 8, 1749

On Wednesday last was solemnized the Funeral of Richard Bennett, Esq. of Wye River, in a very handsome and decent Manner, by the Direction of his sole Executor, the Hon. Col. Edward Lloyd. Mr. Bennett, by his Will, has forgiven above one hundred and fifty of his poor Debtors, and has made Provision for the Maintainance of many of his Overseers, and other Dependents, and settled a Sum of Money to be paid annually to the Poor of a Parish in Virginia; and done many other Acts of Charity and Munificence. He was supposed to be the Richest Man on the Continent; and as he died without issue, he has, after making many large and handsome Bequests to others, left the Bulk of his Estate to his Executor.

43. Planter-Capitalists: The Case of the Carrolls

Two main branches of Carrolls—the Catholic and the Protestant lines —flourished in provincial Maryland. Both were wealthy, and both were studded with the given name Charles. The Catholic Carrolls stem from Charles Carroll the Settler, who came to the province shortly before 1689 and made a tidy fortune as planter, merchant, and land speculator. His son, Charles Carroll of Annapolis, enlarged the family wealth, which eventually passed to his only son, Charles Carroll of Carrollton, famous as a signer of the Declaration of Independence. In the 1760's the matrimonial prospects of young Charles Carroll of Carrollton brought on a discussion of the family fortune, always a matter of importance in arranging dowries and jointures. In the structure of assets discussed in the

Carroll letters, the sum of £25,000 to £30,000 sterling at interest is note-worthy. This was clearly the growth factor, and its management is instructive. Characteristically the Carrolls made loans in connection with any one of several interests: iron manufacture, merchandising, or land dealings. In any case the loan was analogous to a deposit created to cover the cost of the commodity plus a considerable markup in value. As a simple example, a loan to a blacksmith or a farrier of ten pounds might cover the prime cost of a ton or iron at five pounds plus a 100 per cent markup of five pounds. The loan of ten pounds bore interest at 6 per cent, or twelve shillings a year; but it also made possible the sale of iron which yielded an even greater profit.

SOURCE: Kate Mason Rowland, *Life of Charles Carroll of Carroll-ton, 1737–1832, With His Correspondence and Public Papers*, 2 vols. (New York, G. P. Putnam's Sons, 1898), I, 60–61, 87.

Letter of Charles Carroll of Annapolis
to Charles Carroll of Carrollton,
January 9, 1764

DEAR CHARLEY

I hereby give you a short abstract of the value of my estate:

	£.	s.	d.
Forty thousand acres of land, two seats alone containing each upwards of twelve thousand acres would now sell a 20 s. sterling per acre	40,000	0	0
One fifth of an Iron Work consisting of the most convenient furnace in America, with two forges built, a third erecting, with all convenient buildings: 150 slaves, young and old, teams, carts etc., and thirty thousand acres of land belonging to the works, a very growing estate which produced to my fifth annually at least 400 pounds sterling at twenty-five years purchase	10,000	0	0
Twenty lots in Annapolis with the houses thereon	4,000	0	0
Two hundred and eighty-five slaves on my different plantations at £ 30 sterling each, on an average	8,550	0	0
Cattle, horses, stock of all sorts on my plantations, with working tools, etc.	1,000	0	0
Silver household plate	600	0	0
Debts outstanding at interest in 1762 when I balanced my books	24,230	9	7
	88,380	9	7

You must not suppose my annual income to equal the interest of the value of my estate. Many of my lands are unimproved, but I compute I have a clear revenue of at least £ 1800 per annum and the value of my estate is annually increasing by the increase of my lands.

Your most affectionate father,

CHA. CARROLL

Letter of Charles Carroll of Annapolis to Charles Carroll of Carrollton, April 10, 1764

Mr. Baker's letter to you speaks him to be a man of sense and honor. . . . He promises at his death to make his daughter share equal his estate with his sons. I proposed upon your coming into Maryland to convey to you my Manor of Carrollton, 10,000 acres, and the addition thereto called Addition to Carrollton 2700 acres, now producing annually £ 250 sterling and greatly improving as not nigh half of the 12,700 acres is let, and what is let, is let to tenants at will, and my share of the Iron Works producing at least annually £ 400 sterling. If this should be deemed insufficient settlement and gift to you, and security for the lady's jointure, I am willing to add on my death my Manor of Doohoregan, 10,000 acres and 1,425 acres called Chance adjacent thereto on which the bulk of my negroes are settled. . . . As you are my only child you will of course have all the residue of my estate on my death. . . . Your return to me I hope may be in the next fall.

Letter of Charles Carroll of Carrollton to William Graves, January 16, 1768

By the laws or the usage of this Province, widows are entitled to one-third of the personal estate absolutely and negroes are accounted as part of the latter.

The bulk of my estate consists of negroes and money. We have near £ 30,000 at interest and above 300 negroes, worth at least in the average £ 30 sterling each. In case of my death a very large proportion of my estate would probably be carried into another family, the prejudice of my own children or of the heir at law.

The young lady to whom I am to give my hand and who has already my heart, altho' blessed in every good quality, has not been favored by fortune in respect to money, and this among many others is a strong instance of the partiality and blindness of that goddess; or that riches are not always bestowed upon the deserving. I mention not this circumstance as an objection to the young lady. I prefer her thus unprovided to all the women I have ever seen— even to Louisa—but only as a reason inducing the necessity of a settlement, and strongly justifying it.

VII

Portrait of a Society

SOCIAL RELATIONS and the rules that regulate them often prove the most difficult of any aspect of the past to describe in a clear statement. The student finds himself drawn into economic and political matters that are so entwined with the subject that it seems impossible to separate them for analysis. Then after reducing these complex relationships to the fundamental ties and controls that are the essence of a society, he finds he has not so much a portrait as a sketch. Nevertheless a sketch has the merit of simplicity.

The most obvious feature of the planting society is its stratification. The notion of orders or classes in society was a part of the cultural baggage brought to the colonies by the earliest settlers. During these first years, when high and low faced the common problem of taming the wilderness, hardship and danger dulled the sharper outlines of class structure. But the idea never disappeared; and as the decades passed, ancient tradition reasserted itself, though with important modifications.

Of the varieties of stratification the most fundamental was a simple dichotomy: the free and the bond. Although we may begin our analysis of society—of the whole population in the planting colonies—with this neat distinction, the eighteenth century would hardly have accepted this approach, this legal stratification. Indeed, were we able to evoke the shade of an ancestor who lived in those days, we would find him puzzled about this way of dividing the people. Sons of the bond, he might explain, are not a part of "the people." But, of course, he would continue, there are degrees among the freemen: some occupy superior stations, and others inferior stations. And if we were to press him about his adjectives, superior and inferior, he might—surprised at our lack of perception in matters so obvious—try to convey the idea by speaking about the "better sort" and the "meaner sort." For social stratification—though they did not use the term—was a commonplace, almost unanalyzed, notion among men of the seventeenth and eighteenth centuries, a conception which shone through our ancestor's expressions in conversation or writing as naturally as any other received idea that he accepted without too much discussion of its bearings. Doubtless our ancestral shade would be a trifle amused if we tried on him our analytical tools and spoke of kinds of stratification— economic, social, and so on. Of course some people have more money than others, he would rejoin; and naturally, too, some are gentlemen, and others are not.

At least our analysis has the merit of familiarity for students today and helps us in getting to the realities of eighteenth-century society. The most satisfactory scale to apply in an age of quantification is the economic. At the bottom of the scale the men of small estates (those under one hundred pounds) constituted the majority—roughly two thirds of all heads of families. Above them the comfortably well-to-do families (with estates ranging from one hundred to one thousand pounds) made up nearly another third. At the top the great planters, the grandees, whose chattel properties ranged from one thousand to many thousands of pounds, formed the smallest percentage—not more than 5 or 6 per cent, or about one family in twenty.

Variously called the aristocracy, the oligarchy, the squirearchy, the wealthiest planters have become the stereotype of the planting society for students today, as they were in their own day the ideal, the goal to which the ambitious aspired. They had the keenest self-respect, they cultivated the good life, they worked hard, and they gravitated to positions of political leadership just as they had moved into the forefront in business affairs. Their traits appear most clearly in the letters and diaries they left as memorials. They subscribed themselves as gentlemen, or—what comes to the same thing—their neighbors did it for them in court records and newspapers. Yet they never became an exclusive group set apart from the rest of the planters. The lines of demarcation were fuzzy, and the aggressive, ambitious types from below constantly moved up into this favored upper group. In other words, the planting society had a rather high degree of social mobility.

The yeomen and the middle group of planters were scarcely less proud or assertive than the upper group. English travelers to the colonies almost invariably noted the absence of formal tokens of respect among the masses toward the "gentry." To be sure, the lives of these lesser folk lacked something in color—indeed, they were rather drab—but they were voters with power to prefer to honors and to withhold rewards of elective office from even the greatest. A few among them put a foot on the ladder and rose to wealth and position. In the relationship between high and low there were already the seeds of that attitude which later in the age of Jackson destroyed the notion of the "meaner sort," or at least the expression of it.

The grandee with a hundred slaves and the yeoman without even one accepted the idea of the unfree class. Historically in America indentured servitude came earliest. Economically indentured servants were desired as an addition to the labor force. No one questioned the morality of the institution. In his infinite wisdom God had ordained that some be masters and others servants. To implement God's ordinance man developed around the institution of indentured servitude a body of legislation to protect both servants and masters in their reciprocal rights and obligations. The laws enjoined masters to furnish sufficient clothing and diet and forbade undue punishment. Moreover, the terms of service were minutely prescribed to prevent scheming masters from prolonging the period of bondage. On the other side the code protected masters against losses from malingering servants, against runaways, and against female servants who "bastardized."

Negro slavery was at first a sort of extension of indentured servitude. In the middle years of the seventeenth century, court records of the Chesapeake provinces—then the only planting colonies—referred to Negroes as "servants for life." The life term was of course the important advantage to the planter: he did not lose his servant at the end of a few years. Moreover, as slaves multiplied, the children became slaves: the system was self-perpetuating. In time the bondage deepened; the slave became a chattel, his status different in kind from indentured servitude. Court cases show the lights and shadows, and for the most part they do not make pleasant reading.

By the beginning of the eighteenth century the social structure had, like the economic arrangements to which it was articulated, settled into a reasonably permanent pattern. Throughout the century the controls that kept the structure intact were perfected. The legislation on morals and the pronouncements of attitudes in sermons reveal the ideals of the planting society in its heyday.

44. A Gentleman Provides for His Family

THE BONDS of family were strong in the planting society and strongest of all among the squires. Their wills testified unambiguously to their care in providing competences, particularly for male heirs. Augustine Washington had the means to endow his six sons: land, slaves, ironworks, and debts owing him. Befitting his position as gentleman, he paid special attention to the descent of his landed estates, part of which he had acquired by purchase to provide each of his sons a plantation that would answer to their future positions as gentlemen planters. The provision of landed estates for their heirs by men of business lured many of their descendants into the round of plantation life and away from commerce and trading. George Washington, however, continued in his father's tradition of business activity. He was particularly interested in land speculation.

SOURCE: "The Will of Augustine Washington, Sr. (Father of George Washington)," Tyler's Quarterly, IX, 34,038.

The Will of Augustine Washington, Sr.

In the name of god. amen.

I, Augustine Washington of the County of King George, Gentleman, being sick and weak but of perfect and disposing sense and memory, do make my last will and testament in manner following hereby revoking all former will or wills whatsoever by me heretofore made.

Imprimis.—I give unto my Son Lawrence Washington and his heirs forever all that plantation and tract of land at Hunting Creek in the County of Prince William containing by estimate, two thousand and five hundred acres with the water mill adjoining thereto or lying near the same and all the slaves, cattle and stocks of all kinds whatsoever and all the household furniture whatsoever now in and upon or which have been commonly possessed by my said son, together with the said plantation tract of land and mill.

Item.—I give unto my son Augustine Washington and his heirs forever all my lands in the County of Westmoreland except such only as are hereinafter otherwise disposed of together with twenty-five head of neat cattle forty hogs and twenty sheep and a negro man named Frank besides those negroes formerly given him by his mother.

Item.—I give unto my said son Augustine three young working slaves to be purchased for him out of the first profits of the Iron Works after my decease.

Item.—I give to my son George Washington and his heirs the land I now live on which I purchased of the executors of Mr. Wm. Strother deceased. And one moiety of my land lying on Deep Run and ten negro slaves.

Item.—I give unto my son Samuel Washington and his heirs my land at Chotank in the County of Stafford containing about six hundred acres and also the other moiety of my land lying on Deep Run.

Item.—I give unto my son John Washington and his heirs my land at the head of Maddox in the County of Westmoreland containing about seven hundred acres.

Item.—I give unto my son Charles Washington and his heirs the land I purchased of my son Lawrence Washington whereon Thomas Lewis now lives, adjoining to my said son Lawrence's land above devised. I also give unto my said son Charles and his heirs the land I purchased of Gabriel Adams in the County of Prince William containing about seven hundred acres.

Item.—It is my will and desire that all the rest of my negroes not herein particularly devised may be equally divided between my wife and my three sons Samuel, John and Charles, and that Ned, Jack, Bob, Sue, and Lucy may be included in my wife's part, which part of my said wife's, after her decease I desire may be equally divided between my sons George, Samuel, John and Charles, and the part of my said negroes so devised to my wife I mean and intend to be in full satisfaction and in lieu of her dower in my negroes. But if she should insist notwithstanding on her right of dower in my negroes I will and desire that so many as may be wanting to make up her share may be taken out of the negroes given hereby to my sons George, Samuel, John and Charles.

Item.—I give and bequeath unto my said wife and my four sons George, Samuel, John and Charles, all the rest of my personal estate to be equally divided between them which is not particularly bequeathed by this will to my wife and it is my will and desire that my said four sons estates may be kept in my wife's hands until they respectively attain the age of twenty one years, in case my said wife continues so long unmarried but in case she should happen to marry before that time I desire it may be in the power of my executors to oblige her husband from time to time as they shall think proper to give security for the performance of this my last will in paying and delivering my said four sons their estates respectively as they come of age, or on failure to give such security to take my said sons and their estates out of the custody and tuition of my said wife and her husband.

Item.—I give and bequeath unto my said wife the crops made at Bridge Creek, Chotank, and Rappahanock quarters at the time of my decease for the support of herself and her children and I desire my wife may have the liberty of working my land at Bridge Creek Quarter for the time five years next after my decease, during which time she may fix a quarter on Deep Run.

Item.—I give to my son Lawrence Washington and the heirs of his body lawfully begotten forever that tract of land I purchased of Mr. James Hooe adjoining to the said Lawrence Washington's land on Maddox in the County of Westmoreland which I gave him in lieu of the land my said son bought for me in Prince William County of Spencer and Harrison and for want of such heirs then I give and devise the same to my son Augustine and his heirs forever.

Item.—I give to my said son Lawrence all the right title and interest I have to in or out of the Iron Works in which I am concerned in Virginia and Maryland provided that he do and shall, out of the profits raised thereby purchase for my said son Augustine three young working slaves as I have herein before directed and also pay my daughter Betty when she arrives at the age Eighteen years the sum of four hundred pounds which right title and interest on the condition aforesaid I give to my said son Lawrence and his heirs forever.

Item.—I give to my said daughter Betty a negro child named Mary daughter of Sue and an other named Betty daughter of Judy.

Item.—It is my will and desire that my sons Lawrence and Augustine do pay out of their respective estates devised to them one half or moiety of the debts I justly own and for that purpose I give and bequeath unto my said two sons one half of the debts and owing to me.

Item.—For as much as my several children in this will mentioned being of several venters cannot inherit from one another in order to make a proper provision against their dying without issue. It is my will and desire that in case my son Lawrence should die without heirs of his body lawfully begotten that then the land and

Mill given him by this my will lying in the county of Prince William shall go and remain to my son George and his heirs but in case my son Augustine should choose to have the said lands rather than the lands he holds in Maddox either by this will or any settlement then I give and devise said lands in Prince William to my said son Augustine and his heirs on his conveying the said lands in Maddox to my said son George and his heirs. And in case my said son Augustine shall happen to die without issue of his body lawfully begotten, then I give and bequeath all the said lands by him held in Maddox to my son George and his heirs and if both sons Lawrence and Augustine should happen to die without issue of their several bodies begotten then my will and desire is that my son George and his heirs may have his and their choice either to have the lands of my son Lawrence or the lands of my son Augustine to hold to him and his heirs and the land of such of my said sons Lawrence or Augustine as shall not be so chosen by my son George or his heirs shall go to and be equally divided among my sons Samuel John and Charles and their heirs share and share alike and in case my son George by the death of both or either of my sons Lawrence and Augustine should according to this my intention come to be possessed of either of their lands then my will and desire is that said lands hereby devised to my said son George and his heirs should go over and be equally divided between my sons Samuel, John and Charles and their heirs, share and share alike and in case all my children by my present wife should happen to die without issue of their bodies, Then my will and desire is that all the lands by this my will devised to any of my said children should go to my sons Augustine and Lawrence if living and to their heirs or if one of them should be dead without issue then to the survivor and his heirs. But my true intent and meaning is that each of my children by my present wife may have their lands in fee simple upon the contingency of their arriving at full age or leaving heirs of their bodies lawfully begotten or on their dying under age and without lawful issue their several parts to descend from one to another according to their course of descent and the remainder of their or any of their land in this clause mentioned to my sons Lawrence and Augustine or the survivors of them is only upon the contingency of all my said children by my present wife dying under age and without issue living, my sons Lawrence and Augustine or either of them.

Lastly.—I constitute and appoint my son Lawrence Washington and my good friends Daniel McCarty and Nathaniel Chapman— Gentlemen Executors of this my last will and Testament.

In Witness whereof I have hereunto set my hand and Seal the Eleventh Day of April 1743.

AUGUSTINE WASHINGTON

Signed sealed and published in the presence of us
    Robert Jackson   Anthony Strother   James Thompson

Provided further that if my lands at Chotank devised to my son Samuel should by course of law be taken away then I give to the said Samuel in lieu thereof a tract of land in Westmoreland County where Benjamin Wicks and Thomas Finch now live by estimation seven hundred acres.

Item.—I bequeath to my son George one lot of land in the town of Fredericksburg which I purchased of Col. John Walton also two other lots in the said town which I purchased of the executors of Col. Henry Willis with all the Houses and appurtenances thereunto belonging.

And whereas some proposals have been made by Mr. Anthony Strother for purchasing a piece of land where Matthey Tiffy lately lived now if my executors shall think it for the benefit of my said son George then I hereby empower them to make conveyance of the said land and premices to the said Strother.

In Witness whereof I have hereunto Set my hand and seal this eleventh day of April 1743.

AUGUSTINE WASHINGTON

Signed sealed and published in the presence of us
    Robert Jackson   Anthony Strother   James Thompson

At a court held for King George County the 6th day of May 1743

The Last will and testament of Augustine Washington Gentlemen deceased was presented into Court by Lawrence Washington Gentlemen one of the Executors who made oath thereunto and the same was proved by the oath of Anthony Strother and James Thompson [and] admitted to Record

A Copy   Teste

HARRY TURNER
Clerk

45. The Virginia Gentleman: A Self-Appraisal

IN ENGLAND, as in Virginia, William Byrd of Westover found the "better sort" his natural milieu. During his visits "back home" he moved in circles that included noble lords to whom his manner was meticulously correct. Byrd's letter to Charles, Earl of Orrery, on his return to Virginia has that touch of deference due a great nobleman; but it also breathes his sense of satisfaction with his position, analogous to the patriarchs of old, in Virginia and with the society about him, which he found in general very much to his taste.

SOURCE: William Byrd II to Charles, Earl of Orrery, July 5, 1726, Virginia Magazine of History and Biography, XXXII, 26–28.

MY LORD,

Soon after my arrival I had the honour to write to your Lordship to acquaint you that we had happily escaped all the dangers of the sea, and were safely landed at my own house. There was nothing frightfull in the whole voyage but a suddain puff that carried away our topmast, which in the falling gave a very bad crack, but we received no other damage, neither were our women terrified at it. The beautifullest bloom of our spring when we came ashore gave Mrs. Byrd a good impression of the country. But since that the weather is grown warm, and some days have been troublesome enough to make her wish herself back in England. She now begins to be seasoned to the heat and to think more favourably of our clymate. She comforts herself with the thought that a warm sun is necessary to ripen our fine fruit, and so pays herself with the pleasure of one sense for the inconvenience that attends the others. I must own to your Lordship that we have about three months that impatient people call warm, but the Colonel would think them cool enough for a pair of blankets, and perhaps a comfortable counterpain into the bargain. Yet there are not 10 days in the whole summer that your Lordship would complain of, and they happen when the breazes fail us and it is a dead calme. But then the other nine months are most charmingly delightfull, with a fine air and a serene sky that keeps us in good health and good humour. Spleen and vapours are as absolute rarities here as a winter's sun, or a publick spirit in England. A man may eat beef, be as lazy as Captain Hardy, or even marry in this clymate, without having the least inclination to hang himself. . . . Your Lordship will allow it to be a fair commendation of a country that it reconciles a man to himself, and makes him suffer the weight of his misfortunes with the same tranquility that he bears with his own frailtys. After your September is over, I shall wish your lordship a little of our sunshine to disperse that fogg and smoake with which your atmosphere is loaded. Tis miraculous that any lungs can breath in that of dirty London. For my part mine were never of a texture to bear it in winter without great convulsions, so that nothing could make me amends for that uneasiness but the pleasure of being near your Lordship. Besides the advantage of a pure air, we abound in all kinds of provisions without expence (I mean we who have plantations). I have a large family of my own, and my doors are open to every body, yet I have no bills to pay, and half-a-Crown will rest undesturbed in my pocket for many moons together. Like one of the patriarchs, I have my flocks and my herds, my bond-men and bond-women, and every soart of trade amonst my own servants, so that I live in a kind of independence on every one but Providence. However this soart of life is without expence, yet is attended with a gread deal of trouble. I must take care to keep all my people to their duty, to set all the springs in motion and to make every one draw his equal share to carry the machine forward. But then 'tis an amusement in this silent country and a continual exercise of our patience and economy.

Another thing my Lord that recommends this country very much—we sit securely under our vines and our fig trees without any danger to our property. We have neither publick robbers nor private, which your Lordship will think very strange, when we have often needy Governors, and pilfering convicts sent amongst us. The first of these it is suspected have some-times an inclination to plunder, but want the power, and though they may be tyrants in their nature, yet they are tyrants without guards, which makes them as harmless as a scold would be without a tongue. Neither can they do much injustice by being partial in judgement, because in the Supreme Court the Council have each an equal vote with them. Thus both the teeth and the claws of the lion are secured, and he can neither bite nor tear us, except we turn him loose upon ourselves. I wish this was the case with all his [M]ajesty's Subjects, and I dare say Your Lordship has the goodness to wish so too. Then we have no such trades carried on amongst us, as that of housebreakers, highway-men, or beggars. We can rest securely in our beds with all our doors and windows open, and yet find every thing exactly in place the next morning. We can travel all over the country by night and by day, unguarded and unarmed, and never meet with any person so rude as to bid us stand. We have no vagrant mendicants to seize and deafen us wherever we go, as in your Island of Beggers. Thus my Lord we are very happy in our Canaans if we could but forget the onions and fleshpots of Egypt. There are so many temptations in England to inflame the appetite and charm the senses, that we are content to run all risques to enjoy them. They always had I must own too strong an influence upon me, as your Lordship will believe when they could keep me so long from the more solid pleasures of innocence and retirement. I doubt not but my Lord Boyle has learn't at Paris to perform all his exercises in perfection and is become an absolute master of the French language. I wish every Secretary of State could write it as perfectly as his Lordship does, that their performances might not be subjected to the correction of Mr. De La Fay. I am sure that Lord Boyle will in every respect answer the affectionate care your Lordship has taken of him, and I suppose it will not be long befor I shall have the pleasure to hear that he is happily married, for it now seems wholy to depend upon him, to furnish heirs to the noble family of name. I most heartily long to hear from your Lordship, and shall rejoice at every happy accident that befalls you, for I am as much as any man alive, My Lord, your, etc.

W. Byrd

46. A Gentleman's Style of Life

William Byrd's secret diaries strikingly resemble the diaries of Samuel Pepys. Both recorded their days in shorthand safe from prying eyes, and both wrote with the unself-conscious frankness of men savoring their lives and doings. Byrd gives little space to philosophical reflections; he outlines the day from his early rise to bedtime prayers, which he occasionally omitted. The substance is there: the daily menus, a quarrel with his wife, the beating he gave little Jenny for which he was later sorry, the unvarying reading in Hebrew, Greek, Italian, or French. But beyond this round he shows us another Byrd, settling his accounts, supervising his tobacco shipments, and acting the Squire Allgood for his neighbor by calling to order malefactors who debauched her slaves. This is Byrd of private and public business, which reached its peak in the days at the capital in Williamsburg, filled with council sessions, meetings with colleagues, and dispatching letters to England.

SOURCE: Louis B. Wright and Marion Tinling (eds.), The Secret Diary of William Byrd of Westover, 1709–1712 (Richmond, The Dietz Press, 1941), 129–131, 216–222, 369, 377–381. Reprinted by permission of the editors.

January 12, 1710

I rose at 7 O'clock and read a chapter in Hebrew and some Greek in Cassius. I neglected to say my prayers and ate chocolate for breakfast with my company. Then we took a walk and after that played at billiards. I sent my sloop away to Falling Creek. I ate roast swine for dinner. In the afternoon we took another walk about the plantation. Mr. Salle went away. In the evening we played at cards and drank a bottle of wine till 12 O'clock at night. My daughter Evelyn was indisposed and took a purge which did not work very well. My wife was better, thank God, but did not come out to the company. I neglected to say my prayers in form, but said them shortly. I had good health, good thoughts, and good humor, thanks be to God Almighty.

January 13, 1710

I rose at 7 o'clock and read a chapter in Hebrew and some Greek in Cassius. I said my prayers and ate chocolate with the company for breakfast. About 9 o'clock they went away to Williamsburg and I sent some letters by them. My wife was better today. I danced my dance. I took a walk about the plantation. I ate hashed mutton for dinner. My daughter was not well and took a purge which did not work much. My wife was severe to her be cause she was fretful. In the afternoon I danced more dances, and then took a walk again about the plantation with my bow and arrow. In the evening I [reproached] Bannister for his pride. I read some Latin in Terence. I said my prayers and had good health, good thoughts, and good humor, thanks be to God Almighty. . . .

January 17, 1710

I rose at 5 o'clock and read two chapters in Hebrew and some Greek in Cassius. I said my prayers and ate milk for breakfast. Two of my negro children were sick and took a vomit which worked very well. I wrote a letter to the President and read some Latin in Terence. It began to rain a little with an east wind. I ate roast pork for dinner. In the afternoon I played at piquet with my wife and then read some news. It continued to rain so that I could not walk about the plantation. In the evening I read some Latin in Terence. I neglected to say my prayers but had good health, good thoughts, and good humor, thanks be to God Almighty.

January 18, 1710

I rose at 3 o'clock and read two chapters in Hebrew and some Greek in Cassius. I said my prayers and ate milk for breakfast. I danced my dance. It rained much this night and continued almost all day. I settled some accounts and then read some Latin. I ate boiled pork for dinner. In the afternoon I played at cards with my wife. Then I settled more accounts and read more Latin. Then I danced my dance again because it rained that I could not walk out. In the evening I read Latin in Terence. I said my prayers devoutly and had good health, good thoughts, and good humor, thanks be to God's will.

January 19, 1710

I rose at 5 o'clock and read two chapters in Hebrew and some Greek in Cassius. I said my prayers and ate milk for breakfast. I danced my dance. Colonel Kemp [?] came to see me from Mr. Harrison to desire me to have patience about the protested bill of exchange which I agreed to. He went away presently and I walked to my people to overlook them. When I returned I read some Latin in Terence. I ate roast mutton for dinner. In the afternoon I played at cards with my wife. Dick Randolph came and brought me a letter from England by which I learned the Queen's letter was sent to Carolina to forbid them from meddling with our traders. I ordered my people to set him up to Mr. Bland's. I took a walk with my wife about the plantation. In the evening I read some Latin in Terence, and said my prayers and had good health, good thoughts, and good humor, thanks be to God Almighty. . . .

August 12, 1710

I rose at 5 o'clock and read a chapter in Hebrew and some Greek in Lucian. I said my prayers and ate boiled milk for breakfast. I danced my dance. I had a quarrel with my wife about her servants who did little work. I wrote a long and smart letter to Mr. Perry, wherein I found several faults with his management of the tobacco I sent him and with mistakes he had committed in my affairs. My sloop brought some tobacco from Appomattox. Mr. Bland went away and I wrote more letters. I put some tobacco into the sloop for Captain Harvey. It rained and hindered our walk; however we walked a little in the garden. I neglected to say my prayers but had good health, good thoughts, and good humor, thank God Almighty.

August 14, 1710

I rose at 5 o'clock and read two chapters in Hebrew and some Greek in Lucian. I said my prayers and ate boiled milk for breakfast. I danced my dance. I wrote a letter to England. Walter Scott came to offer himself to be my overseer at Burkland but I could not give him any answer till I see Joe Wilkinson. The weather was hotter this day than it had been a good while. I ate some muskmelon before dinner and then I ate some hashed mutton. In the afternoon I settled my library. Then I read some Latin and afterwards wrote another letter to England. In the evening Mr. C——s and I took a walk about the plantation and ate a good many peaches. I said my prayers and had good health, good thoughts, good humor, thanks be to God Almighty. My sloop came from putting tobacco on board Captain Harvey.

August 15, 1710

I rose at 5 o'clock and read two chapters in Hebrew and some Greek in Lucian. I said my prayers and ate boiled milk for breakfast. I sent my flat with several goods to Appomattox. About 11 o'clock Mr. Drury Stith and his wife came to our house and not long after came Colonel Hill and Mr. Anderson with Mrs. Anderson, etc. About 12 o'clock we went to the courthouse where the freeholders were met to choose burgesses. After a great deal of persuading the choice fell on Colonel Eppes and Sam Harwood, notwithstanding Mr. Parker thought he should have carried it. But Colonel Hill used his endeavors to make the people vote for Colonel Eppes and he had it by one vote. Nothing remarkable happened but that the disappointment gave Mr. Parker a fever. We did not dine till 4 o'clock and then had so much company that there was no pleasure. I ate stewed eggs. In the evening the company went away. I walked to the courthouse, where the people were most of them drunk and Mr. Doyley gave me some letters which he brought from Williamsburg, among which was one from Colonel Parke which told us he was going to England but was not put out of his government and though he was dismissed he should not be put out if he could justify himself from the accusation against him. I neglected to say my prayers but had good thoughts, good health, and good humor, thanks be to God Almighty.

August 18, 1710

I rose at 5 o'clock and settled accounts with several people from Falling Creek. As soon as I had done with one, another came, so that I could read nothing this morning. About 9 o'clock Mr. Tom D——k came to renew some bills of exchange. Captain Randolph came over to get some iron and some rope. I said my prayers and ate boiled milk for breakfast. About 11 o'clock Colonel Hill came in order to go on board Captain Burbydge who sent his boat for us about 12 o'clock. My wife and child went with us, and Mr. C——s. When we came there we were equably treated and had a good dinner and I ate abundance of pease porridge. Mr. Platt and his wife and Mr. Cargill came to us; we stayed till 6 o'clock and then went away in the Captain's boat. He gave us nine guns at parting. We went to Mr. Cargill's where we had some syllabub. It was terribly hot. I neglected to say my prayers but I had good thoughts, good health, and good humor, thank God Almighty.

August 19, 1710

I rose at 6 o'clock and read nothing. I ate some milk for breakfast. I neglected to say my prayers. We took a walk about the plantation. I ate two apples and some watermelon. We diverted ourselves till about 11 o'clock and then went to dinner. I ate fowl and bacon. In the afternoon Mr. Hill came to us on his way to preach at [Weyanoke]. Colonel Hill came to us in the morning. About 1 o'clock we rode to Mr. Platt's, in whose field there was a race. There was Captain Burbydge and some other company. Here was another dinner provided but I could eat nothing but a little lamb. About 5 o'clock we went home in our boat, which came for us about 4 o'clock and Colonel took a passage with us. We found all well but old Jane who had a fever. We went into the river. I neglected to say my prayers but had good health, good thoughts, and good humor, thank God Almighty.

August 20, 1710

I rose at 5 o'clock and read a chapter in Hebrew and some Greek in the Greek Testament. It was exceedingly hot. I said my prayers and ate boiled milk for breakfast. About 11 o'clock we went to church and had a good sermon from Mr. Anderson. Cope Dyley died yesterday morning at Mrs. Harrison's of an imposthume in his head. We had some watermelon in the churchyard and some cider to refresh the people. We asked nobody to go home with us, that our servants might have some leisure. I ate roast veal for dinner. In the afternoon I read Grotius' *Truth of the Christian Religion*. About 4 o'clock there happened a small gust with little rain. I heard Mr. Drury Stith was sick and I gave a man some Jesuit's bark. In the evening we took a walk but only in the garden for fear of the rain. I neglected to say my prayers but had good health, good thoughts, and good humor, thanks be to God Almighty.

August 22, 1710

I rose at 5 o'clock and read two chapters in Hebrew and some Greek in Lucian. I said my prayers and ate boiled milk for breakfast. John G—r—l was taken sick of a fever. About 9 o'clock Mrs. Harrison came to ask my advice concerning her overseer and those people who sold them drink. I offered my service to wait on her to her quarters which she accepted of. When we came there we saw the overseer and I threatened him severely so that he promised never to neglect his business more. He promised, very frightened, too, and then we returned home. I ate whole hominy for dinner. In the afternoon I settled some accounts and then read a little in Grotius. In the evening I had a severe quarrel with little Jenny and beat her too much for which I was sorry. I went into the river. I said a short prayer and had good health, good thoughts, and good humor, thanks be to God Almighty. . . .

July 3, 1711

I rose about 5 o'clock and wrote a letter to the Governor and to Dr. Cocke and then sent away the express. I read a chapter in Hebrew and some Greek in Homer. My wife was better, thank God, though her headache continued. Bannister came back with my tobacco and told me Captain S—c—r would not take it in. I sent my sloop away to Appomattox for more tobacco. I found myself out of order, especially in my head. I wrote letters to England till dinner and ate some minced veal. I read some French and then wrote more letters to England till the evening. Then I took a little walk about the plantation. I continued indisposed and had but little stomach. I took great care of my wife, however. I said my prayers and had good thoughts, good humor, but indifferent health, thank God Almighty.

July 23, 1711

I rose at 5 o'clock and said my prayers. Then I drank some chocolate and then took my leave and went into the boat and got to Colonel Ludwell's landing by 8 o'clock where Tom was with my horses and I rode to the house and found them all well. Major Harrison was here and his brother Hal. Here I ate some bread and butter and drank some tea. About 10 o'clock the Governor's coach came for me and Dr. Cocke came in it, and after the horses had rested about two hours we took leave and went to Williamsburg. I was set down at my lodgings and did some business till about 2 o'clock and then to the Governor's where I found Captain P—s—t—n that came from New York for the pork bought up here. This gentlemen [d—b—ch][1] one of Colonel Hyde's [daughters], the Governor of Carolina. I ate some mutton for dinner and then returned to my lodgings and did more business with the naval officers. I did not stir out any more this evening but did my business till 9 o'clock and then went to bed but did not sleep very well.

---

[1] This diary was in shorthand. These are the only letters the editors could decipher. It must mean "debauched."—Ed.

However I said my prayers and had good health, good thoughts, and good humor, thank God Almighty.

July 24, 1711

I rose about 5 o'clock and said my prayers shortly. Then I prepared my public accounts. Several people came to see me which hindered me very much. About 8 o'clock I ate some water gruel. About 10 came Colonel Ludwell and examined my accounts and we did not finish till about 2 o'clock. Then we went to Council where my accounts were passed. There were no more than five members of the Council beside the Governor, and Mr. Blair was one, who looked as if he would be [sick] soon. When the Council was done some of us went to dine at the Governor's lodgings and dispatched a great deal of business and settled several people's accounts till 10 o'clock. Then I said my prayers shortly and had good health, good thoughts, and good humor, thank God Almighty, but I did not sleep very well but sweated much. Dick Randolph copied some letters for me.

July 25, 1711

I rose about 6 o'clock and neglected to say my prayers. I began to write my letters to England and wrote several to Mr. Perry. About 8 I had some water gruel and then wrote more letters. Several gentlemen came to see me, and I did business with Mr. Bland and others. About 11 o'clock I went to the coffeehouse and ate some bread and butter and drank some tea till my room was put in order. Then I returned and wrote more letters and did more business till about 2 o'clock and then I went to the Governor's to dinner where I ate some beef. After dinner I returned soon to my lodgings because I would not hinder the Governor nor my self from writing letters. I wrote several letters to England and went not out any more that night. About 9 o'clock I went to bed. I said my prayers and had good thoughts, good health, and good humor, thank God Almighty. I sent my man home for my horses this morning.

July 26, 1711

I rose about 5 o'clock and neglected to say my prayers. I wrote several letters and settled several accounts. About 8 o'clock I ate some milk and baked pears for breakfast. About 9 my man Tom came from home with my horses and brought me a letter from my wife with an account that all was well, thank God. He brought me some fruit which I sent, some to the Governor and some to Mrs. Bland. About 11 o'clock I went to the coffeehouse and drank some tea and ate bread and butter till 12. Then came Colonel Ludwell and Mr. Custis about business. I wrote a letter to England and about 2 o'clock went to the Governor's to dinner. I ate some fowl for dinner. After dinner I went to my lodgings where I wrote letters till the evening. I went to see Mrs. Bland and from thence to the coffeehouse where I drank some tea and about 9 went home to bed, where I did not sleep very well. I said my prayers and had good health, good thoughts, and good humor, thank God Almighty. It was extremely hot. Captain Posford came and took leave of me.

July 27, 1711

I rose about 5 o'clock and said my prayers. Then I wrote several letters to England till about 8 o'clock and then I ate some milk and pears and then wrote more letters and some accounts. Then I sealed up my letters and at 11 I went to the coffeehouse and made my second breakfast of tea and bread and butter. Then I returned to my lodgings and had several persons come to me so that I could do no business. About 2 o'clock I went to the Governor's where was Mrs. Hyde on her way to the boundaries of Carolina. It was extremely hot so that we sat without our [capes] notwithstanding the ladies. I ate some boiled beef for dinner. Here I stayed till about 6 o'clock and then left my letters with the Governor and took my leave. Then I went and took leave of Mrs. Bland and then went to Colonel Ludwell's where was much company and my cousin Harrison among the rest. I drank some tea and about 10 o'clock went to bed. Major Harrison lay in the same room and we talked almost all night for the heat would not let us sleep. I neglected to say my prayers but had good health, good thoughts, and good humor, thank God Almighty. This was the hottest weather I ever felt.

July 28, 1711

I rose about 3 o'clock and prepared to go home and about 4 got on my horse and by moonshine rode to the ferry and then it began to be day. When I was over the river I drank some warm milk and then proceeded on my journey and got home about 9 o'clock and found everything well, thank God, except John, who had run a nail into his foot. Several of my people had been sick but were recovered. About 10 o'clock came John Woodson and I settled accounts with him. I drank some tea and ate some bread and butter. When John Woodson was gone I found myself tired and laid down to sleep, and slept about two hours which refreshed me much. I ate a pigeon for dinner and in the afternoon took another nap. I said my prayers on the road. I read nothing but only put my things to rights. In the evening came an express from the Falls by which I learned that all was well there, thank God, and I wrote two letters there. In the evening I drank some warm milk and walked in the garden till it was almost dark. I neglected to say my prayers but had good health, good thoughts, and good humor, thank God Almighty. I slept better this night than I had done since I was sick.

July 29, 1711

I rose about 7 o'clock and read a chapter in Hebrew and some Greek in Homer. I drank some warm milk from the cow and about 9 o'clock had some tea and bread and butter. About 10 came an express from Drury Stith to tell me he was sick of fever and desired two bottles of cider, which I sent him. I gave Will Eppes leave to go see his mother. Moll at the quarters was sick of a fever which I gave her a vomit that worked very well. Billy Wilkins was also sick. I ate boiled pigeon and bacon for dinner. In the afternoon we sat and talked till 3 o'clock and then ate some watermelon. Then wrote the entries of my journal and afterwards read some French till the evening and then we took a walk about the plantation. My wife and I had a small quarrel about the trial which made us dumb to each other the rest of the night. I said my prayers and had good health, good thoughts, and indifferent good humor, thank God Almighty.

47. The Education of Young Planters: A Parent's View

SONS of the wealthiest planters frequently had their schooling in England. William Byrd II, Daniel Dulany the younger, Charles Carroll Barrister, and Henry Laurens are representative. Robert Carter entrusted the supervision of his sons to William Dawkins, London merchant, with whom he did considerable business. His letter to Dawkins about their education and the expenses they incurred sounds a very modern note.

SOURCE: Louis B. Wright (ed.), Letters of Robert Carter, 1720–1727: The Commercial Interests of a Virginia Gentleman (San Marino, The Huntington Library, 1940), 25–27. Reprinted by permission of the Huntington Library.

Rappahannock, July 14, 1720

SIR:

Yours of the 5th of April came to hand but yesterday. I shall be glad the shoes, etc., may get to me time enough for my occasions.

The health of my sons and their improvement in learning and manners is one of the greatest blessings I can meet with in this world. Let others take what courses they please in the bringing up of their posterity, I resolve the principles of our holy religion shall be instilled into mine betimes; as I am of the Church of England way, so I desire they should be. But the high-flown up top notions and the great stress that is laid upon ceremonies, any farther than decency and conformity, are what I cannot come into the reason of. Practical godliness is the substance—these are but the shell.

I come now to their expenses. I find you have gone beyond the bounds of your proposal. Your setting down everything in particular is very satisfactory and what I must always desire. The character I have of their master pleases me well enough, and their improvements I hope answers my desire also, but their expenses staggers me very much. Landon hath been there but half a year—I observe nothing paid for his board. How these things comport with your proposals of 40 [pounds] per annum I can [not] reconcile, nor shall be able to hold out at this rate. I have good intelligence that, further from the city, they may have as good an education for less than half the money, and thither they must go if you can be no better husband for them. There is several strange articles in their accounts. Mr. Harrison, the apothecary, a person I know very well, £7 for poor Charles's physic. I dare say 7/ would have paid for it all. The world is strangely altered, sure, since I was young. I lived with old Mr. Baily six years. I never stood my brother in £30 in any one year of the time. 'Tis in vain, I know, to run into particulars. I'm unwilling to order the removal of them at once, but to that it must come, I fear.

All our letters are full of the stockjobbing trade. The South Sea stock to advance so much in so short a time is very surprising. All these things are mysteries to me: I must leave them to clearer heads. Pray God send us a general peace all the world over and the continuance of it through my days, than which nothing can be a greater blessing.

Captain Kent hath made a little more haste than he did last year in loading. If God blesses him with a good passage he will be able to get him into the old tract again.

I am really sorry for the two young Graveses' lying idle so long. For Ben's part, I'm satisfied he deserves as well as anybody at all. Surely, for the sake of their good father as well as their own, you will exert yourself in getting them into some proper business.

The heaviest part of my controversy with Wise is already over. I shall be contented to stay your leisure for the conclusion of what's behind. I take notice of your observations about the bank. For that little interest I have there [I] must expect to meet with no better fate than other men do.

Pinchback Hammerton tells Mr. Walker he's coming over hither to look for his right. Walker, as one of the executors of old Hammerton, still keeps the remaining part of the estate in his hands to secure himself against a protested bill of Hammerton's that is lying out in James River. This is all that I can say about that affair, and pray let Mr. Hollis be acquainted with it. It cannot be expected of me to be young Hammerton's security. If the money were returned for England and the protest afterwards comes to be recovered, what a fine condition will the security be in.

I have lately discoursed Mr. Richard Lee about your debts. He thinks most of your debtors have shipped tobacco to you this year, and I hope there will not much remain unpaid. Your debt with

Mark Atkins will certainly be lost: he was upon the alms of the parish and is later dead, leaving some debts behind him that will never be paid.

I am become a great smoker. You must yearly make me a present of a small box of tobacco. My sister Swan, who for the most part lives with me, tells me she's in your debt 6 or 7 pounds; I think you must charge it to my account. Mr. Lee's draft of an account is here inclosed. It was forgot to be put into the letter relating to your affair with him. I am, Sir,

Your very humble servant

1 doz. brushes to clean the teeth
2 currycombs and brushes

48. The Education of Young Planters: A Son's View

THE SONS *often had to justify themselves to parents back in the provinces. Peter Manigault, only son of Gabriel Manigault, wealthy Charleston merchant, went to England in 1750 at the age of eighteen to complete his education and begin the study of law. Some unfortunate expressions in an earlier, missing letter home had brought down parental wrath on young Peter's head. In reply he justifies his plans for completing his training, including the grand tour on the Continent, a fearful expense to parents. Peter's letter to his father had the desired effect. He remained two more years about the "improvement" he describes to his mother, before returning in 1754 to a distinguished career in South Carolina.*

SOURCE: *The South Carolina Historical and Genealogical Magazine,* XV, 120–123. Reprinted by permission at the South Carolina Historical Society.

Letter of Peter Manigault to His Father,
March 13, 1752

London

HONORED SIR

I should be guilty of ingratitude in the highest degree, if I did not upon all occasions willingly acquiesce in every thing that you think for my good. From this principle it is that I have no manner of objection to continuing with Mr. Corbett, till I am of age, as you are inclined that I should, and as our perfect knowledge of one another, makes it beyond all doubt that we shall agree in every thing. It gives me no small uneasiness to find that anything that ever came from me should, instead of giving you pleasure, have the contrary effect, and I am very angry with myself for giving you cause to reproach me, with omitting to write, not only as tis a neglect of my duty, but as it is also a neglect of what ought to give me, and really does give me, the greatest pleasure. I am sorry to find Sir, that you construe into a demand, which was only meant as a petition far be such presumption from me, as to pretend to teach you your duty! I wrote what I did, because I had never heard any thing from you upon that subject, and I thought you would be glad to know my inclinations. And this I did, not upon the credit of my own opinion, but first took Mr. Corbett's Advice. And as to the reasons I gave for my opinion, was it not natural for me to think that you would be pleased to see that I advanced nothing but what I could give a reason for. But since I see my inclinations do not suit with your desires, I heartily submit myself to what you think proper & shall only add upon this subject that I am concerned to see you were angry because the most distant hint of your dislike to any thing is with me sufficient reason to disapprove of it. As you are so kind to offer me the liberty of returning to Carolina immediately after I am of age or of staying sometime longer abroad I am willing to be directed in that respect, intirely by you; however if my inclinations, provided they are not unreasonable, are in that case to govern, (upon mature deliberation of the many advantages that may accrue from a longer stay here,) I would not, without your desire, leave England, till this time two year, and would imploy all the intermediate time, in a close application to my improvement. But as I presume you would like to know particularly, how I would bestow myself during so long a space, so I ought in duty to inform you, that I would chuse to stick close to my books, all this summer, in London, and in the fall, go the Northern Circuit & then have an opportunity of seeing such relations as I have in that part of England. The next winter, I would also chuse to spend in London, & omit nothing, that can possibly be of any advantage to me. Early in the spring, I hope you won't be against my going to France, & seeing some parts of Holland and Flanders; in this excursion I promise myself that besides other useful attainments, I shall with the help of what I understand already, make myself a compleat master of the French tongue. I should like to return in the spring; chiefly taken up, in preparing myself for my return in the spring; when I could like to take an opportunity of going to Boston, & travelling by land to Charlestown, where I would not propose to be, till the Month of October. This Sir is the scheme I have formed to myself, but submit it entirely to you, & will gladly alter or leave out, any part of it, as you shall think fit, or more, or less necessary, for my improvement. But upon the whole Sir, this you may depend upon, that I don't want to lengthen my stay here, either out of fondness for England, or any dislike to Carolina, but merely for the sake of my improvement, & that if that were out of the case, you could not recall me sooner, than I would be willing to return.

I have written to Mama by Capt. Pearson who sails about the same time with the vessel that carrys this. Capt. Pearson has on board with some things in it for Mama. There is in the box, five magazines, and four volumes of a book called Amelia, all which I hope, will get safe to hand.

Be pleased to make my compliments to Mr. Rutledge, & other inquiring friends, & believe me to be your

Most dutiful Son,
PETER MANIGAULT

Letter of Peter Manigault to His Mother, July 20, 1752

York

HONORED MADAM

I should be at a loss to find an excuse, for not giving you an account of my travels as I know you expect it. I suppose you don't desire I should trouble you with a particular relation of every day's proceeding, as that would be both tedious & unentertaining. I set out then, from London this day fortnight, in company with Mr. Blake, Drayton, & two other gentlemen of [the] Temple whom you know nothing of. I believe there never was a more agreeable party [missing] any scheme in the World. I am sure there never was a more sober one, for we five often found it difficult to de-molish a single pint of wine. We travelled with great pleasure till we got to Stamford in Lincolnshire, where Squire Drayton fell ill.

This detained us two days, & only served to whet the edge of our impatience, & give us greater alacrity to proceed to Hull. The polite Capt. Reaston (for I must upon this Occasion call him so,) waited for us at a place called Barton, & conducted us over a large ferry, of about five miles to Hull. When he got us there, he insisted upon it, that Blake, Drayton, & myself, should lodge with him, as we had before parted with the other two Gentlemen. We all refused, till his mother came in, & made the same request, (which we, being too well bred to refuse any thing to the Lady, immediately granted.) Reaston's mother & his sister too, seem to be mightly good sort of people, & expressed great kindness for you, & all their other relations abroad. While we were with Capt. Reaston, we spent a day at Hornsea; we went thither to see Mr. Acklom, but he was not at home. Our labour however was not lost, for beside a delicious bathe in the Sea, Master Reaston carried us to dine with an old aunt of his, a very ancient woman, who was in perfect possession of all her senses, and could write & read without spectacles, though eighty-nine years of age. We tarried at Hull but three days; we should have spent more time there, but knew it must be inconvenient to the good folks, as they have not been much used to entertain company. We left Hull on the Wednesday sennight after we came from London, & got that very night to York. We are now diverting ourselves with attending the Courts for that is the only diversion we can find tis well tis a good one!

I had almost forgot to tell you our method of travelling. Mr. Blake rides on horseback, & Drayton & I, have a post chaise between us. As none of us had that necessary & indispensable convenience, a servant, we clubbed for one, who proves a very sober honest sort of a fellow, & to borrow an expression made use of among jockeys, he is a knowing one. I shall write to you often while I am upon my journey, as well for my own pleasure, as to satisfy you, which is the business of my life. I hope you will be pleased at my going into the Temple. As I am now of an Age to be able to judge a Little for myself, I must confess I think it the properest place for me. I mention'd this, because some people think, (though tis no credit to their understandings) that the Temple is a very wild place, which is by no means true; however for argument sake allow that tis, yet you can't be against my removing thither from Bow Street, which is situated in the very center of all the bad houses in Covent Garden. Be pleased to assure my good Father of my sincerest duty & affection, & pay my proper respects to all who are kind enough to enquire after, your dutiful Son

PETER MANIGAULT

I am almost ashamed to send you such a letter as this, But as I am at an Inn I am persuaded you will excuse me.

49. Properties of a Lesser Planter

A FEMALE planter is always something of a surprise. Ordinarily the male head of the household was the planter, but occasionally a widow who chose not to follow the custom of immediate remarriage, or, still more rarely, a spinster played the role. Rebecca Royston of Calvert County, Maryland, is a case in point. For many years a widow, Rebecca Royston produced small crops of tobacco with the aid of an indentured servant on the family plantation of two hundred acres. She owed several small debts, about half of them to Quaker merchants. When these were paid by her son and administrator, the remainder of the estate came to £81. 9s. 11d. There is little literary evidence about the style of life among those families whose assets totaled about a hundred pounds, but thousands of inventories of their goods and chattels present a clear picture of their sumptuary situation. Exactly one half of Rebecca Royston's estate consisted of livestock—cattle, sheep, and hogs. For the rest she had a small tobacco crop of about three hogsheads and the furnishings and equipment of a farm household. Clearly the family enjoyed an ample country living; the utensils for the dairy and for food preparation suggest as much. It is also apparent that nothing went to waste when every article from old baskets to a "damnified pott" had value; all broken metal, whether pewter, brass, or iron, was salvaged. The nearest approach to elegance appears in the entry, "a parcel of old table linning."

SOURCE: Inventory of the Goods and Chattels of Rebecca Royston, 1720, Inventories, Liber 4, folios 244–245 (Maryland Hall of Records, Annapolis).

An Inventory of All and Singular the Goods & Chattels
of Rebecca Royston Late of Calvert County
Appraised this 19th Day of September 1720 by the Subscribers

	£.	s.	d.
31 head of cattle	44	17	0
15 head of sheep at 6 s.	4	10	0
29 head of hogs	8	1	6
1463 lbs. tobacco at 10 s. percent	7	6	2
5 old feather bedds	16	2	0

	£.	s.	d.
1 flock bedd	0	10	0
Wearing apparell of the deceased	10	1	0
11 old chests and 1 box	2	6	6
1 old large seal skin trunk	0	12	0
13 old chairs and 1 old couch	1	10	0
4 old tubbs	0	13	6
9 old sickles 4 d.	0	3	0
A parcell of earthen ware and bottles	0	5	9
2 wyre 1 lawn sifter	0	6	10
4 tinn panns 1 callender 1 warming pann	0	7	6
A parcell of plantation old tools	0	12	10
A parcell of old table linning	0	5	2
1 box iron and heaters & a pair of small stillyards	0	7	0
1 old plow & old horse harness	0	7	6
1 pair of large iron doggs	0	18	0
66 lbs. of wool at 4 d. per lb. & 2 pair wool cards	1	3	4
1 bushell of salt	0	2	0
5 old casments 8 d. per	0	3	4
A parcell of old basketts	0	2	0
A parcell of old books	0	18	0
3 old candelsticks 1 flower 1 candelbox	0	1	0
2 pair tongs & fire shovels	0	3	6
50 lbs. old pewter at 7 d. & 2 new basons 1 s.	0	12	2
30 lbs. old brass at 7 d. per lb.	0	17	7
115 lbs. pott iron att 2½ d. per lb.	1	2	4
1 damnified pott	0	5	0
1 pott rack 1 frying pann 1 pestle	0	5	0
1 old spitt & 1 grid iron	0	2	0
2 old gunns	0	10	0
2 pailes 2 pigens 2 bowls 1 cann 1 churn	0	6	10
2 old cyder casques & a parcell of lumber	2	6	0
1 old quern stone & 9 iron wedges	0	8	0
12 lbs. woolen yarn damnified at 6 d. per lb.	0	6	0
1 small looking glass	0	0	8
1 servant boy 8 years to serve	12	0	0
Sterling	114	6	8

Creditors

Isaac Jones	George Harris
Kensey Jones	Joseph Harris

50. Planters in the Lowest Economic Bracket

SOME of the connotations men of the eighteenth century attached to the expression the "meaner sort" will be clearer from inspection of the entries in the inventory of Thomas Collins of Somerset County, Maryland. Collins falls into the lowest economic bracket of planters. In fact he barely misses coming within the legal category of "pauper estates," technically defined as gross estates of twenty-five pounds or less and established for easier administration at the county level of the Commissary General's operations. In the 1750's this element with estates of twenty-five pounds or less made up approximately 10 per cent of the planting families in the Chesapeake area. It would be a mistake, however, to think of Collins as being almost a charity case, for he was a small landowner and had a net worth of £18. 1s. 5½d. after his wife and administratress paid all his debts. But the adjectives—"broken," "raged," "derty," "old"—used by appraisers of the estate leave little doubt about the quality of life and surroundings of families in the lowest economic bracket.

SOURCE: Inventory of the Goods and Chattels of Thomas Collins of Somerset County, 1752, Inventories, Liber 50, folios 155–156 (Maryland Hall of Records, Annapolis).

A Just and True Inventory of the Goods and Chattels and Credits of the Estate of Thomas Collins Late of This County Deceased in Current Money of This Province of Maryland

	£.	s.	d.
To 3 cows and yearlings at 35/0 each 2 cows and calfs at 30/0 each	8	5	0
To 1 old horse £ 4 and 1 yearlen colt 20/0	5	0	0
To 5 very old sows and some pigs at 30/0 10 small shots 20/0	2	10	0
To 136 lbs. of old derty feathers and rotten ticks at 6 d. per lb.	3	8	0
To 3 old broken bed steds 5/0 1 grinding stone 6 d.	0	5	6
To sum very old rag[g]ed bed cloths at 15/0	0	15	0
To 11½ lbs. old pewter at 13 d. per lb. 18 lbs. very old pewter at 6 d. per lb.	1	1	8½

	£.	s.	d.
To 22½ lbs. of old broken pewter at 4 d. per lb.	0	7	6
To 74 lbs. very old pot iron at 9 d. per lb. old cow bell 5/0	1	3	6
To 5 old broken barrels 1/0 each 2 old brace candle sticks 3/0	0	8	0
To 1 pare of old small stillards 2/6 1 pare spoon moles 2/6	0	5	0
To small parcell broken tub and palls	0	7	6
To 10 lbs. derty wool at 9 d. per lb. 12 glass bottels 3/0 [and] 1 old hakel 1/0	0	11	6
To 1 old box iron at 6 d. 1 tap 1/0 1 gun 12/6	0	14	6
To split barral gun 2/6 [and] 1 old gun barral 2/0	0	4	6
To 40 lbs. old iron at 3 d. per lb. To small parcell old lumber 5/0	0	15	0
To 1 old croscut saw 2/6 1 old hansaw 2/6	0	5	0
To 1 old vise eaten out with rust 1/0 [and] to cash 11/6	0	12	6
To 1 old table cloth 3/0	0	3	0
Movables	27	2	2½

Signed as greatest creditors
 JOHN HANDY
 T. DENNIS

Debts due to the deceased disperate by George Jones	0	15	0
Sum totall	27	17	2½

Taken on the 4th day of August 1752
[Signed by Risdon Moor, William Moor, by Nelly Collegs, John Windsor]

51. A Historian on the Carolina Planters

THE ACCOUNT of North Carolina in the 1730's by Dr. John Brickell contains several passages that approach systematic description of the yeoman or small planter. In the first paragraphs Brickell speaks exclusively of this social stratum. When he comes to housing and furniture, he includes the "better sort," though his contrasts make reasonably clear the differences in the two styles of life. The frolic, homemade drink, wrestling, and the like belong to yeoman planter ways.

SOURCE: John Brickell, M.D., *The Natural History of North Carolina* (Dublin, James Carson for the author, 1737), 31–34, 37–42.

The Europians, or Christians of North Carolina, are a streight, tall, well-limb'd and active people; their children being seldom or never troubled with rickets, and many other distempers that the Europians are afflicted with, and you shall seldom see any of them deformed in body.

The men who frequent the woods, and labour out of doors, or use the waters, the vicinity of the sun makes impressions on them; but as for the women that do not expose themselves to weather, they are often very fair, and well featur'd as you shall meet with any where, and have very brisk and charming eyes; and as well and finely shaped, as any women in the world. And I have seldon abserv'd any red-hair'd women, or men, born in this country.

They marry generally very young, some at thirteen or fourteen; and she that continues unmarried, until twenty, is reckoned a stale maid, which is a very indifferent character in that country. These marriages for want of an orthodox clergyman, is performed by the governor or the next justice of the peace, who reads the matrimonial ceremony, which is as binding there as if done by the best divine in Europe. The women are very fruitful, most houses being full of little ones, and many women from other places who have been long married and without children, have remov'd to Carolina, and become joyful mothers, as has been often observ'd. It very seldom happens they miscarry, and they have very easie travail in their child-bearing.

The children at nine months old are able to walk and run about the house, and are very docile and apt to learn any thing, as any children in Europe; and those that have the advantage to be educated, write good hands, and prove good accomptants, which is very much coveted and most necessary in these parts. The young men are generally of a bashful, sober behaviour, few proving prodigals, to spend what the parents with care and industry have left them, but commonly improve it.

The girls are most commonly handsome and well featur'd, but have pale or swarthy complexions, and are generally more forward than the boys, notwithstanding the women are very shy, in their discourses, till they are acquainted. The girls are not only bred to the needle and spinning, but to the dairy and domestick affairs, which many of them manage with a great deal of prudence and conduct, though they are very young.

Both sexes are very dexterous in paddling and managing their canoes, both men, women, boys, and girls, being bred to it from their infancy. The women are the most industrious in these parts, and many of them by their good housewifery make a great deal of cloath of their own cotton, wool, and flax, and some of them weave their own cloath with which they decently apparel their whole family though large. Others are so ingenious that they make up all the wearing apparel both for husband, sons and daughters. Others are very ready to help and assist their husbands in any servile work, as planting when the season of the year requires expedition: pride seldom banishing housewifery. Both sexes are most commonly spare of body and not cholerick, nor easily cast down at disapointments and losses, and seldome immoderately grieving at misfortunes in life, excepting it be the loss of their nearest relations.

By the fruitfulness of the women in North Carolina, and the great numbers of men, women, and children, that are daily transported from Europe, they are now become so powerful, in this and most of the other provinces in the hands of the English, that they are able to resist for the future any attempts the Indians may make on them. Add to this, the several Indian kings that at present are in the Christian interest, who pay some small tribute as an acknowledgement of their subjection, and are ready upon all occasions to assist them when ever they are required to do so; therefore they live at present without any dread or fear of those savages to what they formerly did.

The men are very ingenious in several handy craft businesses, and in building their canoes and houses; though by the richness of the soil, they live for the most part after an indolent and luxurious manner; yet some are laborious, and equalize with the Negro's in hard labour, and others quite the reverse; for I have frequently seen them come to the towns, and there remain drinking rum, punch, and other liquors for eight or ten days successively, and after they have committed this excess, will not drink any spiritous liquor, 'till such time as they take the next Frolick, as they call it, which is generally in two or three months. These excesses are the occasions of many diseases amongst them. But amongst the better sort, or those of good economy, it is quite otherwise, who seldom frequent the taverns, haveing plenty of wine, rum, and other liquors at their own houses, which they generously make use of amongst their friends and acquaintance, after a most decent and discreet manner, and are not so subject to disorders as those who debauch themselves in such a beastly manner. The former sometimes bring their wives with them to be partakers of these Frolicks, which very often is not commendable or decent to behold. . . .

Their houses are built after two different ways; viz. the most substantial planters generally use brick, and lime, which is made from oyster-shell, for there are no stones to be found proper for that purpose but near the mountains; the meaner sort erect with timber, the outside wtih clap-boards. The roofs of both sorts of houses are made with shingles, and they generally have sash windows, and affect large and decent rooms with good closets, as they do a most beautiful prospect by some noble river or creek.

Their furniture, as with us, consists of pewter, brass, tables, chairs, which are imported here commonly from England: the better sort have tollerable Quantities of plate, with other convenient, ornamental, and valuable furniture.

The cloathings used by the men are English cloaths, druggets, durois, green linnen, etc. The women have their silks, calicoes stamp-linen, calimanchoes and all kind of stuffs, some whereof are manufactured in the province. They make few hats, tho' they have the best furrs in plenty, but with this article, they are commonly supplied from New-England, and sometimes from Europe.

Their diet consists chiefly of beef, mutton, pork, venison in abundance, wild and tame fowl, fish of several delicate sorts; roots, fruit, several kinds of sallads, good bread, butter, milk, cheese, rice, Indian corn, both which they concoct like a hasty-pudding: But as I shall treat more particularly of the productions of the country in the succeeding pages, I shall now proceed to their liquors.

The liquors that are common in Carolina at present, and chiefly made use of, are, rum, brandy, mault drink; these they import. The following are made in country, viz. cyder, persimon-beer, made of the fruit of that tree, ceder-beer, made of ceder-berries; they also make beer of the green stalks of Indian corn, which they bruise and boyle: They likewise make beer of mollosses, or common treacle, in the following manner, they take a gallon of molloses, a peck of wheaten bran, a pound of hops, and a barrel of fountain water, all which they boyle together, and work up with yest, as we do our malt liquors; this is their common small-beer, and seems to me to be the pleasantest drink, I ever tasted, either in the Indies or Europe, and I am satisfied more wholsom. This is made stronger in proportion, as people fancy.

It is necessary to observe that though there is plenty of barley and oats in this province, yet there is no malt drink made, notwithstanding all kind of malt liquors bear a good price, nor have any of the planters ever yet attempted it.

Chocolate, teas, and coffee, are as common in Carolina as with us in Ireland, particularly the last, which of late years they have industriously raised, and is now very cheap: These are sober liquors, and take off the better sort from drinking what are hot and spiritous, who are not so addicted to rum and brandy as the inferior sort, caslena or yaupan, an Indian tea, which grows here in abundance is indifferently used by planters and Indians.

The Fireing they use is wood, and especially hickery, though we discovered pit-coal in our journies towards the mountains, yet it is not worth their while to be at the expence of bringing it, timber being so plenty.

The chiefest diversions here are fishing, fowling; and hunting wild beast, such as deer, bears, racoons, hares, wild turkies, with several other sorts, needless to treat of here, 'till we come to describe each particular specie.

Horse-racing they are fond of, for which they have race-paths, near each town, and in many parts of the country. Those paths, seldom exceed a quarter of a mile in length, and only two horses start at a time, each horse has his peculiar path, which if he quits, and runs into the other, looses the race. This is agreed on to avoid jockying. These courses being so very short, they use no manner of art, but push on with all the speed imaginable; many of these horses are very fleet.

It is common for people to come and go from this province to Virginia, to these publick diversions.

They are much addicted to gaming, especially at cards and dice, hazard and all-fours, being the common games they use; at which they play very high, nay to such a pitch, that I have seen several hundred pounds won and lost in a short time.

Cock-fighting they greatly admire, which birds they endeavor to procure from England and Ireland, and to that intent, employ masters of ships, and other trading persons to supply them.

Wrestling, leaping, and such activities are much used by them; yet I never observed any foot races. Dancing they are all fond of, especially when they can get a fiddle, or bagpipe; at this they will continue hours together, may, so attach'd are they to this darling amusement, that if they can't procure musick, they will sing for themselves. Musick, and musical instruments being very scarce in Carolina.

These are the most material observations I have made in respect of their usual diversions.

But they have a particular season, which is only at their wheat-harvest, not to be omitted; this they celebrate with great solemnity, it is the beginning of June—which time the planters notify to each other, that they design to reap the aforesaid grain, on a certain day, some send their Negroes to assist, others only go to partake of the great feasts, etc. Some will frequently come twenty, nay thirty miles on this occasion, the entertainments are great, and the whole scene pleasant and diverting; but if they can get musick to indulge this mirth, it greatly adds to the pleasure of the feast. It must be confest, that this annual revelling is very expensive to the planters, but as its customary, few omit it, nor have they ever those publick diversions at the reaping of any other grain but the European wheat.

I am sensible that many persons, who by their misbehaviour in this country, were obliged to quit it, have maliciously endeavoured to represent, not only the province, but its inhabitants, in a wrong light; but as they intirely take the opportunity to talk either before those who were never there, or before persons incapable of judging, it is to be hoped, that the scandalous reports of such, will not be regarded. Several of those trifling Nusances have to my knowledge, scarcely been out of the town or port where they first arrived, during their residence there: How therefore cou'd they be acquainted with the fertility of the country, the constitution, and temper of the inhabitants; before the learn'd, by whom they can be convicted, they dare not appear? And if the credlous and ignorant will be amused, all the arguments man can produce will not avail.

52. The Yeomanry on Their Rights

HOWEVER mean their estates and mindless their frolics, the small planters were ready to resist what they deemed injustice—a reaction that has associated with yeomen the adjective "sturdy." No more given to niceties of technical law than they were to tidiness about their farm-steads, they quickly scented affronts to their way of life and violations of common-sense equity. Governor Johnston's overreaction to what must have seemed to him slapdash administration of the land system brought instant response from the small planters. Johnston threatened their titles as being based on something less than a true patent. They assured him that intent had been good on both sides when the grants were made and that they had improved their lands in good faith. Equity was on their side. The address breathes the spirit of the later Regulators and the revolutionary patriots who shouldered their muskets in defense of their "laws & liberties."

SOURCE: The Humble Address of the Inhabitants of Bertie & Edge-combe Precincts, October 1735, *The Colonial Records of North Carolina,* IV, 18–22.

To his Excellency Gabriel Johnston, Esq., etc. of North Carolina The Humble Address of the Inhabitants of Bertie & Edgecombe precincts.

Your Excellency in your answer to the grand jurys address seemed to wonder that you should hear any more upon so unreasonable a subject wee hope it will not be thought unreasonable that we should address your Excellency to protect our laws & liberties & that we may not be disquieted in the possessions of our estates, (tho poor & mean) which we first paid for honestly & afterwards settled and improved with much hard labour from the barren woods exposed to the violent heat of the sun most part of the year and many of us trusting to what providence would lay in our way for food: Sometimes a deer or bear & sometimes a racoone & many days nothing, a rare feast for industrious protestants. And that many of our ancestors have fallen by the hands of the savage Indians we believe will not be worth mentioning. The fatigue of settling an estate in this province your Excellency's predecessor might have informed you, for no man living could have taken more pains & fatigue then he did to acquaint himself with this province in general, which his many journeys & travels into the back woods on foot will justifie sometimes accompanied by one man only & often pinched with hunger (nay) in danger of perishing, having but one biscuite for three days to subsist on and sometimes coming amongst the inhabitants without a ragg of cloaths to his back, perhaps 200 miles from the place he set out, often carrying with him considerable sums of money & disposing of it amongst many poor people to encourage & enable 'em the better to settle the back lands. And altho it has been alledged that Mr. Burrington had taken the great quantity of the kings lands to his own use, we say that most part of that land lies so far back that it can be of no service to Mr. Burrington or to any other for 100 years to come & even that he paid ready money for that it might encourage others to settle the back lands. Notwithstanding these many good Offices which that worthy gent has done for the province with many thousands more, he is now mangled with the imputation of violence, tyranny, perjury with many other expressions of indignity & yet stands unconvicted of either of them, all which tho never so pleasing to a few persons at most a dozen which we know to be the whole number of his enemys will never be grateful to the province in general who will for ever (and deservedly) hold even his memory in esteem & veneration. . . . Your Excellency is pleased to call our deed of grant a temporary letter of attorney which subsisted two years only. You may call it what you please Sir but we are persuaded the Lords proprietors meant as they wrote (if so) the proprietors may appear by their deed of grant directed their council here to grant lands to any persons in Albemarle County by reason their lands would not produce tobacco as well as the Virginia Lands. The Quit Rents then became payable in other commodities received at every mans house and the said payments never refused by the Lords proprietors but being content they sent directions in the Year 1712 to their Receiver General here how he should dispose of these commodities which plainly shows that not only the Lords proprietors deputies with the representatives of the people here duly elected have settled the quit rents to be payable in our commodities here at certain prizes but there is also the Lords proprietors assent thereto in directing their Receiver General how to dispose of said commodities which according to the charter is conclusive & makes the payment of the commodities at certain prizes indisputable in our opinion. Your Excellency is pleased to call our laws shamefull collusions betwixt the Lord proprietors servants & their tenants to cheat their masters. If our laws be what you are pleased to call them we may be counted rather fools then cheats for settling on so slippery a foundation. We are persuaded it would be little worth the Lords proprietors or their servants while to make use of any collusions to undo the poor inhabitants of this province which are many degrees poorer than any of his Majesties subjects under heaven. Your Excellency also alledges that we make a great matter of paying the King two shillings per hundred acres sterling and that if we think it a hard bargain that we may leave the Kings Lands for that they are the Kings Lands & not ours & that there are to your Excellency's knowledge thousands of industrious protestants that would come into our places gladly & pay the crown double the rents without clamour or noise (we thank them kindly) & now answer that if the lands we possess belong to the King, we have no bargain either hard or soft. But as we know our lands to be our own, paying his Majesties quit rents, which we mean to do honestly, we are persuaded his Majesty would not desire us to part from our lands & improvements here to any people whatsoever without first satisfying us for our labour which when done we will readily quit the province & seek out lands in our neighbouring collonys where we may call the fruits of our labour our own & where collusions are not studies & if your Excellency be desirous we will leave the blood & carcasses of our ancestors to help manure the ground for them which will some what help their industrye. There is one thing more which we begg leave to lay before your Excellency (to wit) The ill treatment the grand jury of this province met with at the setting of the last general court at Edenton from William Smith, Esquire Chief Justice, who told the grand jury they were perjured and wondered they would not find a bill of indictment against Mr. Tho. Shervin of Edenton when the matter was so fully proved to them & publickly ordered the attorney general to bring all things before him by information for that he would trust nothing with such men & moreover told Mr. William Mackey a responsible free holder & then one of the petty jury that he would perjure himself for a shilling. These are proceedings never before heard of in this province and altogether contrary to the liberty of a British subject and to the power and priviledges of grand juries. This we hope will be worth your Excellency's while to redress seeing it immediately tramples liberty under foot etc.

We are etc.

[Endorsed]

Copy of an address to Gov. Johnston in favour of Capt. Burrington the late Governor and complaining of many hardships they have suffered by the present governor, the Chief Justice, etc.

53. The Balance of Racial Elements

ALL THE PLANTING colonies encouraged importation of white servants by various devices, but none did so with quite the urgency of South Carolina. As rice culture turned planters increasingly to slave labor, the growing racial imbalance raised the specter of black revolts against the dominant whites. By this act, passed in 1698, South Carolina tried to ensure distribution of white servants among plantations where slaves had become numerous enough to get the upper hand. The ratio established was one white servant to six slaves, regardless of whether the planter wished the whites.

SOURCE: Thomas Cooper, Statutes at Large of South Carolina, II, 153–156.

An Act for the Encouragement of
the Importation of White Servants

Whereas, the great number of negroes which of late have been imported into this Collony may endanger the safety thereof if speedy care be not taken and encouragement given for the importation of white servants.

I. Be it enacted by his Excellency, John Earl of Bath, Palatine, and the rest of the true and absolute Lords and Proprietors of the Province, by and with the advice and consent of the rest of the members of the Generall Assembly now met at Charlestowne, for the south-west part of this Province, that every merchant, owner or master of any ship or vessel, or any other person not intending to settle and plant here, which shall bring any white male servants, Irish only excepted, into Ashley River, above sixteen years of age and under forty, and the same shall deliver to the Receiver General, shall receive and be paid by the said Receiver in dollars or pieces of eight, at five shillings the piece, the sum of thirteen pounds for every servant so delivered, and for every boy of twelve years and under sixteen, imported and delivered to the Receiver as aforesaid, the sum of twelve pounds, as aforesaid; Provided that every servant, as aforesaid, hath not less than four years to serve from and after the day of his arrival in Ashley River, and every boy aforesaid, not less than seven years. . . .

II. And be it further enacted by the authority aforesaid, that no servant or boy shall serve longer than such time they have indented and contracted for, and that every servant above sixteen years old which shall be brought into Ashley River without contract or indenture, shall serve five years and no longer; and every boy from twelve years old to fourteen shall serve till they come to one and twenty years old, and from fourteen years old to sixteen years shall serve seven years and no longer.

III. And be it further enacted, that every owner of every plantation to which doth belong six men negro slaves above sixteen years old, shall take from the Receiver one servant, when it shall happen to be his lot to have one, and shall within three months pay the said Receiver so much money for the said servant as the Receiver gave to the ½ person from whom he received the same; and the owner of every plantation to which doth belong twelve negro men, as aforesaid, shall when it shall be his lot, take two servants as aforesaid; and every master of every plantation proportionably; Provided, and it is hereby intended, that every male servant contracted for four years, and not under, shall to all intents and purposes be deemed as good, and supply the room of such as shall be bought from on board of any vessel, or by lot should be appointed him as aforesaid.

IV. And that no master of any plantation may have any servant put unduly and unjustly upon him, but the same it shall be his lot to have, and not till it shall be his lot thereto,

Be it enacted, that every constable, in his division, under the penalty of forty shillings, shall make a lyst of the names of all masters of plantations, to whom six negro men or upwards do belong, and the same shall deliver to the publick Receiver for the time being [and servants shall be assigned to plantations by lots drawn from these lists. Servants shall be allotted first to all plantations with twelve Negroes or more and then to plantations with six negros, until the provisions of Section III shall be met.]

Read three times, and ratified in open Assembly, the 8th day of October, 1698.

54. A Code for Bond Classes

THE NORTH CAROLINA ACT of 1741, Chapter XXIV, has fifty-eight sections and is in effect a code. Those sections on indentured servants provide safeguards against the practice of kidnaping victims into servitude by compelling importers to produce signed indentures, against excessive and degrading punishment, and against masters who withheld necessities of food, clothing, and shelter. The provisions of the law on women guilty of bastardy, though severe, were actually less harsh than those in other colonies, where both whippings and fines were prescribed punishment for such transgressions of morality and waste of the employer's time. In the sections on slaves, the intent was of course to keep Negroes at work, to prevent runaways, and to thwart rebellion. For extreme cases the law revived the ancient doctrine of outlawry, permitting any person to kill the outlaw with impunity.

SOURCE: An Act Concerning Servants and Slaves, chap. XXIV, State Records of North Carolina, XXIII, 191–204.

An Act Concerning Servants and Slaves

I. Be it Enacted, by his Excellency Gabriel Johnston, Esq., Governor, by and with the advice and consent of his Majesty's Council, and General Assembly of this Province, and it is hereby enacted, by the authority of the same, that no person whatsoever, being a Christian, or of Christian parentage, who, from and after the ratification of this act, shall be imported or brought into this province, shall be deemed a servant for any term of years, unless the person importing him or her shall produce an indenture, or some specialty or agreement, signifying that the person so imported did contract to serve such importer, or his assigns, any number of years, in consideration of his or her passage, or some other consideration of his or her therein expressed: and upon any contest arising between the master of any vessel, or other person importing any servant or servants, without indenture, upon any bargain or specialty as aforesaid, the same shall be determined at the next county court to be held for the county where the said servant or servants shall be imported, the justices of which court are hereby impowered to hear and determine the same, in a summary way: and such determination or judgment shall be conclusive and binding on the importer of servant or servants, either for the discharge of the said servant or servants, or to oblige him, her, or them, to serve the importer, or his assigns, as the matter shall appear.

II. And be it further enacted, by the authority aforesaid, that if any christian servant, whether he or she be a servant by importation or otherwise, shall at any time or times absent him or herself from the service of his or her master or mistress, without licence first had, he or she shall satisfy and make good such loss of time by serving after their time of service by indenture or otherwise is expired, double the time of service lost or neglected by such absence: and also such longer time as the county court shall think fit to adjudge, in consideration of any further charge or damage the master or mistress of such servant may have sustained, by reason of his or her absence as aforesaid.

III. And be it further enacted, by the authority aforesaid, that if any christian servant shall lay violent hands on his or her master or mistress, or overseer, or shall obstinately refuse to obey the lawful commands of any of them, upon proof thereof by one or more evidences before any justice of the peace, he or she shall, for every such offence, suffer such corporal punishment the said judge shall think fit to adjudge, not exceeding twenty-one lashes.

IV. And as an encouragement for christian servants to perform their service with fidelity and cheerfulness; be it further enacted, by the authority aforesaid, that all masters and owners of any servant or servants shall find and provide for their servant or servants wholesome and competent diet, clothing and the lodging, at the discretion of the county court, and shall not, at any time, give immoderate correction, neither shall at any time whip a christian servant naked, without an order from the justice of the peace. And if any person shall presume to whip a christian servant naked, without such order, the person so offending shall forfeit and pay the sum of forty shillings, proclamation money, to the party injured; to be recovered, with costs, upon petition to the county court (without the formal process of an action), as in and by this act is provided for servants' complaints to be heard and determined: provided complaint be made six months after such whipping. . . .

XVII. And whereas many women servants are begotten with child by free men, or servants, to the great prejudice of their master or mistress, whom they serve, be it therefore enacted, by the authority aforesaid, that if any women servant shall hereafter be with child, and bring forth the same during the time of her servitude, she shall for such offence be adjusted by the county court to serve her master or mistress one year after her term of service by indenture or otherwise is expired.

XVIII. And be it further enacted, by the authority aforesaid, that if any woman servant shall hereafter be delivered of a child, begotten by her master, such servant shall immediately after delivery be sold by the church wardens of the parish. And if any white servant woman shall, during the time of her servitude, be delivered of a child begotten by any Negro, mulatto, or Indian, such servant, over and above the time she is by this act to serve her master or owner for such offence, shall be sold by the church wardens of the parish, for two years, after the time by indenture or otherwise is expired: and the money arising thereby applied to the use of the said parish; and such mulatto child or children of such servant, to be bound by the county court until he or she arrives at the age of thirty-one years. . . .

XXXIX. And be it further enacted, by the authority aforesaid, that if any negro or other person, who shall be taken up as a runaway and brought before any justice of the peace, and cannot speak English, or through obstinacy, will not declare the name of his or her owner, such justice shall in such case, and he is hereby required, by a warrant under his hand, to commit the said negro, slave, or runaway to the gaol of the county wherein he or she shall be taken up: and the sheriff or under-sheriff of the county into whose custody the said runaway shall be committed, shall forthwith cause notice, in writing, of such commitment to be set up on the court-house door of the said county, and there continued during the space of two months; in which notice a full description of the said runaway and his clothing shall be particularly set down: and shall cause a copy of such notice to be sent to the clerk or reader of each church or chappel within his county, who are hereby required to make publication thereof, by setting up the same in some open and convenient place, near the said church or chappel, on every Lord's Day for the space of two months from the date thereof. And every sheriff failing to give such notice as is herein directed shall forfeit and pay five pounds, proclamation money; which said forfeiture shall and may be recovered with costs in any court of record in this government by action of debt, bill, plaint, or information, wherein no essoign, privilege, protection, injunction or wager of law shall be allowed. The one moiety whereof shall be to the church wardens, for the use of the parish, as well as towards the defraying of the charges that shall arise and become due by virtue of this act, and the other moiety to the person who shall sue for the same. . . .

XLIV. And be it further enacted, by the authority aforesaid, that no slave shall be permitted, on any pretence whatsoever, to raise any horses, cattle or hogs; and all horses, cattle and hogs that six months from the date thereof, shall belong to any slave or of any slave's mark in this government, shall be seized and sold by the church wardens of the parish where such horses, cattle or hogs shall be, and the profit thereof be applied, one half to the use of the said parish, and the other half to the informer.

XLV. And whereas many times slaves run away and lie out hid and lurking in the swamps, woods, and other obscure places, killing cattle and hogs, and committing other injuries to the inhabitants in this government: Be it therefore enacted, by the authority aforesaid, that in all such cases, upon intelligence of any slave or slaves lying out as aforesaid, any two justices of the peace for the county wherein such slave or slaves is or are supposed to lurk to do mischief, shall, and they are hereby impowered and required, to issue proclamation against such slave or slaves (reciting his or their name or names, and the name or names of the owner or owners, if known), thereby requiring him or them, and every of them, forthwith to surrender him or themselves: and also, to impower and require the sheriff of the said county to take such power with him as he shall think fit and necessary for going in search and pursuit of and effectual apprehending such outlying slave or slaves; which proclamation shall be published on a Sabbath Day, at the door of every church or chappel or for want of such, at the place where divine service shall be performed in the said county, by the parish clerk or reader, immediately after divine service: And if any slave or slaves against whom proclamation hath been thus issued, stay out and do not immediately return home, it shall be lawful for any person or persons whatsoever to kill and destroy such slave or slaves by such ways and means as he or she shall think fit, without accusation or impeachment of any crime for the same.

XLVI. Provided always, and it is further enacted, that for every slave killed in pursuance of this act, or put to death by law, the master or owner of such slave shall be paid by the public; and all tryals of slaves for capital or other crimes, shall be in the manner and according as hereinafter is directed.

55. The Accountability of Masters: Indentured Servants

TESTIMONY in the Fincher case exhibits the darker side of master-servant relations and the course of the law in bringing to justice harsh masters. The proceedings in this case are not easy for the novice to follow because it was taken from a county court to the provincial court. When the provincial court met on December 21, 1664, at its capital, St. Mary's, with three justices on the bench, the first order of business was the reading and entry on the record of a transcript from Anne Arundel County court, the court of first resort. This transcript shows that a jury of twelve men had viewed the body of Jeffery Hagman, servant to Joseph Fincher, and found that he had died of disease. Nevertheless the justices of the county court had ordered Fincher held on suspicion of murder. On September 13 the county court had taken testimony of six witnesses. The evidence was clearly against Fincher—with two exceptions: the testimony of Thomas Whyniard and Edward Ladd—and created a presumption of guilt. Fincher's guilt, if established, would have called for the death sentence, a sentence beyond the competence of the county court to pronounce. Consequently, at this point proceedings in the county court terminated and a true copy attested by the clerk was sent to the provincial court.

In the provincial court, proceedings began with the examination of Fincher himself and further examination of witnesses who had previously given testimony in the county court. The grand jurors brought in a true bill, formally presenting Fincher for murder. Fincher pleaded not guilty and asked for jury trial—"by God and his country." Whereupon the court ordered the sheriff to impanel "12 good men and able" for the petit or trial jury. The jury found Fincher guilty; the court sentenced him to hang and directed a writ for his execution to the sheriff of Anne Arundel County. A further interesting development followed when the provincial-court justices directed the sheriff to arrest two witnesses, Whyniard and Ladd, on suspicion of collusion with Fincher to conceal the murder (see their hedging testimony taken before the county court in the transcript of proceedings). Both Whyniard and Ladd were acquitted in a subsequent trial, but Fincher was hanged.

Source: *Archives of Maryland*, XLIX (Provincial Court Proceedings), 303–314.

At a Provincial Court Held at St. Mary's
December 21, 1664

Present: Charles Calvert, Esq., Governor
Philip Calvert, Esq., Chancellor
Mr. Baker Brooke

[The following is a transcript of Anne Arundel County Court Proceeding.]

Wee whose names are hereunder written being required to view the body of Jeffrey Hagman, servant to Joseph Fincher and to the best of our knowledge to returne our verdict how he came by his death, wee being sworne and having viewed the said Hagman's body doe finde no mortall wound about him that did occasion his death but doe unanimously concurr and judge the said Hagman being a diseased person died of the scurvey and an imposthume.

Witness our handes, August the 28th 1664

Thomas Besson, foreman   Dennis N Macconah's marke
Robert Francklin   William W∃ Graye's marke
John Gray   John ∽ Jones' marke
Andrew Roberts   John Kersseake
Robert Lloyde   Thomas TP Parson's marke
Maren Duvall   Theo. Lewys

A true copy, witness myself, Theo. Lewys, Clerk of the Court, Anne Arundel

[Writ] to Captain William Burges, Sheriff of Anne Arundel County

Wee the commissioners Justices of the County of Anne Arundel doe hereby deliver unto you the body of Jodeph Fincher who is suspected have murthered his servant Jeffrey Hagman, by the examination of severall witnesses.

These are therefore in the Lord Proprietor's name to will and require you to take him into Goale and there to keep him safe untill he be cleared by the law hereof. Fayle not as you will answer the contrary at your perill.

Given under our handes September 14th 1664

ROBERT BURLE ROGER GROSE
THOMAS BESSON RICHARD EWEN
RALPH WILLIAMS JOHN NORWOOD

At a Court Held for Anne Arundel County,
September 13, 1664

Present: Robert Burle   Capt. Thomas Besson ⎫ Commissioners
        Roger Grose   Capt. John Norwood ⎬ [Justices]
        Richard Ewen   Ralph Williams   ⎭

Edward Ladd aged 21 yeares or thereabouts sworne in court deposeth as followeth:

That he saw Joseph Fincher strike his servant but not in the tobacco house and those blowes that the said Fincher did at that time give his servant this deponent is sure could doe him no hurt, and further saith not.

EDWARD ◯ LADD his marke

Thomas Whyniard aged 21 yeares or thereabouts sworne in court deposeth as followeth:

That he saw Joseph Fincher strike his servant with a small sticke but not in the tobacco howse and further this deponent saith not.

THOMAS ⊤ WHYNIARD's marke

Sussannah Leeth aged 20 yeares or thereabouts sworne in court deposeth as followeth:

This deponent going to worke saw Joseph Fincher pegging of plants and he called his man out worke, he not comming when he call'd him, he goes in and fetches him and loades him with a burden of plants. The man not able to beare them, the said Fincher followes him and flings him downe plants and all and beate him and kicked him and afterwards sent him into the howse. His wife turnes him back againe and sends him for a paile of water, she following him for another, and goeing to the spring the fellow not goeing soe fast as she would have him, she shuveth him along till he fell downe and afterwards she pull'd him up againe and gave him some blowes. Then coming from the springe the man fell downe with the paile in his hand, but this deponent knowes not whether there was any water in it or noe. She could not gett him up but calls to her husband. The man seeing his master comming getts up and goes toward the howse. His master followeth him and beateth him with a sticke. A while after wee came out againe to worke picking up plants wee heard a great noise in the tobacco howse whereof Joseph Fincher cryed; "gett up, gett up." A while after this deponent saw a little girle belonging to the howse rinning to the dwelling house and presently after Thomas Whyniard and fetcht a bottle of dramms. My master seeing him runn calls to Lawrence Organ and goes to the tobacco house and further saith not.

Susanna Leeth

William Gunnell ages 22 yeares or thereabouts sworne in court deposeth as followeth:

That upon Fryday being the night before Joseph Fincher's man died this deponent saw the said Fincher loade his man with plants and loaded soe much on him that the said servant told his master he could not beare it, who said to his servant, "Sirrah doe or else I will beate you never was dogg soe beaten," who answered his master, "Master I cannot cary them allthough you knock me in the head," and the fellow staggering his master comming to him, kickt him and beate him with his fist saying, "Sirrah, Ille use thee never noe dogg was soe used. Ile either knocke thee in the head or starve thee rather than Ile lead this life with thee," and then Fincher called his servant to him againe and loaded him with some of the plants. The fellow carryed them as well as he could to the old howse. This was done on Fryday night before the fellow dyed. And the next morning this deponent being pegging of plants saw the said Fincher beate his servant againe with a sticke and likewise his fist and all soe kicked him and after this deponent went home and comming out againe from breakfast this deponent saw the said Fincher's wife and the fellow goeing to the spring. The fellow not goeing so fast as she would have him shuved him along and struck him with her hands and haul'd him & pull'd him and gott him up againe and comming from the springe the fellow fell downe againe and she call'd to her husband, and told him that she could not gett the fellow up. Her husband comming, the fellow rise and after he went up to the tobacco howse in the corne feilde and this deponent heard a greate noise and the fellow cryed out, "Lord, Master, if you beate me any more you will knock me in the head," and after this deponent saw a wench goeing downe to the dwelling howse. She not comming soe soon as they expected Thomas Whyniard runn after and brought up a bottle of dramms. Thomas Miles, this deponent's master seeing of him runn called to Lawrence Organ and told him that he thought in his heart the fellow was dead. And this deponent further saith that Joseph Fincher formerly reported he had beate his servant and brake 2 tobacco stickes about the sides of him and declared it to John Kickseeck, Lawrence Organ, and this deponent being in the feilde when the said Kickseeck spoke of it. This Joseph Fincher declared to the Dutchman and the Dutchman to us, and further saith not.

WILLIAM GUNNELL's marke

Lawrence Organ aged 35 yeares or thereabouts sworne in court deposeth as followeth:

This deponent saw Joseph Fincher beate his servant with his hand and kickt him with his feete and likewise saw the said Fincher's servant's nostrills of his nose bloody in the house where he was dead and further saith not.

LAWRENCE L O ORGAN's marke

Thomas Miles aged 45 yeares or thereabouts sworne in court deposeth as followeth:

This deponent being in the feilde saw Joseph Fincher loading of plants upon his man, he being not able to carry them, fell downe plants and all, and Joseph Fincher loaded his maid, soe when she was gone he ran to the fellow saying, "Can you neither carry plants nor walke," turn'd him home. His wife meeting of him turn'd him back againe till he came to the tobacco howse or thereabouts. There the fellow would goe noe further but fell downe. She called to her husband and told him the fellow would not walke. He, the said Fincher throwing downe the said plants that was in his armes and runn up to the tobacco howse and tooke up a stick and gave him foure or five blowes and kickt him and cufft him againe. Then about the 2nd or 3rd hour of the day this deponent being in the feilde with his people heard a greate noise in the tobacco howse like the clatterring of sticks and crying, "Gett up, gett up, why doe you not gett up," soe presently after this deponent saw the wench running home and after her Thomas Whyniard, seeing these thinges this deponent pondering in his minde what was the matter and it rise in his hart that the fellow was dead. Presently this deponent called Lawrence Organ and told him what he thought, who answered your deponent, "Come, let's goe and see," soe when we came to the tobacco howse dore wee saw the fellow upon the ground leaning against his master's knee, he being blooddy about the nose. This deponent askt Joseph Fincher how it came, who answered this deponent that he fell downe against the tobacco sticks and further this deponent saith not.

THOMAS MILES

A true copy, witness myself, Theo. Lewys, Clerk of the court, Anne Arundel county

Record of Trial in the Provincial Court

EXAMINATIONS TAKEN BEFORE THE GOVERNOR AND COUNCIL

Joseph Fincher confess that Jeffrey Hagman dyed on the 27th day of August 1664.

Thomas Miles being further examined upon oath saith that when he came into the tobacco howse the said Jeffrey Hagman was dead and further saith he saw black spotts upon his body and hinder parts. Joseph Fincher was urgent with the said Myles to bury him before any body saw him and further saith that upon report he was beaten with 2 tobacco sticks by the said Joseph Fincher.

Lawrence Organ further saith that the very same day he dyed he saw the said Joseph Fincher beat the aforesaid Hagman.

Susanna Leeth further examined saith in the beginning of her deposition the words relates to the day that Jeffrey Hagman was slaine, and by these words he called his man Jeffrey Hagman was ment and by the words heard a greate noyse like the rattling of tobacco stickes.

William Gunnell further examined saith, being askt what Fincher's mans name was he saith Jeffrey, which said Jeffrey is since dead, Fincher and two freemen pegging of plants and saith he saw Thomas Whyniard come out of the howse and he goeing into the howse presently found the said Jeffrey dead.

Robert Loyde, surgeon, sworne saith being demanded if he

viewed the body of the deceased person answered yes, and being demanded if he did see blew spotts upon the forepart and hinder parts, answered, "yes, I saw two stroakes and a sore on his side that was formerly under my cure. . . ."

Let it be inquired for the Right Honorable the Lord Proprietary whether Joseph Fincher in Rhode River in the county of Anne Arundel the 27th day of August in the yeare of our Lord God 1664 in the river and county aforesaid upon Jeffrey Hagman, servant to the said Joseph Fincher, by force and arms an assault did make and with certaine sticks of no vallue which he the said Joseph Fincher in his right hand then and there did hold, divers blowes on the body of the said Jeffrey Hagman did strike, soe that of the said blowes the said Jeffrey Hagman the day aforesaid did dye and soe if the said Joseph Fincher the said Jeffrey Hagman then and there feloniously and of malice forethought did kill and murder, contrary to the peace of his said Lordship his rule and dignity.

WILLIAM CALVERT

The witnesses names
SUSANNA LEETH
THOMAS MILES
The mark of WILLIAM Z GUNNELL
The mark of LAWRENCE L O ORGAN
The [grand] jurors having theire charge given departs the court by themselves to consider of the indictment with the evidences.

The jurors returnes into court answering all to theire names being demanded who should speake for them, answered the foreman, who delivers theire verdicts endorsed on the bills. . . .

On Joseph Fincher: A true bill. Uppon which the said prisoner was call'd to the barre and the presentment read to which the said Joseph Fincher pleads not guilty. Hee being demanded how he would be tryed, answered by God and his country.

The presentment as followeth:

The jury for the Right Honorable the Lord Proprietary doe present Joseph Fincher of Rhode River in the county of Anne Arundel, for that the said Joseph Fincher on the 27th day of August 1664 upon Jeffrey Hagman servant to the said Joseph Fincher in his right hand then and there did hold, divers blowes on the body of the said Jeffrey Hagman did strike soe that of the said blowes the said Jeffrey Hagman the day aforesaid dyd dye,

And soe the said Joseph Fincher the said Jeffrey Hagman then and there feloniously and of malice forethought did kill and murder contrary to the peace of his said Lordship his rule and dignity. . . .

Summons to sherriffe to impannell 12 good men and able for the petty jury. Sheriffe returnes his writt and warrant:

Foreman Samuel Chew	John Watkins
Francis Holland	Philip Allumbey
Robert Peca	John Bayley
John Burrage	Robert Blinckhorne
Samuel Garland	Thomas Hopkins
John Ewen	William Evans

The indictment againe read, and the evidences called, examined, and sworne as before sett downe.

The jurors withdrew to consider of the said bille with the charge. They returne and being called answered every one to his name. The foreman delivers in theire verdict endorsed on the back side of the bill with this word (viz.) Guilty.

The prisoner call'd to the barre. Joseph Fincher hold up thy hand.

Are you agreed of your verdict? Answer: yes.

Who shall say for you? Answer: the foreman Mr. Samuell Chew.

Gentlemen of the jury, you say Joseph Fincher is guilty of the murder whereof hee stands indicted? Answered: yes.

You all say soe? Answer: Yes.

Joseph Fincher hold up thy hand. You doe remember upon your indictment you have been arraigned and have pleaded not guilty and for your tryall you have put your selfe upon God and country, which country hath found you guilty, for cann you now say for your selfe, why according to law you should not have judgment to suffer death? What saist thou, Joseph Fincher? Answered: that if he deserv'd it, he must dye. Being askt if there bee all he hath to say for himselfe, answered yes.

The judge gives sentence in these words following:

Joseph Fincher, you shall be carryed to the place from whence you came, from thence to the place of execution, and there be hanged by the neck till you are dead. . . .

[*To the High Sheriffe of the County of Anne Arundel*]

These are in the name of the Right Honorable the Lord Proprietary of this province to will and require you to see the body of Joseph Fincher (who att our last court of session held at St. Mary's the 22nd of this instant December was arraigned and convicted of murder) carryed to the place of execution within three dayes after your receiving the said Fincher into your custody, and betwixt 8 and 9 of the clock in the morning there to hang by the neck till he be dead according to the judgment given on the day abovesaid, and for soe doeing this shall be your warrant.

Given under my hand this 27th day of December 1664.

CHARLES CALVERT
[Governor]

[*To the High Sheriffe of Anne Arundel County*]

Whereas Thomas Whyniard and Edward Ladd late of your said county, planters, hath been arrested for suspition of felony by them as is said committed, wee will and command you therefore to receive into your custody the said Thomas Whyniard and Edward Ladd there to remaine untill by due course of law they shall be delivered.

Witness our deare brother Philip Calvert, Esq., Chancellor of our province of Maryland.

Given att St. Mary's this 23d day of December 1664.

PHILIP CALVERT

56. The Accountability of Masters: Slaves

CASES involving slaves came less frequently to court than those concerning indentured servants. Reasons are not far to seek. Restrictions on punishment did not extend so far with slaves as with indentured servants. Masters might, for example, whip a slave naked without infraction of the law. And masters were not enjoined minutely to furnish necessities of food and clothing to slaves—on the assumption presumably that their self-interest would lead them to take adequate care of their investment. Nonetheless neither public opinion nor the court allowed slave owners complete license. The attorney general of Maryland indicted one Symon Overzee for "correcting his negro servant, so that "the said negro dyed under his said correction." The case has several points of interest. First, the victim was a "negro servant." The law as it stood in 1658 had not yet demoted blacks to the status of chattels. Second, the indictment carefully avoids mention of murder. Third, the testimony reasonably clearly establishes a connection between the punishment, which was surely cruel and unusual, and the Negro's death. Apparently the case perplexed the judges, who overruled Overzee's motion for acquittal and ordered further inquiry by the grand jury. The whole matter came to a dramatic end the following February after the grand jury heard testimony that Antonio, the slave, was a rogue and a persistent runaway. Overzee was acquitted by proclamation.

Source: *Archives of Maryland*, XLI (Provincial Court Proceedings), 190–191.

Att a Provincial Court Held att St. Clement's Manor, December 2, 1658

Present: Josias Fendall, Esq., Governor
Philip Calvert, Esq., Secretary
Thomas Gerard
Col. John Price
Thomas Cornwalleys, Esq.

ATTORNEY GENERAL v. OVERZEE

Mr. William Barton informes the court against Mr. Symon Overzee, for that the said Overzee correcting his negro servant the said negro dyed under his said correction.

The examination of Hannah Littleworth aged 27 yeares or thereabouts taken the 27th of November 1658, before Philip Calvert, Esq.

This Examinant sayth that sometime (as shee conveives) in September was two yeares, Mr. Overzee commanded a negro (commonly called Tony) formerly chayned up for some misdemeanors by the command of Mr. Overzee (Mr. Overzee being then abroad) to be lett loose, and ordered him to goe to worke, but instead of goeing to worke the said negro layd himselfe downe and would not stirre. Whereupon Mr. Overzee beate him with some peare tree wands or twiggs to the bigness of a man's finger att the biggest end, which hee held in his hand, and uppon the stubbernes of the negro caused his dublett to be taken of, and whip'd him uppon his bare back, and the negro still remayned in his stubbernes, and feyned himselfe in fitts, as hee used att former times to doe. Whereuppon Mr. Overzee commanded this examinant to heate a fyre shovel, and to bring him some lard, which shee did, and sayth that the said fyre shovel was hott enough to melt the lard, but no soe hot as to blister anyone, and that it did not blister the negro, on whom Mr. Overzee powr'd it. Immediately thereuppon the negro rose up, and Mr. Overzee commanded him to be tyed to a Ladder standing on the foreside of the dwelling howse, which was accordingly done by an Indian slave, who tyed him by the wrist, with a piece of a dryed hide, and (as shee remembers but cannot justly say) that hee did stand uppong the grownd. And still the negro remayned mute or stubborne, and made noe signes of conforming himselfe to his masters will or command. And about a quarter of an howre after, or less, Mr. Overzee and Mrs. Overzee went from home, and [she] doth not know of any order Mr. Overzee gave concerning the said negro. And that while Mr. Overzee beate the negro and powred the lard on him, there was nobody by, save only Mr. Mathew Stone, and Mrs. Overzee now deceased. And that from the time of Mr. Overzee and his wife going from home, till the negro was dead, there was nobody about the howse but only the said Mr. Mathew Stone, William Hewes, and this examinant, and a negro woman in the quartering house, who never stir'd out. And that ofter Mr. Overzee was gone, uppon the relation of Mr. Mathew Stone, in the presence of William Hewes that the negro was dying, this examinant desyred Mr. Mathew Stone to cutt the negro downe, and hee refused to doe it, William Hewes allso bidding him let him alone and within lesse then halfe a howre after the negro dyed, the wind comming up att northwest soone after hee was soe tyed, and hee was tyed up betweene three and fowre o'clock in the afternoone, and dyed about six or seaven, and was kept till next morning before he was buried.

Uppon the reading this examination (Hannah Littleworth being present in court) when shee came to that particular concerning the tying of the negro up by the wrists (viz) Whither hee stood uppon the grownd Yea or Noe? Shee declareth that now shee very well remembers that hee stood uppon the grownd.

William Hewes sworne in upon court sayth that hee was present, att the time when Mr. Overzee beate the negro, and saw him allso powre lard uppon him, and that as hee conceaves and remembers, he saw noe blood drawne of the negro, and this deponent being willing to help the negro from the grownd, Mr. Overzee haveing his knife in his hand, cutting the twigs, threatened him to runne his knife in him (or words to that effect) if he molested him, and that the negro (as he thinks, but cannot justly say) stood uppon the grownd, and sayth further that the negro did commonly use to runne away, and absent himselfe from his Mr. Overzees service.

The governor requests the councell, then present, to declare their opinions, whither it was in the power of the court to judge this business now, Yea or noe? Mr. Overzee humbly requesting the court to end it, and that he may be acquitted, and uppon consideration that Mr. Mathew Stone was allsoe present as is declared whose examination is not yett taken, may evidence some things materiall in the business, it is agrad by the board, and ordered that Mr. Overzee putt in bond of one hundred pownds of tobacco, to the Lord Proprietary for his appearance att the next Provinciall Court, and there to attend the finall determination of the same.

57. Slave Crimes

SLAVES *indicted for crimes ranging from theft to murder stood trial in the courts of law, just as did indentured servants and freemen. And the punishments meted out to convicted slaves were likewise the same as for whites, free or bond. At least this was true of the seventeenth century. During the eighteenth century the courts began adding touches designed to impress, and sometimes to terrorize, slaves. The Negro Hannah, convicted of a brutal ax murder in 1723, was sentenced by the court to hang, "and that after she is dead she be hanged up in chains on the said gallows there to remain until she be rotten." Whites were spared these indignities. Mary Reed, indentured servant convicted at the same court session of stealing a nightgown, French brandy, and other goods to the total value of £4. 8s. 0d., was sentenced to hang for grand larceny. In Maryland at least, killing of his master by a slave went beyond the usual definition of murder and became "petite treason."*

SOURCE: Lord Proprietor v. Jacob the Negro, *Archives of Maryland*, XLIX (Provincial Court Proceedings), 490–491.

Called to the bar Jacob the negro. The presentment read, which is as followeth:

The [grand] jury for the right honorable the Lord Proprietary doe present that Jacob a negro slave and servant to Nathaniel Utie of Spesutia in Baltemore county and to Mary his wife the 29th of September 1665 in the howse of the said Nathaniel Utie in Spesutia aforesaid in the county aforesaid by force and armes, to witt, with a drawne knife of two pence value, which the said Jacob then and there in his hand did hold, uppon the aforenamed Mary, the wife of the said Nathaniel Utie then his mistresse then and there in the Peace of God, and his said Lordship, being voluntarily and of his malice forethought an assault did make, and the same Mary then his mistresse then and there with the said knife felloniously and trayterously upon her right arme strongly did strike and stabb, gyving her a mortall wound fowre fingers broad, in the upper part of her right arme, of which mortall wownd shee the said Mary the wife of Nathaniel Utie uppon the fowrth day of October did dye, and soe the aforenamed Jacob, att Spesutia aforesaid of his malice aforethought the same Mary Utie his mistresse aforesaid in manner and forme aforesaid, willingly, wittingly, felloniously and trayterously did kill, against the peace of his said Lordship his rule and dignity.

WILL CALVERT

Anthony Brispo aged 20 yeares or thereabouts sworne and examined in open court this 11 of October 1665 sayth

The hee see Jacob the negro stab Mrs. Mary Utie uppon Saturday the 30th of September last, about ten of the clock in the night, that hee stabbed her with a knife produced in court, that in outward appearance shee was in perfect health before he wounded her, that hee the said Jacob gave her two wounds in the right arme, one whereof was fowre fingers wide, and that shee dyed uppon the Wednesday att night following, and further that hee doth believe that shee dyed of those wounds having bled a day and a night.

[Deposed on oath] PHILIP CALVERT

Francis Stockett aged 31 yeares or thereabouts sworne and examined this 11th of October 1665 sayth

That hee dressed the wounds gyven by Jacob the negro to Mrs. Mary Utie viz, two wounds in her arme, whereof one was fowre fingers wide, and that hee doth varily believe shee dyed of those wounds.

[Deposed on oath] PHILIP CALVERT

The names of the jury men impannelled and sworne to view the corps of Mrs. Mary Utie, and have as is here underwritten gyven in their verdict of the cause of her death:

Mr. Francis Stockett	Thomas Symonds
Mr. John James	Samuel Bennett
Mr. Henry	George Elthringham
Mr. William Thurrell	Richard Woolfe
William Perce	Richard Leeke
John Royland	Cornelius Beice

That the wounds which shee received in her arms was the cause of her death.

JOHN COLLETT
sheriffe

The foregoeing oaths being read, and that verdict of the jury shewen in court, and demanded whither guilty or not guilty, hee stands in a manner mute.

Judgment of the board is guilty of petite treason. Uppon this matter, these things being heard and seene and by the court fully understood it was considered that the said Jacob is guilty of petite treason.

Then the Governor gave sentence in these words, You shall be drawne to the gallows att St. Maries and there bee hanged by the neck 'till yow are dead.

58. Dr. John Brickell on North Carolina Negroes

IN Brickell's day (the early 1730's) the slave codes had already pretty much developed their final form. The Negro slave had become a chattel; his testimony could be taken only in cases involving another Negro, never against a white. Already, too, some of the more debasing practices had appeared—for example, slave breeding. Brickell's second paragraph sounds like the beginnings of lynching.

SOURCE: John Brickell, M.D., Natural History of North Carolina, 272–275.

The Negroes are sold on the coast of Guinea, to merchants trading to those parts, are brought from thence to Carolina, Virginia, and other provinces in the hands of the English, are daily increasing in this country, and generally afford a good price, viz. more or less according to their goodness and age, and are always sure commodities for gold or silver, most other things being purchased with their paper money. Some of them are sold at sixteen, twenty five, or twenty six pounds sterling each, and are looked upon as the greatest riches in these parts. There are great numbers of them born here, which prove more industrious, honest, and better slaves than any brought from Guinea; this is particularly owing to their education amongst the Christians, which very much polishes and refines them from their barbarous and stubborn natures that they are most commonly endued with. I have frequently seen them whipt to that degree, that large pieces of their skin have been hanging down their backs; yet I never observed one of them shed a tear, which plainly shows them to be a people of very harsh and stubborn dispositions.

There are several laws made against them in this province to keep them in subjection, and particularly one, viz, that if a Negroe cut or wound his master or a christian with any unlawful weapon, such as a sword, scymiter, or even a knife, and there is blood-shed, if it is known amongst the planters, they immediately meet and order him to be hanged, which is always performed by another Negroe, and generally the planters bring most of their Negroes with them to behold their fellow Negroe suffer, to deter them from the like vile practice. This law may seem to be too harsh amongst us, to put a man to death for blood-shed only, yet if the severest laws were not strictly put in execution against these people, they would soon overcome the christians in this and most of the other provinces in the hands of the English.

Notwithstanding the many severe laws in force against them, yet they sometimes rise and rebel against their masters and planters, and do a great deal of mischief, being both treacherous and cruel in their natures, so that mild laws would be of no use against them when any favourable opportunity offered of executing their barbarities upon the Christians, as hath been too well experienced in Virginia, and other places, where they have rebelled and destroyed many families.

When they have been guilty of these barbarous and disobedient proceedings, they generally fly to the woods, but as soon as the Indians have notice from the Christians of their being there, they disperse them; killing some, others flying for mercy to the Christians (whom they have injured) rather than fall into the others hands, who have a natural aversion to the Blacks, and put them to death with most exquisite tortures they can invent, whenever they catch them.

When any of these Negroes are put to death by the laws or the country, the planters suffer little or nothing by it, for the province is obliged to pay the full value they judge them worth to the owner; this is the common custom of law in this province, to prevent the planters being ruined by the loss of their slaves, whom they have purchased at so dear a rate; neither is this too burthensom, for I never knew but one put to death here for wounding, and after attempting to kill his master, who used all means he could to save his Life, but to no purpose, for the country insisted on having the law put into execution against him

The Negroes that most commonly rebel, are those brought from Guinea, who have been inured to war and hardship all their lives; few born here, or in the other provinces have been guilty of these vile practises, except over-persuaded by the former, whose designs they have sometimes discovered to the Christians; some of whom have been rewarded with their freedom for their good services; but the reader must observe, that they are not allowed to be witnesses in any cases whatever, only against one another.

There are some Christians so charitable as to have the Negroes born in the country, baptized and instructed in the Christian Faith in their infancy, which gives them an abhorance of the temper and practice of those who are brought from Guinea. This freedom does not in the least exempt them from their master's servitude, whatever others may imagine to the contrary, who believe them to be at their own liberty as soon as they have received baptism. The planters call these Negroes thus baptized, by any whimsical name their fancy suggests, as Jupiter, Mars, Venus, Diana, Strawberry, Violet, Drunkard, Readdy Money, Piper, Fidler, etc.

Their marriages are generally performed amongst themselves, there being very little ceremony used upon that head; for the man makes the woman a present, such as a brass ring or some other toy, which if she accepts of, becomes his wife; but if ever they part from each other, which frequently happens, upon any little disgust, she returns his present these kind of contracts no longer binding them, than the woman keeps the pledge given her. It frequently happens, when these women have no children by the first husband, after being a year or two cohabiting together, the planters oblige them to take a second, third, fourth, fifth, or more husbands or bedfellows; a fruitful woman amongst them being very much valued by the planters, and a numerous issue esteemed the greatest riches in this country. The children all go with the mother, and are the property of the planter to whom she belongs. And though they have no other ceremony in their Marriages than I have represented, yet they seem to be jealously inclined, and fight most desperately amongst themselves when they rival each other, which they commonly do.

Their children are carefully brought up, and provided for by the planters, 'till they are able to work in the plantations, where they have convenient houses built for them, and they are allowed to plant a sufficient quantity of tobacco for their own use, a part of which they sell, and likewise on Sundays, they gather snake-root, otherwise it would be excessive dear if the Christians were to gather it; with this and the tobacco they buy hats, and other necessaries for themselves, as Linnen, Bracelets, Ribbons, and several other toys for their wives and mistresses.

There are abundance of them given to theft, and frequently steal from each other, and sometimes from the Christians, especially rum, with which they entertain their wives and mistresses at night, but are often detected and punished for it.

59. An Abortive Slave Uprising

FEAR of slave risings was constantly in the minds of planters. Fed by rumors and occasionally fulfilled by an actual incident, these apprehensions gave birth to laws against assemblages of Negroes and to the establishment of patrols, systems of passes, and the like. The conspiracy Bordley describes in his letter to an Eastern Shore friend exhibits instructive aspects of the syndrome, particularly of the preoccupation with the designs of Negroes on "young white women." Doubtless the story had grown with much discussion and retelling as the posse comitatus organized and drilled for service. The planting society never deluded itself that the Negro enjoyed his lot.

SOURCE: Stephen Bordley to Matthias Haris, dated Annapolis, January 30, 1740, Stephen Bordley Letterbook, 1738–1740 (Maryland Historical Society, Baltimore).

We have lately discovered a conspiracy among the negroes in Prince George's county to rise and massacre all the inhabitants on this shore; and the scheme was as well laid as any of the kind that I ever heard of: They were on a Sunday appointed, to meet at a particular place, to the number of two hundred, and after having chosen their several officers (the first stirrer of this mischief having been all along agreed by them to be their king) they were to disperse every one to their several homes and there to stay till after the families in the country were abed, when they were to destroy all those of their several families Negro women and all except the young white women only whom they intended to keep for their wives, and by help of the several arms which they could pick up in each family and their masters horses and furniture, they were immediately to repair to the field where the consultation was to be held, and when a sufficient number of them was gott together, they were to ride in the night immediately up to Annapolis, and dividing themselves into two parties, one was to secure the powder house, and the other the council room which when they had done and sufficiently fortified themselves, with arms and ammunition, they were to disperse in several bodies over the town and cutt the throats of men women and children excepting none but the white young women; which when they had done, as they expected, (and no doubt but they would) all the negroes farr and near would flock in to them, they were then to disperse again in to the country in large bodies and to cutt of all the surviving familes there, and when they had done this jobb they intended to return to town with their young white wives and dividing the houses among themselves were to settle their government here, and upon the first opportunity to dispatch all the boats they could over to your shore to bring over such Negroes as were willing to join them; and in case they heard of any considerable head being made against them from your shore, or elsewhere so that they could not keep these parts, they were to pace up all worth carrying, to drive the country, and with their white wives to settle back in the woods: the first Sunday appointed for the undertaking was so rainy that few mett, and among the rest wanting were their chiefs, and the same cause providentially put it off for two other Sundays, and the mean time a negroe fellow of the number belongong to Mr. Brooke finding they were resolved to kill his master among the rest, informed him of it which blew up the design and six of them, (among whom is their king and they say a clever sinsible fellow between 40 and 50 years old) are now in the county goal, and the sheriffe daily expects 8 or 10 more: this affair had been 8 months in agitation: this happy discovery has putt us all upon our guards here, and will no doubt produce some good effects among us: We are now at last contriving ways and means to secure the council house and magazine by a nightly watch, and one likewise for the town of four sturdy fellows; arms and ammunition are now dispersed into every one's hands, and the time is come (alas the day which I never thought to see!) of my being made a soldier: Col. Gale is the captain of our Independent Troop, and Rogers of the foot. Sir, We can muster 40 good horse at 1/4 of an hours warning with as many bold daring fellows on the backs of them, and 60 foot all compleatly armed: It is said, before the Appointment of any day for the execution of the design a negroe woman lying abed in a quarter overheard several of the negroe fellows talking in their country language, concerning this very affair, and she accordingly told her mistress of it next morning, but could not gain relief; foolish woman! that sooner than give herself the trouble of looking into the affair would run the hazard of having her throat cutt; but perhaps she had a mind for a black husband.

60. Propagandizing the Slaves

THOUGH the planters did not indulge in the delusion that the slaves liked their bondage, they had a few other resources beside naked force as social controls. The resort to persuasion was by no means a hypocritical pose, for the planting society accepted the notion of bond and free as it accepted governors and governed or superior and inferior. Among the few examples of practicing persuasion on the slaves themselves, the sermons of Thomas Bacon link the status quo with the plan and dominion of Almighty God. Bacon's intentions further appear in the social and educational work he carried on for several years among slaves in his parish on the eastern shore of Maryland. If God had ordained bond and free, man was obligated to make the ordinance as tolerable as possible.

SOURCE: Thomas Bacon, *Sermons Addressed to Masters and Servants and Published in the Year 1743* (Winchester, Virginia, c.1813), 111–135.

Sermon II

Ephesians 6:8. Knowing, that whatsoever good thing any man doeth, the same shall he receive of the Lord, whether he be bond or free.

My well-beloved Black Brethren and Sisters,

When you were last here, I endeavoured to shew you: that God made you and all the world, and that he made you and all mankind to serve him, that it is he who places every man in the station or rank which he holds in the world, making some kings, some masters and mistresses, some tradesmen and working people, and others servants and slaves. That every one of us is obliged to do the business he hath set us about in that state or condition of life in which he hath been pleased to call us. And that whoever is doing his business quietly and honestly in the world and living as a christian ought to do, is serving of God, though his condition be ever so low and mean, and will be as much taken notice of and as highly favoured by God at the last day as the greatest prince upon earth. For God is no respecter of persons. I also laid before you that you ought to serve God for your own sake, because you have souls to be saved, and if you should lose them, you are undone forever. That every one who dies and goes into another world must go either to heaven or hell. . . .

I then went on to shew you what duty you owe to God in particular. . . . That if the love of God is not strong enough to keep you from doing what is bad, and vexing and offending him thereby, you ought at least to dread his terrible judgments. For that he is able not only to destroy your bodies and strike you dead in a moment, but also to cast both body and soul into hell, which will certainly be the portion of all such as provoke him to anger by leading wicked lives. That you ought to worship God both in public and in private, in public by coming to church as often as you have leave and opportunity, and in private by praying to him for every thing you want and giving him thanks for all his goodness to you, which you may easily do when you are walking or working in the house or in the field. That you ought to reverence and honour Almighty God and keep from all cursing and swearing or making any light foolish vain use of his great and holy name. And that you must keep from all lying, because God hates all such as tell lies and will give them over to the devil, who is the father of all lies and liars.

In the next place I endeavored to shew you how you ought to behave towards your masters and mistresses, and to make it plain to you that as God himself hath set them over you here in the nature of his stewards or overseers, he expects you will do every thing for them as you do for yourself. That you must be obedient and subject to them in all things and do whatever they order you to do unless it should be some wicked thing which you know that God hath forbidden, in which case you are to refuse, but in no other. That you must not be eye servants, that is such as will be very busy in their master's presence, but very idle when their backs are turned. For your head master, Almighty God, is looking at you and though you may escape being found out or punished by your owners for it, yet you cannot deceive God, who will punish you severely in the next world for your deceitful dealing in this. That you must be faithful and honest to your masters and mistresses, not wasting their substance or letting anything belonging to them perish for want of your care. Because that is next to stealing, for the master's loss is the same as if he had been robbed of it. And that you are to serve your owners with cheerfulness, respect, and humility, not grumbling or giving any saucy answers, but doing your work with readiness, mildness, and good nature. Because your rudeness and grumbling is not as much against your owners, as it is against God himself, who hath placed you in that service and expects you will do the business of it as he hath commanded you.

I now come to shew you, as I promised in my last sermon, what is the duty and behaviour you owe to your fellow servants and others.

And you are to take notice that the great rule which Almighty God hath given us in this case is to love one another. . . .

To make this rule as plain as I can to you, do but think within yourselves what you would do for any person you really had a love and affection for. Would you not do them all the good and shew them all the kindness you could? Would you not be very sorry to give them any trouble or vexation? Would you not keep from doing them any sort of harm yourself, and hinder other people from doing them any wrong or hurt? And would not your love to them make you so careful of them and so unwilling to hurt them as if they were your nearest relations. This consideration will lead you into a true notion of what is meant by those rules in the holy scriptures, where God Almighty commands us to love one another. . . .

Your fellow servants are more particularly to be looked upon as your brethren. Your common station, as slaves, your complexion, and your marriages one among another in different families make you nearer to each other than all the rest of the world, except your owners. And poor and ignorant as you are, you may do much good and prevent much harm, by behaving one towards another as brothers and sisters ought to do and as God requires of you. . . .

Take care that you do not fret or murmur, grumble, or repine at your condition. For this will not only make your own life uneasy, but will greatly offend Almighty God. Consider that it is not yourselves, it is not the people you belong to, it is not the men that have brought you to it, but the will of God, who hath by his Providence made you servants, because no doubt he knew that condition would be best for you in this world, and help you the better towards heaven, if you would but do your duty in it.

61. Catechizing the Soldiery

THE IMPORTANCE of the sermon in colonial America is easy to underrate. For the many families without books, the pulpit was almost the only contact with ideas above the level of casual talk about crops, weather, and neighborhood doings. The minister's text and his exegesis furnished topics for rumination and nearly unending discussion on the porch and at the fireside. Hardly an important occasion passed without its special sermon: muster days, openings of legislative sessions, elections. And the sermons were designed to influence conduct in socially desirable directions. It is small wonder that the established church jealously guarded its position, for much more was at stake than mere salaries and sinecures. The Great Awakening heightened the importance of preaching and produced sermons more relevant to personal experience, especially to the experience and understanding of the less educated groups in the provinces. Ministers like Samuel Davies, a dissenter and a light of the Great Awakening, must be counted as forces directing their hearers toward social goals. Davies' sermon "Religion and Patriotism the Constituents of a Good Soldier"—preached to Captain Overton's Independent Company of Volunteers raised in Hanover County, Virginia, in 1755—places the sanction of Christianity on war. The background was the beginning of the last and bitterest conflict between the British and the French in North America, known to history as the French and Indian War.

SOURCE: "Religion and Patriotism the Constituents of a Good Soldier," in Samuel Davies, Sermons on Important Subjects, 3 vols. (fifth edition, London, 1803) III, 345–366.

I cannot begin my address to you with more proper words than those of a great general, which I have read to you: *Be of good courage, and play the men for your people, and for the cities of your God: and the Lord do what seemeth him good.*

My present design is, to illustrate and improve the sundry parts of my text, as they lie in order; which you will find rich in sundry important instructions, adapted to this occasion.

The words were spoken just before a very threatening engagement by Joab, who had long served under that pious hero king David, as the general of his forces, and had shewn himself an officer of true courage, conducted with prudence. The Ammonites, a neighbouring nation, had frequent hostilities with the Jews, had ungratefully offered indignities to some of David's courtiers whom he had sent to condole their king upon the death of his father, and congratulate his accession to the crown. Our holy religion teaches us to bear personal injuries without private revenge: but national insults and indignities ought to excite the public resentment. . . .

There are some men who naturally have this heroic turn of mind. The wise Creator has adapted the natural genius of mankind with a surprising and beautiful variety to the state in which they are placed in this world. To some he has given a turn for intellectual improvement, and the liberal arts and sciences; to others a genius for trade; to others a dexterity in mechanics and the ruder arts necessary for the support of human life. The generality of mankind may be capable of tolerable improvements in any of these: but it is only they whom the God of Nature has formed for them, that will shine in them: every man in his own province. And as God well knew what a world of degenerate, ambitious, and revengeful creatures this is; as he knew that innocence could not be protected, property and liberty secured, nor the lives of mankind preserved from the lawless hands of ambition, avarice, and tyranny, without the use of the sword; as he knew this would be the only method to preserve mankind from universal slavery; he has formed some men for this dreadful work, and fired them with a martial spirit, and a glorious love of danger. Such a spirit, though most pernicious when ungoverned by the rules of justice and benevolence to mankind, is a public blessing when rightly directed: such a spirit, under God, has often mortified the insolence of tyrants, checked the encroachments of arbitrary power, and delivered enslaved and ruined nations: it is as necessary in its place for our subsistence in such a world as this, as any of the gentler geniuses among mankind; and it is derived from the same divine original. He that winged the imagination of an Homer or a Milton; he that gave penetration to the mind of Newton; he that made Tubal-Cain an instructor of artificers in brass and iron, and gave skill to Bezaleel and Aholiah in curious works; nay, he that sent out Paul and his brethren to conquer the nations with the gentler weapons of Plain Truth, miracles, and the love of a crucified Saviour; he, even that same gracious power, has formed and raised up an Alexander, a Julius Caesar, a William, and a Marlborough, and inspired them with this enterprising, intrepid spirit; the two first to scourge a guilty world, and the two last to save nations on the brink of ruin. There is something glorious and inviting in danger to such noble minds; and their breast beat with a generous ardour when it appears. . . .

Though nature be the true origin of military courage, and it can never be kindled to a high degree where there is but feeble spark of it innate; yet there are sundry things that may improve it even in minds full of natural bravery, and animate those who are naturally of an effeminate spirit to behave with a tolerable degree of resolution and fortitude in the defence of their country. I need not tell you that it is of great importance for this end that you should be at peace with God and your own conscience, and prepared for your future state. . . . We are obliged to defend our country: and that is a sneaking, sordid soul indeed that can desert it at such a time as this. But this is not all; we are also obliged to take care of an immortal soul; a soul that must exist, and be happy or miserable through all the revolutions of eternal ages. This should be our first care; and when this is secured, death in its most shocking forms is but a release from a world of sin sorrows, and an introduction into everlasting life and glory. But how can this be secured? Not by a course of impenitent sinning; not by a course of stupid carelessness and inaction; but by vigorous and resolute striving; by serious and affectionate thoughtfulness about our condition, and by a conscientious and earnest attendance upon the means that God has graciously appointed for our recovery. But "we are sinners, heinous sinners against a God of infinite purity and inexorable justice." Yes, we are so; and does not the posture of penitents then become us? Is not repentance, deep, broken-hearted repentance, a duty suitable to persons of our character? Undoubtedly it is; and therefore, O my countrymen, and particularly you brave men that are the occasion of this meeting, Repent: fall down upon your knees before the provoked Sovereign of heaven and earth, against whom you have rebelled. Dissolve and melt in penitential sorrows at his feet; and he will tell you, *Arise, be good cheer; your sins are forgiven you.* . . .

It is also of great importance to excite and keep up our courage in such an expedition, that we should be fully satisfied we engage in a righteous cause—and in a cause of great moment; for we cannot prosecute a suspected, or a wicked scheme, which our own minds condemn, but with hesitation and timorous apprehensions; and we cannot engage with spirit and resolution in a trifling scheme from which we can expect no consequences worth our vigorous pursuit. This Joab might have in view in his heroic advice to his brother: *Be of good courage,* says he, *and let us play the men for our people, and for the cities of our God.* q.d. We are engaged in a righteous cause; we are not urged on by an unbounded lust of power or riches, to encroach upon the rights and properties of others, and disturb our quiet neighbours: we act entirely upon the defensive, repel unjust violence, and avenge national injuries; we are fighting *for our people, and for the cities of our God.* We are also engaged in a cause of the utmost importance. We fight for our people; and what endearments are included in that significant word! our liberty, our estates, our lives! our king, our fellow-subjects, our venerable fathers, our tender children, the wives of our bosom, our friends, the sharers of our souls, our posterity to the latest ages! and who would not use his sword with an exerted arm when these lie at stake? But even these are not all: we fight *for the cities of our God.* God has distinguished us with a religion from heaven; and hitherto we have enjoyed the quiet and unrestrained exercise of it: he has condescended to be a God to our nation, and to honour our cities with his gracious presence, and the institutions of his worship, the means to make us wise, good, and happy: but now these most invaluable blessings lie at stake; these are the prizes for which we contend; and must it not excite all our active powers to the highest pitch of exertion? Shall we tamely submit to idolatry and religious tyranny? No, God forbid: *let us play the men,* since we take up arms for our people, and the cities of our God.

My first and leading advice to you is, Labour to conduct this expedition in a religious manner. Me thinks this should not seem strange counsel to creatures entirely dependent upon God, and at his disposal, as you are an independent company of volunteers under officers of your own chusing, you may manage your affairs more according to your own inclinations than if you had enlisted upon the ordinary footing: and I hope you will improve this advantage for the purposes of religion. Let prayer to the God of your life be your daily exercise. When retirement is safe, pour out your hearts to him in secret; and when it is practicable, join in prayer together morning and evening in your camp. How acceptable to Heaven must such an unusual offering be, from that desart wilderness Maintain a sense of divine Providence upon your hearts, and resign yourselves and all your affairs into the hands of God. You are engaged in a good cause, the cause of your people, and the cities of your God! and therefore you may the more boldly commit it to him, and pray and hope for his blessing. I would fain hope there is no necessity to take precautions against vice among such a select company: but lest there should, I would humbly recommend it to you to make this one of the articles of your association, before you set out. That every form of vice should be severely discountenanced; and if you think proper, expose the offender to some pecuniary or corporal punishment. It would be shocking indeed, and I cannot bear the thought, that a company formed upon such generous principles, should commit or tolerate open wickedness among them; and I hope this caution is needless to you all, as I am sure it is to sundry of you.

And now, my dear friends, and the friends of your neglected country, In the name of the Lord lift up your banners; be of good courage, and play the men for the people and the cities of your God: and the Lord do what seemeth him good. Should I not give vent to the passions of my heart, and become a speaker for my country, methinks I should even overwhelm you with a torrent of good wishes, and prayers from the hearts of thousands. May the Lord of hosts, the God of the armies of Israel, go forth along with you! *May he teach your hands to war, and gird you with strength to battle!* May he bless you with a safe return and long life, or a glorious death in the bed of honour and a happy immortality! May he guard and support your anxious families and friends at home, and return you victorious to their longing arms! May all the blessings your hearts can wish attend you wherever you go! These are wishes and prayers of my heart; and thousands concur in them: and we cannot but cheerfully hope they will be granted, through Jesus Christ. Amen.

62. Restraint of Vagrancy and Idleness

THE surest antidote to any lingering suspicion that the planting society took a tolerant view of idleness and neglect of honest employment is the legislation in every colony against rogues and vagabonds. The rhetoric of these acts may have roots in the English poor law, but the purpose in the colonies, where there were never enough for all the work, was to guard against the effects of idleness, vagrancy, and abandonment of family ties in a country yet lacking the tight social fabric of Europe. On the matter of an idle mind being the devil's workshop, planters were at one with their Puritan brethren in the north. They began by seeing that at least the hands were busy.

SOURCE: Act of 1755, chap. VI, State Records of North Carolina, XXIII, 435–437.

An Act for the Restraint of Vagrants,
and for Making Provision for the Poor and Other Purposes

I. Whereas divers idle and disorderly persons, having no visible estates or employments, and who are able to work, frequently stroll from one county to another, neglecting to labor; and either failing altogether to list themselves as taxables, or by their idle and disorderly life, rendering themselves incapable of paying their levies, when listed: For remedy thereof,

II. Be it Enacted by the Governor, Council, and Assembly and by the authority of the same, that it shall not be lawful for any inhabitants of this government, to entertain, hire, or employ, in his or her house, above the space of forty eight hours, any such person or persons whatsoever, being taxable, and removing from the parish where he or she formerly resided, unless such person shall first produce a certificate, under the hand of the sherrif, or some magistrate of the county from whence he or she came, that such person paid levy there for the preceding year, or that he or she came into this government since, or was a servant at the time of taking the last list of taxables; and if any one shall entertain, hire, or employ, any such person or persons whatsoever, being taxable, not having such certificate as aforesaid, he or she so offending, shall forfeit and pay twenty shillings, proclamation money, for every such offence, to the informer; recoverable before any justice of the peace of the county where the offence shall be committed: and if any taxable person, not having such certificate, shall be liable to the like penalty of twenty shillings, proclamation money, to be recovered and applied as aforesaid.

III. And be it further enacted, by the authority aforesaid, that all able bodied persons, not having wherewithal to maintain themselves, who shall be found loitering and neglecting to labour for reasonable wages: all persons who run from their habitations, and have wives and children, without suitable means for their subsistence, whereby they are like to become burthensome to the parish wherein they inhabit; and all other idle, vagrant, or dissolute persons, wandering abroad, without betaking themselves to some lawful employments, or honest labour, or going about begging, shall be deemed rogues and vagabonds.

IV. And be it further enacted, by the authority aforesaid, that if any such vagabonds shall be found in any county or place, wandering, begging or misordering him or herself, it shall be lawful for any justice of the peace of that county, and he is hereby impowered and required, by warrant under his hand, to cause such vagabonds to be brought before him, and to examine and inform himself, as well by the oath and examination of the person apprehended, as of any other person or persons which oath or oaths the justice is hereby impowered to administer, and by any other ways or means he shall think proper, of the condition and circumstances of the person or persons so apprehended; and if it shall appear that he or she is under the description of vagabonds within this act, the said justice shall, by his warrant, order and direct him or her to be conveyed and whipt, in the same manner as runaways are, from constable to constable, to the county wherein his wife or children do inhabit, or where he or she did last reside (as the case may be) and there delivered to a justice of the peace, who is hereby required to cause every such vagabond to give sufficient security for his or her good behavior, and for betaking him or herself to some lawful calling, or honest labour; and if he or she fail so to do, then to commit him or her to the common goal of the county, there to remain until such security be given, or until the next court; which court is hereby impowered, if no security be then offered, to bind such vagabond to service, on wages for the term of one year; and such wages, after deducting the charges of the prosecution, and necessary cloathing, shall be applied towards supporting the family of such servant (if any) or otherwise paid to the person so bound after his or her time of service is expired, in full of all other recompence or reward: But if any such vagabond be of such evil repute, that no person will receive him or her into service, in such case the court shall order him or her to receive thirty nine lashes on his or her bare back, well laid on, at the public whipping post, and then to be discharged; and in both cases every such vagabond shall be guilty as aforesaid; and when any such vagabond shall be brought before a justice of the peace and it shall not appear to the said justice that he or she has acquired a legal settlement in any parish the said justice is hereby required to cause such vagabonds to give security for his or her good behavior, and for betaking him or herself to some honest calling or employment; and on failure thereof, shall commit him or her to the jail of the county, there to remain and be dealt with as is before herein directed.

63. Suppression of Sabbath Breaking and Immorality

"BLUE LAWS" figured in the public law of the planting colonies almost as prominently as in New England. The statute books are studded with acts against breaking the Sabbath, profane swearing, adultery, and fornication. Court proceedings give fullest evidence of the serious efforts by law enforcement officers to restrain offenders. Whippings, fines, bonds for good behavior were the common punishments that judges meted out to transgressors, but the pillory and jail sentences were not unknown. The stewards of the planting society had no more use for loose living than they had for idleness.

SOURCE: Act of 1741, Chap. XIV, State Records of North Carolina, XXIII, 173–175.

An Act for the Better Observation
and Keeping of the Lord's Day, Commonly Called Sunday;
and for the More Effectual Suppression of Vice and Immorality

I. Whereas in well regulated governments, effectual care is always taken that the day set apart for publick worship, be observed and kept holy, and to suppress vice and immorality: Wherefore,

II. We pray that it may be enacted, and be it enacted, by his Excellency Gabriel Johnston, Esq., Governor, by and with the advice and consent of his Majesty's Council, and General Assembly of this province, and it is hereby enacted, by the Authority of the same, that all and every person and persons whatsoever shall, on the Lord's Day, commonly called Sunday, carefully apply themselves to the duties of religion and peity and that no tradesman, artificer, planter, labourer or other person whatsoever, shall, upon the Land or Water, do or exercise any labour, business or work, of their ordinary callings (works of necessity and charity only excepted), nor employ themselves either in hunting, fishing or fowling, or use any game, sport, or play on the Lord's Day aforesaid or any part thereof, upon pain that every person so offending, being of the age of fourteen years and upwards, shall forfeit and pay the sum of ten shillings, proclamation money.

III. And be it further enacted, by the authority aforesaid, that if any person or persons shall prophanely swear or curse, in the hearing of any justice of the peace, or shall be convicted of prophanely swearing and cursing, by the oath of one or more witness or witnesses, or confession of the party before any justice or justices of the peace, every such offender shall forfeit and pay the sum of the two shillings and six pence, of the like money, for every oath or curse. And if any person executing any public office, shall prophanely swear or curse, being first convicted, as aforesaid, such person shall forfeit and pay the sum of five shillings, of the like money, for each and every oath or curse.

IV. And be it further enacted, that if any person or persons shall prophanely swear or curse, in the presence of any court of record in this government, such offender or offenders shall immediately pay the sum of ten shillings, of the like money, for each and every oath or curse: to be deposited in the hands of the chairman of the said court and by him accounted for and paid, as hereinafter is directed: or to sit in the stocks, not exceeding three hours, by order of such court.

V. And be it further enacted, by the authority aforesaid, that every person convicted of drunkeness, by view of any justice of the peace, confession of the party, or oath of one or more witness or witnesses, such person so convicted shall, if such offence was committed on the Lord's Day, forfeit and pay the sum of five shillings of the like money; but if on any other day, the sum of two shillings and six pence, for each and every such offence.

IX. And be it further enacted, by the authority aforesaid, that if any persons commit fornication, upon due conviction, each of them shall forfeit and pay twenty five shillings proclamation money, for each and every such offence: to be recovered and applied to the same use as the other fines in this act.

X. And be it further enacted, that any two justices of the peace upon their own knowledge, or information made to them, that any single woman within this county is big with child, or delivered of a child or children, may cause such woman to be brought before them, and examine her, upon oath, concerning the father: and if she shall refuse to declare the father, she shall pay the fines in this act before mentioned, and give sufficient security to keep such child or children from being chargeable to the parish, or shall be committed to prison, until she shall declare the same, or pay the fine aforesaid, and give security as aforesaid. But in case such woman shall, upon oath, before the said justices, accuse any man of being the father of a bastard child or children, begotten of her body, such person so accused shall be adjudged the reputed father of such child or children, and stand charged with the maintenance of the same, as the county court shall order, and give security to the justices of the said court to perform the said order, and to indemnify the parish where such child or children shall be born, free from charges for his, or her, or their maintenance, and may be committed to prison until he find security for the same if such security is not by the woman before given.

XI. And be it further enacted, that the two said justices of the peace, at their discretion, may bind, to the next county court, him that is charged on oath, as aforesaid, to have begotten a bastard child, which shall not be then born, and the county court may continue such person upon security until the woman shall be delivered, that he may be forthcoming when the child is born.

XII. And be it further enacted, by the authority aforesaid, that this act shall be publicly read, two several times in the year, in all Parish churches and chappels, or for want of such, in the place where divine service is performed in every parish immediately after divine service; that is to say, on the first or second Sunday in April, and on the first or second Sunday in September, under the penalty of twenty shillings, proclamation money, for every such omission or neglect: to be levied by a warrant from a justice, and applied to the use of the parish where the offence shall be committed: and the church wardens of every parish are hereby required to provide a copy of this act, at the charge of the parish.